Praise for *Pastoral Imagination*

"The world cries out for justice and healing. It desperately needs pastors, chaplains, and activists who embody a vibrant *pastoral imagination*. And Eileen Campbell-Reed's new book is just what we need in theological education to form religious leaders and public theologians who can speak and act with a robust pastoral imagination, bringing leadership and care to the demanding situations of life. Based in a decade of carefully gathered qualitative research, Campbell-Reed's book is ideal for giving both professors and students a vision, rich stories, and deep questions to accompany them as they *learn in practice* how to speak love, enact hope, and demand justice in our broken and beautiful world."

SERENE JONES, president at Union Theological Seminary

"Encyclopedic in scope yet pulsing with heart in every word, Eileen Campbell-Reed's *Pastoral Imagination* is a compendium of wisdom and a companion for ministry. Pastors will turn to it again and again for encouragement and guidance."

GEORGE A. MASON, senior pastor, Wilshire Baptist Church, Dallas, Texas, and author of *Preparing the Pastors We Need: Reclaiming the Congregation's Role in Training Clergy*

"Through story and scholarship alike, Eileen Campbell-Reed has given us all a generous invitation to ponder anew what makes for faithful leadership today. Rooted in a ten-year research project studying the shape of pastoral imagination, this book offers a litany of accessible openings to larger conversations about the shape of ministry in a world marked by the pandemic of 2020 while also addressing the skills and questions that have always made a difference in ministerial leadership. Whether you are a seminary student or an experienced leader, a lay volunteer or an ordained clergy person, you will find here a treasure trove of insight, learning, and wisdom in which you can rediscover the imagination, hope, and grace that nurtures a lifetime of ministry."

ERIC D. BARRETO, Weyerhaeuser Associate Professor of New Testament, Princeton Theological Seminary, and editor of *Reading Theologically*

"Strange as it may seem, this has not been done before: a look at the practice of ministry as it unfolds over time in the lives of pastors. Campbell-Reed offers a portrait into the lives of fifty ministers as they emerge from seminary and live into their callings. Through their stories, she gives us a look at what pastoral imagination is and how it emerges over time. Evocative, discerning, and insightful—this book will give seminary students as well as pastors, denominational leaders, and theological educators a travel itinerary for how ministers become engaging leaders of communities of faith today."

KATHLEEN A. CAHALAN, professor of practical theology, Saint John's University School of Theology and Seminary, and project director, Collegeville Institute Seminars

---

"*Pastoral Imagination* is a book of wisdom. Eileen Campbell-Reed distills ten years of her research on how one learns pastoral imagination and draws on her own ministerial experience to expertly mentor the reader in the habits, disposition, and reflective ways of being that catalyze growth in the special kind of intelligence that is pastoral imagination. *Pastoral Imagination* will spark joyful discoveries for ministers at every age and stage of their lifelong journey of formation, starting in seminary."

MATTHEW FLODING, director of ministerial formation at Duke Divinity School, coeditor of *Reflective Practice: Formation and Supervision in Ministry*, and former chair of the Association for Theological Field Education

---

"Gaining wisdom in the pastorate typically takes decades of trial and error and lots of support and advice from colleagues. In *Pastoral Imagination*, Eileen Campbell-Reed does us a great service by distilling decades of developed intuition into 'ministry minutes,' giving us the mentor that we need."

CAROL HOWARD MERRITT, pastor of Bedford Presbyterian Church and author of Healing Spiritual Wounds

PASTORAL
Imagination

PASTORAL
Imagination

BRINGING THE PRACTICE
OF MINISTRY TO LIFE

Eileen R. Campbell-Reed

FOREWORD BY CHRISTIAN SCHAREN

FORTRESS PRESS
MINNEAPOLIS

PASTORAL IMAGINATION
Bringing the Practice of Ministry to Life

Print ISBN: 978-1-5064-7006-1
eBook ISBN: 978-1-5064-7008-5

Cover art: Amber Simpson
Cover design: Tory Herman
Interior design and typesetting: Scribe Inc.

To all the participants in the
Learning Pastoral Imagination Project:
an abundance of gratitude

Contents

Foreword

I began my first pastorate in a former manufacturing town in central Connecticut just three months before September 11, 2001. In the week that followed that infamous day, information about both what had happened and who was behind it came to light. Shock turned into a spasm of patriotic fervor. The worship committee chair planted an American flag in the pulpit and told me I'd be a hero for allowing it. I'd learned the flag was an issue my second week on the job when, on Flag Day, June 14, I'd been approached by members bitterly objecting to the interim pastor who preceded me unilaterally deciding to remove the flag from the sanctuary. I said I'd put it on the agenda for an upcoming June congregational meeting. At the meeting, only two people spoke against returning the flag to the sanctuary. As if making a closing argument for the case, an older member, a World War II veteran shot down over France and held prisoner of war, stated emphatically, "I have never seen love of God and love of country to be in conflict."

I was, as Eileen puts it in chapter 39, "pulled up short." I didn't know what to do. Not wanting to draw a line in the sand my first month but feeling very strongly about the dangers of nationalism and flags in the sanctuary, I decided to push back. I negotiated that we place the flag in the foyer, inside the front doors but not in the sanctuary. But after 9/11, in the throes of a national crisis unlike any I'd experienced, I caved, weakly saying we should put the flag on one side of the pulpit with a Christian flag on the other side, as indeed they had been arranged in old photos of the sanctuary. Little did I know then, but the conflicts of those early months and my handling of them sowed the seeds of my departure just a few years later.

Near the end of my time in my first pastorate, I received an invitation from Dorothy Bass and Craig Dykstra to join a project initiated by the Lilly Endowment focusing on practical theology, theological education, and Christian ministry. Although I was an academic, I was serving as a pastor of a congregation and was invited to participate in the three-year seminar from that perspective. My task, as the seminar unfolded, was to write an essay that laid bare how I'd learned to do what I do as a pastor. In the process, I drew on a theory of learning I'd been exposed to while in seminary in Berkeley, articulating the journey from novice to master. Writing about my learning journey thus far helped me notice what I still did not (and could not, given my relative beginner status in ministry) know. The piece turned into a chapter in the seminar's eventual book,

For Life Abundant, and I called it "Learning Ministry over Time: Embodying Practical Wisdom."

During the seminar, conversations with Craig Dykstra about "the long arc of learning ministry" led to the idea of a project following seminarians as their careers unfolded, seeking to understand how one learns pastoral imagination. We thought at the time that such knowledge could help ministers and the communities they lead thrive. Eileen Campbell-Reed was the perfect partner for launching the project, and the ten years following the lives and careers of our national cohort of pastoral leaders continue to represent some of the most exciting and meaningful work I am fortunate to do.

When I began my first pastorate almost twenty years ago, I had a newly minted PhD in theology and sociology, focusing on the dynamics of urban churches just like the one I was called to serve. However, I didn't have pastoral imagination, and boy, could I have used it. Short of that, I could have used a book like the one you hold in your hands, chock-full of wisdom for ministry. I'm grateful for the decade of exploring how one learns pastoral imagination with Eileen. And I'm even more grateful she has offered this path to bringing the practice of ministry to life. May it be so for you!

Christian Scharen
September 11, 2020
New York, NY

Introduction

THE TIMES

What a time it is to be a minister, an activist, a chaplain, a seminarian, a youth worker, or a spiritual leader. In 2020, many pastors and priests had to learn a whole new set of skills, including how to move their congregations into an online environment while people in the United States and around the world stayed home to prevent the spread of COVID-19. Other ministry leaders learned the unavoidable lessons of taking their convictions to the streets in protest of police brutality and in support of justice for Black lives. The call for action in the streets and in the halls of government had to be balanced with more outbreaks of the coronavirus.

Chaplains who have long been heroes of spiritual and pastoral care in medical, military, and long-term care settings suddenly made news headlines as they became lifelines connecting us with our loved ones at the very last moments of their lives. Seminaries and ministry internships were thrown into uncertainty about how to continue. Youth and campus ministers were flung into figuring out how to connect with young people, who depend so utterly on being with peers, in a season when we all needed to be apart for the health and safety of everyone. The worldwide pandemic became the time of universal homeschooling, drive-by birthday parties, pastoral visits shouted from cars to porches, socially distanced or majorly delayed funerals and memorials, and weekly worship streamed on Facebook or posted on YouTube.

These dire and dramatic moments were also punctuated with comedic ones. There were priests who filled squirt guns with holy water to baptize at a distance, the pastor who didn't know about filters and broadcast himself wearing a helmet and then a pink wig, and Zoom performances of hilarious new songs reflecting the creativity of human beings. We all needed haircuts, and some undertook near holy-grail quests in search of toilet paper. Yet it was also a *kairos* kind of moment as we figured out new ways to practice the rituals of faith and grief together while we were apart. And even as the coronavirus took more than 115,000 lives in three months, protests over the value and dignity of Black lives grew, and individuals continued to die in the streets, we began to see a world changing in irrevocable ways.

As I complete this book in the spring of 2020, the entire world is upside down and burning. We are facing more waves of a coronavirus pandemic with no vaccine and no clear end in sight. Economic repercussions are massive. Also, enormous numbers of people have returned to life as if nothing is happening. The numbers of COVID-19 cases have surpassed two million, and deaths keep climbing in the United States and globally. The number of deaths due to the coronavirus has revealed (again) the massive health disparities in this country that favor wealthy, white, privileged people and unfairly disadvantage people with fewer means, people who are indigenous to this continent, and those who live as descendants of enslavement. The high rate of deaths of African Americans, Indigenous Peoples on tribal lands, immigrants to the United States, and people of color by percentage is far out of balance with the racial-ethnic breakdown in the general population. Compounding the crisis is the fragility in systems that should care for elders but instead are revealing social, spiritual, and health disparities for the elderly who are dying of COVID-19 at alarmingly high rates.

In May, three murders of Black Americans took center stage in the national headlines. Protests over the deaths of Breonna Taylor, Ahmaud Arbery, and George Floyd spread through more than 140 cities in the United States and many cities around the globe. Just this evening, there is literally a fire burning in Nashville's City Hall following an afternoon of peaceful protesting. Minneapolis, where the murder of George Floyd was captured on camera, was the epicenter of protests that would stretch into the summer. In multiple cities, antiracist protesters were injured, gassed, bulldozed with cars, shot with rubber bullets, and killed at the hands of police. The situation is complex: there were multiple parties acting, and some groups set out to undermine the peaceful protests in support of Black lives and Black dignity.

These events and seismic shifts in the social and political landscapes are challenging what it means to be a person of faith in this country and what it means to lead. The need for pastoral imagination is urgent. Whether you are leading communities of faith or people protesting in the streets, holding the hand of a dying person, leading worship in an overcrowded prison, or praying with a traumatized soldier, how you see and respond to the situation can make a difference between life and death. The practice of ministry is not for the faint of heart. The learning required is for people who are willing to endure the disorientation and reorientation of their knowing, doing, and being for the sake of bringing the practice of ministry to life.

What needs our focused attention at this moment in order to teach and learn the practice of ministry? How does one become a minister, chaplain, activist, children's or youth pastor, community nonprofit leader, or liturgist? What skills, knowledge, imagination, and improvisation are needed for leading a church steeped in social transgressions or for taking the church beyond its own limits to the world crying out in grief, lament, and pain? How will you make the shift from imagining ministry to a wise and supple pastoral imagination that is ready to meet life?

When Chris Scharen and I launched the Learning Pastoral Imagination (LPI) Project in 2009, some of our colleagues wrung their hands and furrowed their brows. They wanted us to worry more about what kind of lifeworld ministers were launching out into. We were indeed concerned about it, but I had seen the religious world I knew best fall apart fairly dramatically—and in its place, a new world grew and flourished. I've written about how ministry was redefined by clergywomen who came to their calling in the Southern Baptist Convention and departed it with thousands who formed new progressive Baptist groups.[1] So I really was not too sure that there was anything new under the sun. Every age has its newness and its drama, and it carries forward the residue of past traumas, griefs, and sorrows. I believe most of our colleagues were wringing their hands in anxiety over their own crumbling institutions.

It turns out that the decline of the mainline church is indeed real. Sociologists of religion Mark Chaves and David Voas have demonstrated with precision a very slow and certain decay.[2] Simultaneously, the church is growing, blossoming, and spreading in other places and in groups newer to the United States.[3] Even where the numbers of churchgoers are declining, a closer look reveals a vibrant presence of faithful, engaged Christian churches and leaders. A careful study of this moment in time highlights the flourishing of faith values that are driving protests and calls for the dismantling of injustice in governments and industry. Theresa is one of our LPI study participants who spent two years as a pastoral resident in the Pacific Northwest, a region of the country known for its lack of churchiness. She says it was like seeing what the country might look like in a decade or two: "I've been to the future . . . and it's fine! It's different, and you probably won't be able to do it as your full-time job, but you'll be great, and Jesus is still there!"

The world will keep shifting and changing, and communities of faith will continue to need leaders. New forms of community and activism and engagement with the world will keep emerging out of convictions about what God is calling people to do. New pathways will continue to open up, and the real question becomes, "How will we take from the past what we know about how practices are learned and what conditions make that possible?" The changes in this moment of history are critical and profound, and yet how human beings learn practices like ministry has a particular kind of consistency across time. This book enters into the conversation and offers a way to think about how we learn to practice ministry and the crucial skills of improvisation for the moments here at hand.

THE PRACTICE OF MINISTRY

When I get on my bike for a ride, I don't actually think through all the steps that I take: Left leg over bar. Stand on my right foot. Hold hands on brakes. Shift weight to left foot. Back to right foot. Put up kickstand with left foot. Spin right pedal. Turn handlebars to face the direction I want to go. Walk a little forward. Spin the right pedal again. Place right foot on the pedal. Lift up onto seat. Place left foot on the pedal. Balance body. Look right and left. Pedal harder and go a little faster. Balance again. Pedal faster, then slower. Calculate and shift gears.

No. More typically, I simply jump on my bike and ride. Away I go fluidly, perhaps wobbling slightly, yet mostly without deliberative, conscious thinking about it. I just ride my bike, something I learned to do at eight years old.

Ministry is not unlike this. We take dozens of steps and do multiple sequences of activity without thinking through them step by tiny step. But in the beginning, things are different. We need guidance to think through each step. We need people who will hold the seat or help us put on the "training wheels," as Bishop Carlos in the LPI study puts it. And then we need some help taking off the training wheels later. Having mentors who will show us and support us as we learn is a great gift in ministry, just as it is in learning to ride a bike.

In our first paper on pastoral imagination, Chris Scharen and I wrote about this early stage of learning in practice as "imagining ministry." As a novice and beginner, one is preoccupied with the rules, pulling up buckets from deep wells of knowledge, worrying a lot, and asking, "Am I getting this right?" Gradually with time and experience, we begin to know more, grow in confidence, and take more risks with how to respond.

Once we learn to really ride a bike, it's something that stays with us for a lot of our lives, stored as muscle memory, balance, and posture. Only certain kinds of aging, memory loss, or injury take it from us. Also, with ministry, if we take the several years to learn the skills, tasks, and postures and integrate them with knowledge and pastoral ways of assessing situations, we begin to lodge our ministerial knowing in our bodies and in habits of thinking, speaking, and responding. We may not, however, want to push the metaphor too far. One of the differences is that biking may be more akin to a skill than a full professional and spiritual practice. As the 2010 *Clergy Effectiveness* study suggests, there are dozens of different skills, tasks, and aptitudes involved in the work of ministry.[4]

As a minister reaches a stage of confidence about reading situations, knowing how to respond, leading with risk and responsibility, and relating to the world in its holy and relational depths, we can say this minister is coming to embody a pastoral imagination. A subtle and fluid pastoral imagination grown through years of experience takes on the patina of wisdom in knowing how to approach situations, lead people, and make meaningful change. The concept of pastoral imagination was first coined by Craig Dykstra in the late 1990s, and it has become a common way to describe the situated knowing of the pastoral life.[5]

The practice of ministry is a unified and holistic practice. Becoming a minister, activist, chaplain, or pastor usually entails a sense of calling—an affirmation that is simultaneously personal, communal, and holy. In times prior to the twentieth century, almost all ministry was thought of as an identity. One was born a priest. One's family gave one over to the priesthood.

In the first half of the twentieth century, a new expanded and professionalized understanding of ministry emerged. And in the second half of the century, it took hold such that ministry came to be thought of as a matter of gifts, calling, skills, *and* identity. Both Kathleen Cahalan's work and the "Learning Pastoral Imagination Project: Five-Year Report" detail some of the history and theological significance of this shift to understanding ministry as more of a practice.[6] Although the shift comprised many changes, among the most notable is the expanded possibility of women's entry into the practice of ministry. Before the mid-twentieth century, women could never meet the identity criteria of a male priesthood. In the twenty-first century, a growing number of lesbian, gay, bisexual, transgender, queer-identifying, intersex, and asexual-identifying (LGBTQIA) people are finding places that openly embrace their callings. This new welcome is making space for LGBTQIA folks to serve the church and world with their gifts, skills, and knowledge as ministers. They, too, were excluded from ministry defined by a singular identity. Still, equity in ministry is far from complete.[7]

✎ THE RESEARCH SUPPORTING THIS BOOK

"So you are doing pastoral development work in the LPI Project?"

"Well, no. We're doing research, learning how the practice of ministry develops over time."

Some of our colleagues worried that we were leaning a little much into development work and not enough into research. We patiently staked out a different claim, showing how our work is based on qualitative inquiry that has been otherwise neglected by researchers and that considers the life and work of pastors and ministers, chaplains and activists, youth workers and lay ministers. On the other hand, it turned out that our colleagues were not too far off. We quickly discovered that our research method of making space for stories and conversation turned out to be its own kind of good pastoral practice. Participants in our study not only helped us learn; they also felt supported by the research process.

Developing a practical theology of ministry meant we were involved in what we were doing. We were not keeping our work at arm's length. I can say without reservation that it has been some of the most generative and life-giving work I have ever undertaken. How does the profile of the LPI Project fit into a research landscape?

Research about ministry, starting in the early twentieth century, tends to take one of the following approaches: (1) tracing the history of clerical education and professional practice, (2) examining the roles and tasks of clergy, (3) measuring the effectiveness of people doing ministry as a profession, or (4) interpreting ministry as a theological and spiritual calling. More recently, a new approach is emerging in which qualitative studies of ministry take a more ethnographic approach.

Studies of theological education in the early twentieth century, between the World Wars, assessed schools preparing ministers and the work of the clergy. One study of Black ministry preparation and another of predominantly white ministry preparation helped establish the Association of Theological Schools.[8] In the intervening years, additional histories of ministry appeared, and many focused on particular aspects of the work, such as pastoral care, Christian education, preaching, and the priesthood, again addressing professional development and educational delivery systems. Not only were these early studies of theological education the predecessors of other histories of ministry; they were also a fountainhead of various qualitative studies of congregations, theological education, and ministry.[9] Research centers emerged at Hartford Seminary and Auburn Seminary that, together with the Roman Catholic Church–sponsored Center for Applied Research in the Apostolate (CARA) at Georgetown University, have taken on many research initiatives, assessing churches and ministers in the United States.

Beginning in the 1950s, a series of denominational and more ecumenical studies of ministry began focusing on the roles and tasks of clergy. These tended to be quantitative and descriptive studies that tried to dissect the discrete components of what a minister does.[10] They often resulted in a list of five to ten main roles or tasks of the congregational pastor. Building on the earlier studies, Richard DeShon and his colleagues published a study of United Methodist Church (UMC) clergy in 2010. They started with a pilot project, shifted to focus groups, and finally surveyed 341 UMC clergy. Throughout the process, the project identified sixty-five items of knowledge, skill, ability, and personal characteristics (KSAPs) needed by ministers to do their work effectively.[11] In a summary of the research, DeShon identified thirteen distinct cluster competencies, each with multiple skills, that were necessary for the work of congregational pastors. The following competencies are listed in their ranked order, starting with the most important: communication, preaching and public worship, self-development, caregiving, management, other-development, evangelism, fellowship, administration, relationship-building, rituals and sacraments, UMC connection, and facility construction.[12]

One interesting fact that emerges from this assessment of United Methodist pastors is that congregational ministry needs people who can be *expert generalists*. Even among specialty positions of ministry (i.e., age-level or affinity group pastors), ministerial leaders need to be good at many things, integrate multiple skills, have a range of relational capacities, and access ancient and contemporary knowledge as well as bring it all together in a decisive way.

More recently, Matt Bloom and a team of researchers at Notre Dame decided to bring together the social science literature on labor and work with assessments of human flourishing from the research labs of positive psychology. They are interested in seeing beyond "effectiveness" to assess how ministers might be flourishing, experiencing well-being, and finding happiness in their vocations.[13]

In addition to these historical, quantitative, and social science studies of pastors, priests, and clergy, the last seventy years have also included a steady stream of spiritual and theological studies of ministry. These studies have come primarily from scholars in pastoral and practical theology, beginning with Seward Hiltner's *Preface to Pastoral Theology* and including the work of Edward Farley, Christie Cozad Neuger, Edward Wimberly, and Jaco Hamman, among others.[14] Along the way, many ministers and authors have published pastoral memoirs and fictional accounts of pastors that also serve to point the way to the complexity, subtlety, and beauty of the pastoral life.[15]

More recently, studies of ministry have taken not only a turn to practice but also a definite pivot to ethnographic forms of study. Inspired by congregational studies and practical theology more broadly speaking, a small but growing number of qualitative studies are focusing on the pastoral life. The studies that bring life to this book are all based on a method of theological ethnography. Going beyond historical accounts, lists of ministerial tasks, theological prescriptions, or assessments of flourishing, ethnographic accounts help us see how ministry is practiced and how ministers change over time.[16] The main study that funds the insights and stories of this volume is the LPI Project.[17]

The LPI Project, begun in 2009, is the first longitudinal, national, and ecumenical study of ministry in practice. The project follows fifty pastoral leaders transitioning from seminary into ministry, using daylong group interviews as well as follow-up congregational visits and member interviews to deepen our understanding of the long arc of learning ministry. The project also learns from group interviews with twenty-five pastors who have fifteen to thirty-five years of experience in ministry. The rich diversity of the participants—in terms of denomination, race and ethnicity, gender, region, sexual orientation, and age—offers compelling insight into how, in a variety of contexts, ministers learn and embody pastoral imagination.[18]

Ministers in the LPI Project serve in traditions including Orthodox, Pentecostal, Evangelical and Baptist, mainline Protestant, nondenominational, and Roman Catholic. We sought denominational diversity, with more than twenty denominations among the members; however, our sample was never intended to be representative. The ministers, split evenly between male and female, live in every region of the United States, and a few did, or currently do, live outside the United States. The cohort of fifty includes ministers who are Black, Hispanic, Asian, and white. Participants include those who identify as straight, gay, single, and partnered. At the start of the study, the seminarians ranged in age from midtwenties to midsixties. They had a median age of thirty-four. They are all now a decade older. Twelve of the participants are in clergy couples, although some partners are in the study and some are not.

All the participants of the seminary cohort remain in the study to date. Full retention is surprising and rare.[19] As one participant who has also completed degrees in public health research put it, "That's amazing!" She returned to the theme later in our interview day, remarking on the high participation rate: "When you come, it's so life-giving and helpful . . . that I wouldn't miss the meet-up again."[20] At the five-year mark, approximately half of the LPI study participants worked full time in congregations. Another 35 percent worked as chaplains or nonprofit ministry leaders or were serving part time in congregational ministry. Ten years into the study, 88 percent of the participants were involved in professions (paid or volunteer) of ministry. We maintain regular contact with the ten cohorts, and as of fall 2020, participants in the study were serving as follows: 68 percent in full-time ministry positions, 12 percent in volunteer ministry positions (including one retired volunteer), 4 percent in part-time positions, 8 percent not working due to family care or disability, and 4 percent currently working in nonministry positions. Types of ministry positions include work as congregational priests and pastors; church staff ministers; chaplains in military, higher education, and health care; and ministry educators.[21]

By studying *pastoral imagination*, we are seeking to articulate a minister's capacity for wise and insightful perception and judgment that is both embodied and embedded in particular situations. This capacity integrates skill and know-how, making use of multiple kinds of knowledge about self, context, relationships of power, and ritual practices of ministry. The improvisational character of pastoral imagination strengthens the capacity of ministers to meet the challenges of the cultural complexity of congregational and religious life in the United States. Articulating how ministers learn pastoral imagination over time presses theological education toward deeper integration of classroom learning and ministry practice and better preparation of students for shifting from imagining ministry to pastoral imagination.[22]

KEY LEARNINGS

Over the ten years, we have learned a great many things about how people learn ministry in practice. With care, we published findings in a series of academic articles and reports (see the bibliography). For the purpose of this book, a few key discoveries are worth highlighting. Each of the following insights were always underlying the launch of Three Minute Ministry Mentor (3MMM), an online series of weekly episodes featuring stories from the LPI study, my work with students, other studies of ministry, and my own learning over time as a pastoral leader.

Seeing ministry as a practice that is learned by trial and error, through recognizable stages of growth, and through many rounds of experience allows us to take seriously the reality that learning ministry is a lifelong endeavor and not a three-year process of seminary and internships. As we approached our research by asking questions about learning itself, we saw how the stories and insights confirmed that learning is indeed at the heart of pastoral imagination. And although seminary is an important way station on the path to learning the practice of ministry, it is neither the first, the only, nor the last one.

By following the same group of ministers over time, we see how important integration is for the complex work of ministry. That integration is both vertical and horizontal. In other words, some integration needs to happen between topics and various aspects of knowledge that one learns in seminary. Integration also needs to happen between the acquisition of knowledge and the use of knowledge. And far too often, seminary classes still put a tremendous amount of emphasis on students acquiring knowledge without asking students to integrate what they *know* with what they *do*. Additionally, there is a kind of integration that happens between who a person is (identity) and what that person does (skill) and what that person knows (knowledge and understanding). These various kinds of integration can truly only happen over time.[23]

Closely related to this important facet of integration is the insight that what needs to be known and done in ministry cannot be reduced to any kind of formula or list of steps to take. As our advisor and friend Patricia Benner used to remind us, ministry, like nursing, is open-ended and underdetermined.[24] That means the day-to-day practice of ministry is one continuous effort at improvisation. With each new situation, one needs to draw on skills and knowledge, understanding, and spiritual grounding in order to know how to proceed.

Ministry is similar to nursing in this way; it also resonates with other professional and spiritual practices. Learning ministry has family resemblances with how one learns a sport, a musical instrument, a practice of prayer or yoga, or one of the many everyday skills of life like bicycling, driving a car, or cooking for a family. Thus ministry is aligned with multiple kinds of adult human learning and mastery. Across many different practices, we acquire skills and expertise in very similar ways. Yet ministry remains unique because of its particularity of purpose and context.

THE AHA MOMENTS

In the first round of interviews, we had two significant surprising moments. They accumulated with each unfolding interview of seminarians who were on their way to becoming ministers. The first surprise was that *participants shared more commonalities than differences.* Whether our participants were Pentecostal or Orthodox, Roman Catholic or Reformed, United Methodist or Lutheran, they told us very similar stories about learning in practice. Everything that has been written about how adults learn professional practice pointed in this direction. However, we and those with whom we shared our early findings had a lingering question as we started the study: Would denominational differences be so starkly distinctive as to be incomparable?

Of course denominational differences matter. And the particularity of the pathways is just that—particular. But the contours of ministry itself as a practice and many of the significant way stations along that learning trajectory were very similar from group to group and from person to person. The more significant differences in the pathway to learning were what we came to call "interruptions to the birth of pastoral imagination" or what some of our participants called the "brick walls" they faced in ministry.[25]

Here's what these differences looked like on the ground: Women across all the denominations struggled in particular ways regarding gender. They ran into roadblocks, poor assumptions, stereotypes, and implicit and explicit bias. On the whole, it is fair to say that women, who make up half the study, have made slower advances than men have made. What do I mean by advances? First, finding jobs. A number of women in our study struggled to find sustainable employment as ministers, although some continued to offer ministry without compensation. Some of these pathways for women are denominationally determined or shaped, yet the consistency across the cohort is notable. Nonwhite men also experienced more job changes, work-related conflicts that impacted longevity, and health issues.[26]

This is not to say that the white men have not struggled in any way to find work. Some of them have. Nearly a dozen members of the cohort are or have been part of a clergy couple. This also offers a bit of insight about the gendered challenges on the ministry pathway. For example, when a couple enters a ministry setting, sometimes the community places traditional expectations on a husband and wife team, leading to inequity in their pay, benefits, and/or responsibilities. To be clear, a number of women in the study found stable first, second, and third calls in ministry, yet women of color in our study have been less likely to find paid employment related to their practice of ministry. However, some women of color have clearly "made a way out of no way," as womanist theologian Monica Coleman says.[27] They have defied everyone's expectations for them, overcome many obstacles, and found ways to serve God and their communities with purpose.

Many women in the study struggled with traditional expectations related to family responsibilities. Some women have been less supported or encouraged by family and friends to pursue their work in ministry. And in the present pandemic moment, the inequities are further revealed. For example, when we surveyed the full cohort in the summer and fall of 2020, women reported more struggles under the demands of the pandemic. And more women than men reported taking leaves of absence from full-time ministry during this period, including three white women who ended long-term ministry positions during the summer or fall of 2020. The full impact of the global pandemic on the sustainability of ministry will not be visible for some time to come.

Our second aha moment in the first round of interviewing was that *learning in practice does indeed happen in practice and not so much in classrooms.* In the first round of interviews, we heard stories about aha moments of learning coming at the point of being a camp counselor or clinical pastoral education (CPE) student, serving on internships, and participating in field education. We heard very few stories about learning for ministry that happened while a participant read a textbook, took a test, wrote a paper, or listened to a lecture. While this finding seems incredibly obvious to say, it goes against the ethos of many seminaries. Theological educators still largely emphasize knowledge *acquisition* and pay far less attention to knowledge *use.* The most powerful stories of theological educators we heard about in the study were the ones who taught by sharing their own experiences as ministers. Other teachers who left a strong impression made a point of integrating skills of leadership and practice with the deep knowledge of their discipline(s). A few of the most exemplary theological educators had a way of teaching cases or models that captured the dynamics of ministry and brought them into their classrooms.

Studies of the best teachers in higher education reveal that this is the kind of teaching that really sticks with students. It is the kind that brings together powerful understanding and its usefulness in almost any classroom. Medicine, law, engineering, and other professional schools, including ministry, prepare their students best when they set a high bar of integration among knowledge, skill, and character. Whether schools are able to do this successfully is only truly evidenced in their students. And yet students will find a way once in practice to integrate what they know, how to act, when and where to respond, and why things matter. They are able to do this better when they've had a well-integrated educational experience.[28] But the practice itself has no substitute. For example, Malinda learned from a CPE educator to "hold the baby" when making a pastoral care visit to a new family. Yet that saying came to have an entirely different and deeper meaning when she saw through the experience of preaching how embodied presence, *holding the baby*, is a part of every aspect of ministry.

🪶 SURPRISES IN LATER ROUNDS OF INTERVIEWS

In the second round of interviewing, we came to a surprising moment in gathering after gathering. We noticed it immediately with the first group, graduates of Luther Seminary, then in each succeeding group. No longer were these people nervous, slightly anxious, tension-filled students. They were calmer. They spoke more deliberately. They were no less present, no less funny, and possibly more engaging. But their way of seeing and being in the world had changed. My field notes include phrases like "Everyone seemed really relaxed and at ease ... much more mature ... calmer and wiser." The word we found ourselves using most when debriefing was *gravity*.

The second and the third rounds of interviewing brought a fresh set of stories about classroom learning. Now when we asked ministers what prepared them for the practice of ministry, they were able to reach back to moments from their seminary education as one of many important aspects of preparation. They also talked about other jobs they had held, such as Trong's experience of managing a bookstore, which taught him about managing people by caring for them, or Greg's place on the seminary video production team, which was coming in handy as he created short videos for his church. During their first five years of ministry, pastors and chaplains and educators were able to tell us about how they learned from missteps, such as Grace's lesson to show up in person to pray when her parishioners were having surgery. And they also told us about how they recovered from more substantial mistakes, such as one pastor's failure to recognize or affirm his wife's call to ministry. Many pastors recalled what professors and mentors said to them years earlier.

In the third round of interviews, when most ministers in the study had been out of seminary for five years, we began to hear more about the struggles, isolation, and relational challenges of ministry. This was also the stage when ministers began to tell us about how they learned the essential practices of prayer, or Sabbath, or training a hawk, or therapy, or long walks, or forgiveness. The spiritual grounding of ministry became utterly clear at this round of interviewing. As researchers, we could begin to make out the contours of ministry *as a spiritual practice*. Some ministers such as Malinda came to that reality quickly, finding a rhythm of work and surviving a storm of congregational dissatisfaction in her first call.[29] For others like Fr. Lucas, it took several years of sinking into a deep pit of isolation and "erosion" before he saw the spiritual path he might take out of that lonely place. What he says he learned is that praying, finding a mentor, and gaining a profound level of acceptance were in fact the *only* pathway out of being merely the "priest who would close the church."

We also focused in the third round of interviewing on asking study participants to share with us how specific aspects of their pastoral work changed over time. They talked us through the ways that they shifted their approach to weekly preaching, teaching the confirmation class, visiting hospital patients, leading a building project, and recruiting volunteers. Many of these stories from each stage of the project now fill the pages of this book.

THE STORIES AND CONVERSATIONS

One of my own aha moments as I put this book together was how much of my own learning in practice was woven into the narratives. When we began the research, Chris Scharen and I thought carefully, and we decided to present stories from our own ministry experience as examples of the kind of depth and complexity we were hoping to hear from participants. Some ethnographic and qualitative researchers might find this method questionable. But we were not after objective facts or disembodied data. We wanted shared wisdom and narratives of learning. We could not somehow set ourselves apart from that wisdom because both Chris and I brought our full experience as ordained ministers, researchers, professors, parents, and people of faith into the rooms where we met study participants.[30]

Interview days typically began with coffee, tea, and some breakfast foods. We gathered over the food and with informal greetings and catching up with each other. Then we would sit down and make a frame for our conversation that would last all day—with lots of breaks and food and even short walks. Interview days were typically held in retreat centers or churches. When we gathered with each small cohort of five people for the first round of interviews, Chris and I both shared personal stories from our time in congregational and nonprofit ministry with the group. In them, we tried to reflect the complexity, messiness, and beauty of the work of following God's calling into a practice and profession. We also talked about the roadblocks, complications, and brick walls we found ourselves up against at times. We also prayed with every group, and we have prayed for them as individuals consistently and relationally over the last ten years.

Looking back on this early research choice and also the way I work in my seminary classrooms, I should not be surprised that my own stories found their way into this book as part of a conversation about learning in practice. Putting our own stories into the research helped us create an environment of trust and willingness to risk. We were not dispassionate, distant, and "objective" researchers but fellow ministers, spiritual pilgrims, and learners. My hope is that the same will be true for the ways this book weaves stories of the study participants with my stories and provocative questions to draw out *your* stories.

Neither should it surprise me that teaching and writing about experience would cause one to draw on experience. But in the first book I wrote on ministry, I chose intentionally and completely to focus on the clergywomen whom I had interviewed in order to renarrate a story of Baptists.[31] This book is far more dialogue between my life and the lives of fifty new seminary graduates, twenty-five seasoned ministers and priests, and a host of students and mentors I've worked with over the last ten years. From multiple angles, I have been attempting to understand the character, shape, course of trajectory, and necessary conditions for cultivating the rich and complex practice of ministry.

THE CONDITIONS AND CONTEXT

With this book, I want to introduce to you a variety of stories, insights, and questions that can support you in your cultivation of pastoral imagination. And in the process, I hope it will help you become more improvisational, resourceful, and empathic to yourself and to others. Only you can learn these things *in practice* and with time and experience. I also hope this book helps you ground yourself in prayer and spiritual practice and be intentional about choosing mentors, thoughtful in your self-reflection, and willing to look back at your missteps and your growth. When you have engaged in learning the practice of ministry in these ways, I hope you might be able to say to yourself something like "Look! I have changed. I have moved from one way of doing things to another, and it is part of a long pathway of growth that resonates with many ministers, and yet it is also uniquely my own."

This process is of course not all up to you alone. The spirit of God and calling of Jesus are at the heart of this process if you are a Christian minister. And to be clear, your practice of ministry will also take shape in a way that is poured into and shaped by a particular context. Perhaps your bishop sends you to a declining church, or the only congregation in your free-church tradition that will hire you is in a town where the mill closed twenty-five years ago, or you are queer-identifying and you have waited more than a year to get an interview. Factors like context, injustice, and stereotypes will shape your ministry in ways that are beyond your control. In these very difficult and demanding circumstances, the need for a thoughtful and courageous pastoral imagination is essential.

One of our advisers in the LPI Project, pastor and director of the Transition into Ministry program David Wood, regularly posed this question: *What conditions are necessary for the growth and flourishing of pastoral imagination?*

It took time for me to understand the significance of this question. After a couple of full rounds of interviewing, I shifted my focus from individual

ministers on their own pathways, and I could see how much of a role local conditions play. People end up in circumstances that sometimes allow growth and
flourishing. But they can also end up in circumstances that may not make room
for much growth at all. In those poor conditions or toxic contexts, ministers
may struggle simply to survive.

With any and every circumstance of ministry, there will be aspects of the
situation, some obvious and also more hidden, that are definitely going to be
beyond your control. There will be some things that are deeply entrenched and
resistant to change or even grace. That is when the power of pastoral imagination is most needed. You will be called on to see the situation before you
and work with the people and the circumstances to see the presence of mercy,
grace, and divine energy so that you might lead with *situated possibility*. Learning what to do in any given moment is a matter of bringing together everything
you know, drawing on each capacity and skill, leaning into trusted relationships, and grounding yourself in the particularity of the situation. As social
learning theorists Jean Lave and Etienne Wenger say, "In our view, learning is
not merely situated in practice—as if it were some independently reifiable process that just happened to be located somewhere; learning is an integral part of
generative social practice in the lived-in world."[32]

The way you enter into a new ministry context will be conditioned and shaped
not only by the geographical and historical locations of the place but also by
your social location and that of the people you serve. My first call to ministry
out of seminary was shaped by the geography of North Georgia and the small
town where the church was located. It was a new building sitting on formerly
Indigenous land within sight of the Etowah Indian Mounds and surrounded
on three sides by cotton fields. My failure to understand fully that geography of
the erasure of Indigenous Peoples and the subsequent history of enslavement
and later Jim Crow laws in Bartow County diminished what I could offer as a
minister in that place.

My early work in becoming a minister was also shaped by the history of
being a particular kind of Baptist at a particular time in history. I was much
more aware of the effects of that condition on my development as a pastoral
presence. I have written at length about that history and its impact.[33] I was
also shaped by my social location as a cisgender, white-identifying, educated,
middle-class, married woman. I was aware of my social location, but at that
stage of my life, I was still far from conversant in how white privilege shaped my
identity or my ministry. I was highly aware of how I had suffered as a woman
excluded from full humanity. I was less aware of how my social location allowed
and encouraged me to participate in systemic and personal racism, which
caused many harms to my neighbors who identified as Black, Indigenous, and/

or persons of color (BIPOC). My socialization as a white person made me complicit in a system that attempts to define these neighbors as less than fully human. It is an ongoing lifetime of work for me as a white-identifying person in this country to come to terms with my social location and change my commitments at their roots.

Readers of this book will come from many different social locations. Can we connect and learn from each other without erasing these differences? The ten years of this project help me say *yes*. Not with boldness or certainty but with humility. People whose stories make up the content of this book live in multiple and widely varied geographical, historical, and social locations. I work with each study participant, student, and mentor to ensure that the ways I interpret and tell their stories show up in a way they recognize and that they encounter in writing as faithful to their lived experiences. The book strives to create a space much like an interview day or a classroom where a variety and range of experiences come into the moment. Unlike the one-way communication of television and movies, this book is designed to evoke and invoke a conversation. It aspires to host an exchange between ministers on many pathways, and me and you, as we walk patiently together through listening, thinking, and imagining how these stories help us bring a practice to life.

As we think of the conditions that make pastoral imagination possible, we can consider how certain conditions are universal in the way they make space for adult human learning. But the conditions of ministry in the United States (and other places) are grounded in white ownership of space and privileges of money and power. And because ministry has primarily been a paid calling for communities with means and social capital, and because of the politics of respectability, in which marginalized groups get caught up in adopting the values of the dominant group, the *ideal* of ministry and the *profession* of ministry are deeply complicit in the racist structures of US society. By implication, the structures are rooted in European ways of life and colonialism that spanned the globe, reshaping communities and people into subjects of white domination. We have so normalized and embraced uncritically these privileged and racist structures of ministry that we are convinced they are biblical, spiritual, and wise. Similarly, the structures of patriarchy also continue to reinvent themselves, finding new ways to marginalize women and BIPOC.

How do we get out of this trap? There are no quick fixes or easy ways out. Committing to the equality, justice, and significance of Black lives in a society built on the labors, bodies, blood, and sorrow of enslaved people is critical as a starting point. Prioritizing the voices, experiences, and insights of people who have been marginalized in ministry is another important step toward commitment. In particular, moving the voices and experiences of Black women and LGBTQIA people into the center of our conversations and learning will be key to unsettling the dominant structures of power. Working to shake loose the racist ideologies and assumptions from white churches and religious groups is yet another crucial and hard-to-accomplish step. To do antiracist, antisexist work and to include the intersections of resisting ableism, homophobia, and transphobia, long-term commitments of solidarity are needed. We have a moral obligation both to hope and to work toward becoming part of redemptive change (see Appendix: Questions for Redemptive Change).

THE POSSIBILITIES FOR USING THIS BOOK

Given the times we are living in, there is a clear and present need for faith leaders to lead with moral responsibility and renewed vision. We need pastoral imagination to extend into every part of life. This book takes slices of learning on the ground in practice and offers them up in brief presentations to unfold the ways that learning ministry happens in actual lives.

This book has been coming to life for many years now. Going back to my early studies of clergywomen more than fifteen years ago, my interest in understanding the lives of ministers and helping them learn from one another runs deep. I was fortunate that my first academic job, co-directing the LPI study, allowed me to pursue this love. Two years ago, I knew that I wanted to get these stories out to the world in a way that was both easily available and accessible. During a vacation in the summer of 2018, I opened up my journal and made a list from A to Z two times. If I could make a list of topics that filled fifty-two weeks, I was ready to begin. I think it took me about thirty minutes to make that list. That was the birth of 3MMM, an online platform that makes the stories of ministry and my reflection on them as a researcher, professor, and minister available to people who need inspiration and information to support their practice of ministry. Many stories from season one of 3MMM fill the pages of this book.[34]

Although there is no map that shows a single route to learning the practice of ministry, a multilayered map is a good metaphor for the fifty chapters of this book. Each chapter is like another layer of the landscape. One shows the topography and water table. Another shows the plants and trees and animal trails. Yet another layer indicates different historical boundaries across time. Another layer of the map fills in the current streets and dwellings. Yet another slice highlights the businesses and pricing of gas, hotels, and restaurants. Another layer might show live traffic or weather, and still another shows a particular route to a particular destination. All the maps together are telling you about a single place, and together they are giving you a richer understanding of that place. Only you can go to the place itself and experience it. But these thin slices of the map will help you prepare for what you will experience for yourself. They will give you language, stories, and possibilities to help you cultivate your own pastoral imagination for life and leadership.

Chapter topics address indispensable concepts such as defining moments, navigating conflict, brick walls, future stories, being there, and failing creatively.

Each one of the chapters explores a single concept through a story or several stories from actual lives of seminarians, pastors, priests, activists, ministers, and chaplains gathered from the LPI study and other qualitative studies of ministry. The chapters can also be treated like small case studies that reveal important issues, concepts, perspectives, and ways to approach the challenges that come with ministry. They deal alternately with mundane and crisis moments.

The stories in each chapter are also accompanied by resources to help you take the ideas deeper, including a set of provocative open-ended questions. The questions are addressed directly to you—the teachers and learners who will use the book. They are designed to spark conversation between you and other classmates or ministry friends. They can be used to give structure to a discussion with your field education supervisor or mentor. They can also be a guide for exploring the practice of ministry with your peer group. Or they can simply be a launching point for your journal reflections. Together, the stories, resources, and questions will support you in exploring how each aspect of ministry practice might flourish and grow in your own life.

Students, I hope this book comes to you at a time when you are soaking up everything you can about how to understand and imagine the practice of ministry becoming your own. I think the book will be an encouragement and support for your learning. I hope the questions will provoke you to reflect deeply on yourself and the places you are serving. I also hope the resources that make up the syllabus of this book will give you conversations that carry on beyond it for years to come. I believe you will see a bit of your own experience somewhere in these pages, and I encourage you to borrow from the learning of others who have gone before you and are just a bit ahead on the pathway.

Professors, this book is for you if you hope to teach your college or seminary students about the practice of ministry and how to bring the learning to life for them. The questions make excellent conversation starters for classrooms. The brief chapters can be assigned to jump-start online or face-to-face discussions. The bibliography is like a syllabus for teaching and learning the practice of ministry. I hope the book will help you deepen your imagination for your own teaching of any subject or field by inviting you to think about how what you teach really matters. I also hope it will help you hold these ministry learners in your mind as you plan courses for future students.

Supervisors and mentors, this book is especially for you in your work of supporting and walking alongside novices and beginners to the practice of ministry. I hope the questions will be seeds for important conversations that you will have with seminarians, CPE students, and new ministers. My hope is that the stories herein, which are grounded in the love and sacred presence of God that infuse the world, will help you as you bear witness honestly to suffering and brokenness and also do the work of midwifing new ministers in the possibilities for healing, compassion, and delight that come with the work of ministry.

Seminary graduates, ministry apprentices, social justice activists, interns and residents, and new priests and ministers, this book is made up of stories from people just where you are right now. Their experiences are wildly different and unique to them. However, they, like you, are learning the complex and beautiful practice of ministry with all of its giant leaps and baby steps, trip-ups and fumbles, and recoveries and grace along the way. I hope this book will draw out your wisdom while also encouraging you to keep pressing on with each new experience that comes your way.

Experienced clergy, chaplains, and nonprofit community ministers, this book is an invitation to think about how you are supporting and nourishing the next generation of ministers. When you have been in the work for many years, it can be challenging to remember what it is like to be *new in ministry*. The stories and insights of this book may help you regain your sense of empathy and compassion for what it is like to begin. And if you are supervising, teaching, or working alongside ministers who are still getting their feet on the ground, this book will help you ask thoughtful questions and listen actively and supportively.

Perhaps the very ideas of *ministry as a practice* and *pastoral imagination* are new to you. If so, then the questions and stories herein may evoke new possibilities for how you integrate knowledge, skill, gifts, and experience as you bring ministry to life each day. Wherever you are on your pathway of learning ministry, see this as your invitation to pause and think and hopefully talk to some of your peers about your practice of ministry. I urge you to connect with others around meaningful questions that make the demands of pastoral life more sustainable.

From whatever place you enter this conversation, I trust that you are carrying with you your communities and your callings in your heart. This work of serving the world and serving a holy purpose means you are cultivating a richness of knowing about the world and its brokenness. You are also discovering the potential for grace, humility, and—though I always feel reluctant to use the word—transformation. To see this practice and the wisdom of pastoral imagination unfurl over years of time and through tragedies and life changes is a truly profound gift.

Pentecost 2020

50 Ministry Topics

1

Ministry as a Practice

Ministry is a verb: it is something people do. We can understand ministry as a practice that is social and communal, expressed within a historical tradition, embodied, relational, spiritual, and professional.

—Kathleen Cahalan, *Introducing the Practice of Ministry*

Stepping into that first hospital room as a CPE student. Getting that first call in the middle of the night to show up for a family whose father just died. Standing up to preach my first public sermon to fewer than a dozen people with a video camera at the back of the chapel broadcasting the service to patient rooms all over the hospital. Having to lead the hymns myself. Ugh.

Three years later. Sitting surrounded by boxes and to-do lists and Sunday coming at me like a freight train. Realizing there is a whole big thing the search committee forgot to tell me about my new ministry job: I need to design and direct a children's camp for six churches next summer. Feeling the crush of exhausted volunteers who want my support and others who wish I would just take over their jobs. The unfilled roles in the church nursery. The policies that must be reevaluated. The children's time, the newsletter article, and the pastoral prayer, all to be written over the next three days.

Seven years later. Prepping to preach on the first night as youth-camp pastor. Feeling the weight of expectation. Wondering if I can bring my best self to the hundreds of young people and their leaders. Doubting myself. Sitting in silence cross-legged on the dorm-style bed, hands resting on my knees, trying to let everything go into the vast presence of the holy. Breathing deeply to take in God's mercy.

Three beginning moments in ministry at three different seasons of my life: each one is fraught with expectation, a mix of anxiety and trust, the newness that is simultaneously exhilarating and overwhelming. In each of these moments, I was embarking on a new ministry, and while I could draw on past experiences, I was in every way a beginner each time.

Ministry itself, like most professions and complex practices, is dogged and driven by a rush to *achieve*. Yet to focus on achievement can be disastrous, especially if we skip over the steps for learning. To learn the practice of ministry—a multifaceted professional and spiritual practice—takes time and preparation, risk and responsibility, support and feedback.

When we build on prior experience to take on a new aspect of ministry, the practice as a whole expands and deepens. However, we cannot really avoid the beginner phase of learning something new.

Wherever you are on the journey of learning the practice of ministry—at the beginning, somewhere in the middle, or near the end—it can serve you well to pause and consider your own ministry *as a practice learned over time* and enter into a conversation with yourself and your colleagues, your peers and mentors, about how your learning is unfolding.

✦✦✦

Eventually, I stepped with confidence into the rooms of hospital patients and preached with less trepidation and more of a sense of delight. Over time, I managed the daily life of ministry with volunteers and projects, camps, fundraisers, and weekly worship. I grew and changed and matured. But I did not have the language to describe what was happening or how it worked. I did not really know what conditions would help me best grow or learn effectively.

Like many ministers in our time, I simply went to seminary, pressed hard to learn everything put in front of me, and hoped I would be ready for the work when it finally came. Like many women in the last fifty years, I had a clear calling and gifts but not a clear path to serve. After completing a unit of CPE, graduating from seminary, sending out stacks of résumés and letters, and interviewing with a dozen different churches and agencies, I received a call.

I was ready, right? But immediately upon arriving at the North Georgia church and starting to unpack, I saw how unready I was.

The problems were several. I did not know what I did not know. I had lots of ideas and the beginnings of a sense of my identity as a pastoral presence. I said to all who asked me why I did not stay in school for another graduate degree, "I want to know what I've learned in seminary *all the way down*." I did not know for sure what knowing "all the way down" might look like or how it would come to pass. But I did have an inkling that it would take me out of my head full of ideas and into some kind of embodied and emotionally rich kind of knowing.

Perhaps what I lacked most in those years of CPE, congregational ministry, and even the summer of being a camp pastor was a framework that helped me see myself as learning a practice that would unfold and blossom over years. Long after these experiences, and in retrospect, I came to see how my ministry was indeed a practice and something I learned gradually with more and more experiences.

⌘

After five and a half years of serving the congregation in North Georgia, with more learning than I could name or fully process, I returned to graduate school. While I was in the doctoral program at Vanderbilt, I learned about the "novice to expert" continuum of adult learning from the literature of pedagogy and psychology. However, it was not until I began my first academic job that I learned more fully about how this framework could be useful for understanding one's growth in ministry practice.

Just a few months into my first full-time academic job, I found myself sitting in a large conference hall in Indianapolis. The room was filled with round tables. At each table sat groups of ministers from the newest and brightest to the wisest and most seasoned. We were meeting together to think about the transition from seminary into ministry.

The plenary session was led by senior nursing scholar Patricia Benner and my new research partner and practical theologian, Chris Scharen. They shared stories about becoming a nurse and becoming a pastor, respectively. Step by step, Benner and Scharen sketched out an arc of learning that moved from novice, through advanced beginner, to competency and proficiency, and finally to wise expert.[1]

As I witnessed the presentation, it welled up in me with clarity that until that moment, I had no such vision of ministry *as a practice*. Nor could I see how learning ministry might unfold over a time beyond seminary. The really stunning moment landed with a thud: my early years of ministry lacked any strong sense of support for this kind of learning in my congregation.

Don't get me wrong—as far as first assignments for Baptist clergywomen in the South go, my call to North Georgia was a good one. And in those early years of ministry, I learned about reflecting theologically in the moment and on the fly. I witnessed my own gifts blooming, and I found some of my limits and those of others. I learned about leading people of all ages, recovering after letdowns, attending to grief, proclaiming good news, and navigating conflict.

All this was more than I could possibly have imagined on that first day of CPE or the day I stepped out of my car and surveyed the brick church surrounded by a Georgia cotton field three years later. It was more that I could have ever imagined sitting on the college dorm bed getting ready to preach to campers seven years after that. But when the thud of realization finally sounded fifteen years later, a lot of pieces of learning a practice began to fall together.

Nevertheless, I surely do wish that somewhere along the way someone might have suggested that each of these beginnings were truly beginnings and the learning was still yet to come. I wish someone might have shared a book like Kathleen Cahalan's *Introducing the Practice of Ministry*. But it did not exist yet.

Fortunately, it does now, and the book brings to life many aspects of how ministry is indeed a practice, starting with a biblical framework for ministry rooted in the stories, actions, and words of Jesus. Cahalan articulates a theological foundation and vision for ministry as a gift coming from the "two hands of God," one hand being the life of Jesus, the other hand being the charisms (gifts) of the Spirit.[2] And she also draws on the novice-to-expert developmental framework as a process and pathway of learning ministry over time.[3]

Not only does Cahalan introduce ministry as a form of discipleship and leadership. She also develops multiple important aspects of Christian ministry. She says ministry as a practice is

+ made of intentional actions (but not all actions are practices) with human goods as the aim;
+ shaped in communities with shared traditions, meanings, and purposes;
+ expressed through identity, embodiment, knowledge, and convictions;
+ open to corruption, brokenness, and sin; and
+ expressed as a spiritual exercise, attending to God's presence.[4]

Ministry *as a practice* is a complex and rich way to see your own beginnings, midpoints, and ends of learning and vocation. The framework and the many facets of practice are also an invitation for you to explore and understand your work in ministry.

QUESTIONS FOR REFLECTION AND CONVERSATION

Consider the following to guide your journaling or spark conversation with mentors and friends:

+ How can I see ministry not only as a matter of skills and knowledge or identity? How can I also see ministry as a practice?
+ How have my experiences so far changed how I understand and practice ministry?
+ What is still out on the horizon to be learned about bringing ministry to life?

THREE MINUTE MINISTRY MENTOR

Watch episode 1, "Ministry as a Practice," https://3mmm.us/Episode1

2

Seeing Holy Depths

But at the edge of these otherwise everyday, commonplace, ordinary occasions, comes an invitation by some irresistible force, by God, to come closer and listen more attentively.

—Renita Weems, *Listening for God*

Each time we gather with a group of seminarians or new pastors or experienced ministers in the LPI Project, we spend a full day hearing their stories about learning, life, and vocation. Over the course of the interview day, I find myself drawn in and standing in the holiest of spaces. Giving patient, careful attention to the stories of another person is itself a holy experience.

What do I mean by *holy*?

It is not simply an emotional experience, yet I am moved emotionally when I step on holy ground. It is not simply an intellectual experience. Neither do I leave my thinking brain behind when I enter holy depths. Having a sacred or holy experience is one that engages my whole embodied self and my fully relational self as well.

Certain seasons of the year put me in the frame of holy space and time. Advent is one of those seasons. It gives me a quiet resting place in the middle of the headlong rush to the end of the school term, the end of the calendar year, the urgency of balancing the books, and planning for holidays. All of that can be exhausting, even if it is completely necessary.

Yet Advent brings me everyday reminders of the holy. Breaking in all around me is a sense of the utter silence and sacred presence that upholds all of creation. From breath to breath, I can reconnect to that ground and source of being.

When I am interviewing ministers, chaplains, activists, and pastors at every stage of the journey, I also find myself surrounded by a sense of sacred presence, as if my feet are touching holy ground.

When we met Eve, she was a young Lutheran minister just out of seminary and not yet ordained. As we sat together in one of the LPI interview circles, Eve shared stories from her full year of internship as well as completing a unit of CPE. Both experiences gave her many "firsts" in the practice of ministry. Eve told us a CPE story about her own moment of stepping into holy depths and encountering the sacred in the very midst of her work:

> Eve was on call one weekend for a hospice facility. Just after going on a run, she was called in. She had to clean up quickly and drive twenty minutes to the care facility. The crisis was with an elderly couple Eve knew from prior visits. The wife was suffering from severe dementia, and the husband, a hospice patient, had a stroke that afternoon and was dying.
>
> The couple's daughter, Nancy, a Methodist minister, had not yet arrived. Their son Jim asked Eve: "What should I do? Should I bring Mom in? Will that make her worse? Will she go into a panic attack?" Eve helped Jim clarify his desire to help his mom be with her husband. They wheeled his mom down and gathered in Dad's room. Eve prayed at the bedside. As she remembers it, the man died just as she said, "Into your hands we commend his spirit."
>
> "He died right there," she told us in the group interview. "It was a definite growing moment, like, holy cow, this stuff is real!"
>
> Reflecting on the experience, Eve remarked that she had to shift from worry about what her role was, to confidence that she could actually step in and be a resource for the family, helping with a concrete decision to take the wife in and leading a prayer around the dying husband.
>
> Nancy, the daughter, arrived shortly after the death. She went into the room with her dad and sobbed in grief. Eve recalls, "To stand outside that door and witness that was kind of beautiful, but just really hard, too. I was there for like five hours while we were waiting. It was a long day."[1]

There is so much to be noticed in what we encounter in the holy depths as pastors and ministers. So whether you're out leading a protest or at a bedside like Eve was or if you are in your church office or at a youth retreat, wherever you find yourself, the holy is already present. Learning how to be present to that and how to speak to it is one of the great challenges of learning to inhabit a pastoral imagination.

Eve has been featured in other publications of the LPI Project. You can read more of her story in "The Learning Pastoral Imagination Project: Five-Year Report."[2] One of the main findings explored in that report is that pastoral imagination is needed for inhabiting ministry as a spiritual practice, opening up self and community to the presence and power of God.

❧❧❧

Let us be clear. There are no guarantees when it comes to holiness. And no formula can deliver the holy to your doorstep, your prayer life, or your sermon. Holiness can surprise you as it surprised Eve. It can elude you for years, as it did for pastor and professor Renita Weems.

In her beautiful and honest book *Listening for God: A Minister's Journey through Silence and Doubt*, Weems describes her long and winding journey of struggle and disillusionment with God, the church, and faith itself.[3] Even while she was preaching, teaching, parenting, and writing, Weems felt "lost and disoriented."[4] The book describes a long season she calls in retrospect "a spiritual breakdown—questioning seriously my belief in God, prayer, religious texts, and rituals to such a degree that I couldn't bear to talk or read about anything having to do with the sacred."[5]

Weems recalls an encounter with a young, professional woman who was angry, disappointed, and smoldering in her own crisis of faith and doubt. She drove Weems around a city following the author's keynote address. In what should have been a fifteen-minute delivery to a hotel, the car ride turned into an hour-long discussion, with the younger woman pelting Weems with questions about God, family, faith, and prayer.[6] When Weems could not make a stellar defense of the faith, the young woman demanded, "So, why the hell don't you just walk away from it and stop being a hypocrite?"[7]

Weems, who was deep in her own spiritual crisis, heard herself responding, "For the same reason I don't walk away from any of the myriad of things I've committed myself to. I don't want to live my life based solely on my feelings. Feelings change from one moment to the next."[8] The conversation continued a little further, and the young woman remained unconvinced. But Weems says, looking back, it was an encounter that "permanently changed" her own trajectory.[9]

Being pushed into a theological and spiritual corner, Weems says, "I remembered something I had forgotten. I remembered what prompted me to become a minister in the first place."[10] Her endless curiosity about the holy had drawn her into the work of ministry. And that night in the car, driving around an unfamiliar city, she said she remembered that "whatever spirituality is, it is not something to be discovered. It is something to be recovered—something you misplace and recover a thousand times in a lifetime."[11]

No matter where you are engaged in ministry—from leading protests to preparing for Sunday communion, from distributing diapers to preaching about peace—attention to the holy depths of the moment is a part of the practice of ministry. Learning to attend and speak to the sacredness of a moment is one of the postures of ministry that takes careful, patient attention. And even when a sense of the holy escapes you entirely, the discipline of asking the question "How is God showing up in the space, this moment, this situation?" remains your work.

QUESTIONS FOR REFLECTION AND CONVERSATION

Consider the following to guide your journaling or spark conversation with mentors and friends:

- How will I enter into each holy moment of my day this week?
- How will I speak into that moment as a pastor and invite those with me to notice the sacredness of the space?
- When I find myself bereft of the holy, where do I turn? What do I do? What questions can I ask?

THREE MINUTE MINISTRY MENTOR

Watch episode 2, "Seeing Holy Depths," https://3mmm.us/Episode2

3

Self-Reflection

> Collective care, reciprocity, and love are the forces that
> reshaped my understandings and actions. And self-reflection
> was key to a long, everyday process of internal transformation.
>
> —Darnell L. Moore, *No Ashes in the Fire*

I remember early in the planning stages of the LPI Project that Chris Scharen and I had several thoughtful conversations about whether *self-reflection* was essential for a robust pastoral imagination. Remember that pastoral imagination is the capacity to see into a situation in all its embodied, spiritual, and relational depths and then be able to make a fitting pastoral response. My long years of observing and reading and practicing pastoral theology, care, and counseling told me that self-reflection was a crucial if not universal component of pastoral practice.

As I recall, in that moment at the start of our research, Chris was not so certain. We tried to think of examples in which pastors perhaps acted in the best interests of their congregations but without self-reflection. The examples we found were unclear. We did not at that point have enough data to know if any of those pastors were in fact able to reflect on themselves. Nor did we have a measure or guideline to judge effectiveness.

In the ten intervening years, my thoughts about self-reflection and ministry have solidified. In these years, and over hundreds of interviews, I cannot recall an instance of wise pastoral practice or a person of whom I would say *they really just exercised some profound pastoral imagination* that did not include the minister's very credible ability to be self-reflective.

To be clear, no one can be *fully* self-reflective. We all carry implicit biases and unconscious stories with us that are hard to unearth for examination. And there are parts of us that are never fully available to our own perception or assessment. For example, we can never experience our own face as it reacts to other humans. We cannot see ourselves walking through a room, nor can we sit in a congregation and hear ourselves preach. Technology that records and captures images can lead us into thinking that we are able to perceive our-selves, but in fact we are not in real time and real presence able to see ourselves as anyone else does. So we rely on feedback from others, and we embrace a willingness to be *self-reflective*.

We can also acknowledge that *self-reflection* is not self-indulgence. It is not self-preoccupation. Nor is it selfish. Self-reflection, when you are try-ing to cultivate the practice of ministry, is a crucial element of shifting self-preoccupied worries (i.e., *How am I doing?*) into the background of your thinking. What comes into the foreground of thinking? The situation immedi-ately before you comes into focus. That very important shift is at once a greater self-awareness and also a greater freedom to pay careful attention to the people and situations right in front of you.

⟨❧⟩

In one of my first seminary teaching opportunities, I remember a student com-ing to me and through conversation begin to make a self-reflective shift in his thinking. Jake was studying to become an Episcopal priest.[1] He stopped me one day after a pastoral care and theology class and said, "I'd like to come by and chat with you one day."

"Of course," I responded. A couple of days later, we got together in the sem-inary cafeteria, and he began to vent about his concerns about another student in the class. He said, "She is really bugging me, especially during discussion time. She talks too much, interrupts, gets off topic. She's driving me crazy!"

He continued, "She's either not really paying attention to what's going on, or she's talking too much." He continued to complain for a while, and I lis-tened. Within my own thoughts, I also commiserated. She was a challenge. But I kept quiet and let him say what he needed to say. And after a while, he ran out of steam. Clearly what he wanted was for me to do something about her. He wanted me to change the situation.

I asked him this question: "Jake, do you think that there might ever be anyone in your parish who will be anything like the student in our classroom?"

A look dawned on his face. "Oh, right!" he said. "This is my chance, isn't it? To start thinking about how to relate to this person now."

"That's right! This is not just about what you want to fix about the situa-tion or how you wish it could be different. It's about how you see yourself differ-ently and find ways to respond pastorally—starting now." We talked through a few possible responses and also why the situation made him feel so anxious.

This was an important turning point for Jake. "You can start here," I reminded him. "You don't have to wait until you're in the parish. You can begin thinking about *how you reflect on yourself* and *how you're responding to this person right in front of you, right now.*"

⟨❧⟩

Not everyone entering into the work of ministry has the privileges that Jake did. Both the church and seminary made a space for Jake to show up as a person called to ministry, which in turn made room for his self-reflection. Being white, middle-aged, and male meant being seen, with few questions or doubts, as a potential religious leader.

To engage in self-reflection requires a hospitable space where one is seen and recognized as belonging. Not everyone has that experience with seminary or church. Far from it. In his beautiful and vulnerable memoir, *No Ashes in the Fire*, activist and author Darnell Moore tells the painful and poignant story of growing up in Camden, New Jersey, in the 1980s and 1990s. Moore says his stories reveal "all the invisible, and not-so-hidden, forces that rendered my blackness criminal, my black manhood vile, my black queerness sinful, and my black city hood."[2] Much of his life he says he lived on the "edges of the margins."[3]

After many disappointments, traumas, and a persistent yet mostly covert and frustrating search for identity and belonging, Moore found himself giving up one night. He attempted to take enough pills to end his suffering, but as he says, "I won by failing."[4] Early the next morning, his friend Warren called and then came to his aid. It was Easter weekend, and Warren took Darnell to church on Sunday. There he followed Christ and was baptized. In his remaining years as a student at Seaton Hall, Moore says, "I poured my love into a god I worshipped while slowly denying love to myself." He became a campus ministry leader yet continued to hide his queerness and the fullness of his humanity from those he led in song and prayer. The church, he says, was a complicated place, both attracting and repelling him: "The church had harmed me more than it healed me."[5]

Moore says, "Faith in God can be a powerful tool on the route to self-discovery and healing, but people can't be healed by God if they don't fervently believe their bodies and souls are also worth loving."[6] Gradually, Moore embraced self-acceptance and moved into social spaces that allowed him the profound self-reflection that fills his book. Yet more often than not, the church was a hindrance to his process. If churches want self-reflective leaders, then collectively, they must do their own work of fully recognizing, embracing, and loving the humans who make up and lead the church. Self-reflection is both individual *and* collective.

⚜

Self-reflection in ministry is critical if we want to become good listeners and wise ministers. We have to be able to accept ourselves and also to understand why we're reacting to something in a particular way. And then we need to be able to step back from the moment and really let the other person or situation in front of us present itself for who or what it is.

A pastoral theologian who helps us think about self-reflection is Dr. Carrie Doehring. In her wonderful book *Practice of Pastoral Care: A Postmodern Approach*, Doehring brings forth many ideas on both listening and self-reflection.[7] In one exercise, she suggests that as ministers, we can take time to reflect on the ways that our personal narratives prepare us for coping with "jarring moments" that can decenter us as we offer care to others.[8]

Doehring invites us to think first about our own personal experiences that are called forth by the present moment. Second, she invites reflection by asking us to consider how our stories may help us connect, empathize, and find compassion for the person(s) seeking care. And finally, she invites us to reflect on how we may get caught up in feelings or thoughts that diminish empathy and compassion. She asks,

> How might each similarity or difference [with a care seeker] make it likely that you will:
> (1) become emotionally merged with or disengaged from the care seeker;
> (2) become helpless because of feeling overpowered; and/or
> (3) become directive because you need to be in control?[9]

No matter where you are engaged in ministry—in a hospital or health care setting, on the streets as an activist, or in a congregation—you need the skills of self-reflective listening and deeper awareness about how you are responding so that you are not getting in the way of hearing what others are saying or doing. When your self-reflection is honest, then you are also better able to respond pastorally and compassionately with your best self.

QUESTIONS FOR REFLECTION AND CONVERSATION

Consider the following to guide your journaling or spark conversation with mentors and friends:

- How can I become a more self-reflective pastor or minister?
- How does my ministry setting make space to welcome my full humanity and that of all people who approach?
- What ministry situation or person has been irritating or anxiety-producing lately? What does my reaction tell me about myself?
- What are my tendencies when I hear stories or see behaviors in others that tap into my own experiences? Do I pull back, try to control, or lean in with empathy and compassion?

THREE MINUTE MINISTRY MENTOR

Watch episode 3, "Self-Reflection," https://3mmm.us/Episode3

4

Collaboration

And the word became flesh and lived among us.

—John 1:14

The December snow was drifting down around me, piling up on every surface. I had a bit of free time on my hands. My boots crunched in the snow as I walked across the St. John's University campus in Collegeville, Minnesota. My destination was the Hill Museum in the basement of the campus library. I was going to see some of the original manuscripts of the St. John's Bible.

In 1998, the university and the brothers of St. John's Abbey commissioned a new, fully illuminated text of the Scriptures: Hebrew Bible, Apocrypha, and New Testament. They engaged Donald Jackson, calligrapher to the Queen of England, to head the project. They wanted a text for the twenty-first century.

As I wandered at my own pace through the museum, the project was twelve years in and nearing completion. I was awed by the magnificent illustrations, the carefully and beautifully written text, the details and care that filled every two-foot-by-three-foot double-page spread of the St. John's Bible. The illustrations and embellishments felt both emotionally present and contemporary, reflecting the flora and fauna of Minnesota. At the same time, each carefully illustrated page looked timeless and rich with texture, meaning, and wisdom.

Perhaps the part of the story that struck me most profoundly was how the calligraphers worked. I learned that there was an entire team of calligraphers who were writing (the words) and illuminating (embellishments and decorations) the Scripture text. As head of the project, Donald Jackson designed the alphabet and engineered the layout of the entire Bible. He used computer technology to plan every page. He also brought together a team of skilled artists and calligraphers to share the tasks of writing, illuminating, and illustrating the text with elaborate designs.

As the writing team worked together, they honed the alphabet in such a way that they could all reproduce it just so. They worked together in Wales, where Jackson makes his home and keeps his studio.

When the team returned to their home studios to work separately, an interesting thing happened. It turns out that when they were apart from one another for too long, they lost their ability to write the text consistently and precisely. They literally had to come back together and work in the same space in order to maintain their collaborative project and shared artistic style.

This story of collaboration in art offers a beautiful insight into the significance of collaboration in ministry. When we come together, we can craft a shared purpose, idea, and direction. If we separate and do our work solo, we may begin to go in different directions. In a shared ministry, a collection of independent directions may not be as strong or effective as a well-supported sense of shared purpose, our sense of being with one another. Collaboration is essential for doing the work of ministry together.

During the 2020 pandemic, the work of collaboration in ministry took on both new strains and a new sense of urgency. For long stretches of time, people were unable to do the work of most kinds of ministry in close proximity to one another. The need for collaboration was never greater in living memory. Because of social distancing to try to reduce the harms and deadly impact of the coronavirus, churches and their leaders had to find new and creative ways to work together. Chaplains became bridges of collaboration, connecting families and their loved ones through life-and-death situations. They showed us that collaboration is not just extra icing on the cake but a central feature of pastoral imagination.

❧

Collaboration in ministry is both a necessity and a joy. Yet it can also be messy for sure. In the season of Advent, we collectively remember a moment in the church year that celebrates one of the most beautiful collaborations by God with humanity. The entire nativity story that the church rehearses in the four weeks of Advent bears witness to the beauty of God's co-laboring with all of creation. It's also full of surprises and plot twists that resonate with everyday life.

When we read the biblical stories about the preparation and birth of Jesus, we find them crowded with both divine collaboration and partnership and also with unlikely characters, shocking invitations, and bizarre directions from God's designated messengers. Teenaged Mary is startled by an angel announcing a divine collaboration to give birth to a holy child. Her intended spouse, Joseph, is surprised by a dream instructing him to flee with his beloved and their firstborn.

Elizabeth and Zachariah are surely surprised. And Zachariah is even struck silent by Elizabeth's very-late-in-life pregnancy. For a time, collaboration between the two of them breaks down entirely. Innkeepers and shepherds, choirs of angels, Roman kings, and messengers from far away show up in the story bringing holy announcements, strange news, and curious gifts. Collaboration in this sacred saga is punctuated by drama and movement, praise songs, and quiet pondering.

God's collaboration with creation and especially with humanity is, in short, a holy mess. And in ministry, we know the shape and drama of this mess oh so well. When we start planning special holy-day services, reach out to people for collaboration on a great variety of tasks, or gather with families in crisis and grief, we see just how many ways human beings can head off in our own directions and make a jumble of things. In these moments, collaboration can seem anything but obvious or holy. Missed communications, misunderstood meanings, and a plethora of differing expectations can fill the air, making ministry feel chaotic and disjointed if not impossible.

Where is the redemption in these moments? First, God is present in them, even when we are all thrashing around in the messes of our own making. Second, when we can slow down and, with Mary, ponder in our hearts the purpose and serendipity of our lives, we may find that God's collaboration in the ministry and life we share with our families, friends, and peers is indeed full of grace.

When human collaborations are at their best, when we take the time to understand each other and work patiently like the calligraphers of the St. John's Bible, we may find ourselves caught up in a drama of wonder at God's presence and a sense of shared purpose in our work.

The practice of ministry will often be a holy mess. And it may also be a sacred drama that punctuates our lives with grace.

The resource to take you deeper in the work of collaboration is, of course, the St. John's Bible. On that snowy morning when I walked into the museum, the first text that I actually encountered was the Gospel of John. The powerful and poetic word from John is one of collaboration. *And the word became flesh and lived among us.*

QUESTIONS FOR REFLECTION AND CONVERSATION

Consider the following to guide your journaling or spark conversation with mentors and friends:

- How am I making time and space to notice the collaborations with the holy?
- How am I making space for collaboration in my ministry?
- With whom do I share purpose and creative work in my practice of ministry?

+ How are my collaborations in the practice of ministry both a sacred drama and a holy mess?

THREE MINUTE MINISTRY MENTOR

Watch episode 4, "Collaboration," https://3mmm.us/Episode4

5

Being There

Awaken to the mystery of being here.

—John O'Donohue, *To Bless the Space between Us*

The first time we met Grace, she and her cohort were gathered in a circle on comfy couches. Patchy sunlight filtered in through the windows of a Pacific Northwest retreat center. She was just finishing her master's degree, on track to be ordained as an elder in the UMC. Grace was already working with a small congregation and learning the ropes of pastoral life even before she graduated.

Over the first two years of the LPI Project, we interviewed fifty people who were, like Grace, right at that endpoint of their time in seminary. These beginning ministers had studied at ten different seminaries across many Christian traditions and geographical regions of the United States.

One thing we noticed in the early interviews was that many seminarians expressed some level of concern or anxiety about the things they did not yet know. They felt differing degrees of being prepared or unprepared for the practice of ministry. However, with the benefit of looking back from a vantage point two and half and then five and then ten years later, we can see something else clearly. Most new ministers in our study simply didn't yet know what they didn't know.

While a few seminarians we interviewed already had some years of experience behind them, the majority were genuine beginners. They had experienced field education or CPE or perhaps a half or full year of internship. Yet standing at the brink of entering into ministry, they did not know all they needed to know or even understand fully what they did not yet know.

This is the norm when starting a complex practice like ministry. Training in classrooms and even simulations like field education—when done well—can take you a long way. However, to learn a practice, you have to be immersed in the practice. Some aspects of pastoral work come only through trying, not getting it quite right, or even falling on your face and then trying again.

Being there for the people we love and serve as ministers is one such concept that can be difficult to grasp until real situations present themselves. *Being there* is the essential idea in ministry that we bring ourselves fully into the lives of those we serve. Showing up and being there is so important, especially when those in our care most need to know the presence of the holy.

⟨⟩

In our third interview with Grace, she was about five years out of seminary and ordained fully as an elder in the UMC. She was serving a growing parish in the Northwest. And she told us this story, which unfolded over multiple years, about how she learned the profound value of what it means to *be there*.

In her first tiny pastorate in the UMC, while Grace was still a seminary student, she said she would mysteriously learn about a crisis or a major surgery that someone in her congregation had experienced. She would learn about it after the fact. Someone would say, "Oh, did you know that so-and-so had surgery a few months ago?" And Grace would respond, "Oh, no, I didn't know anything about that!"

This pattern continued, Grace said, throughout the time she served that small church, and then she went to another church. Occasionally, she would learn about someone's surgery in advance. She asked Mrs. Morris about her husband's surgery: "Do you think . . . your husband wants me there?" Mrs. Morris said, "Oh, that would be really nice." So Pastor Grace went to the hospital and prayed with Mr. Morris. She recalled the moment as a really great experience.

Other people told her about surgeries. She would ask if she should come and pray. They would say, "Oh, no, no, no. It's too far. It's too early in the morning. Don't worry about it."

So Pastor Grace would say, "Oh, okay."

Three years into her ministry, nothing much had changed. One day Grace was on a neighborhood walk with her friend Jenny, also a pastor at a nearby congregation. Pastor Grace mentioned to Jenny that a mutual friend and member of Grace's congregation, Laura, was having cancer treatment soon. Jenny said, "So you're going to see her, right?"

And Pastor Grace said, "Well, no. Probably not. It starts at five o'clock in the morning, and I'd have to get up even earlier. And rearrange things with my kids' schedule, and it would almost be impossible for me to get there. I can see her any time."

Grace says in that moment, she thought to herself, *You just don't get it!*

Then Jenny stopped, looked her straight in the face, and said, "You're kidding! You've got to be there! Even if you're just there for ten minutes. It matters!"

Grace thought about it and decided that maybe her friend Pastor Jenny was right, so she got herself up early on the appointed morning and went to visit with her parishioner Laura at her first cancer treatment. Pastor Grace walked into the room full of cancer patients, and the moment that Laura laid eyes on her pastor, she welled up with emotion.

Grace remembers watching this woman who had tears streaming down her face. And there was no space for praying. There were thirty people in that room. It would have been awkward and weird. She asked Laura if she wanted to pray.

"No, no," said Laura. "Your being here is enough."

"That," recalls Grace, "changed everything."

From that moment on, Pastor Grace said that she knew this was a very important part of her ministry. She had to be there for people.

❧❧❧

As ministers, we do not simply bring the holy. Nor are we the primary representatives of the holy. Rather, the holy is already present in all situations. However, it is our calling to notice, to name, and to point out the sacred in the situation. And that work is a purpose shared by most (if not all) who are called to the practice of ministry. It is a purpose, however, that is not always self-evident. Often it must be learned.

A resource that captures and connects with this aspect of ministry—so crucial yet hard to learn—comes from a book by John O'Donohue, *To Bless the Space between Us*. Here is his poem "For Presence":

> Awaken to the mystery of being here and enter the quiet
> immensity of your own presence.
> Have joy and peace in the temple of your senses.
> Receive encouragement when new frontiers beckon.
> Respond to the call of your gift, and the courage to
> follow its path.
> Let the flame of anger free you of all falsity.
> May warmth of heart keep your presence aflame.
> May anxiety never linger about you.
> May your outer dignity mirror an inner dignity of soul.
> Take time to celebrate the quiet miracles that seek no
> attestation.
> Be consoled in the secret symmetry of your soul.
> May you experience each day as a sacred gift woven
> around the heart of wonder.[1]

🪶 QUESTIONS FOR REFLECTION AND CONVERSATION

Consider the following to guide your journaling or spark conversation with mentors and friends:

- How can I think about showing up more fully for those in my care, offering the fullness of my presence so that together we can more fully attend to God's presence?
- What aspect of practicing ministry surprised me or took some time to figure out?
- Which important people helped me figure out subtle aspects of the art of practicing ministry?
- What key ways of *being there* for people have I learned or am I learning now?

🪶 THREE MINUTE MINISTRY MENTOR

Watch episode 5, "Being There," https://3mmm.us/Episode5

6

Supporting Peers

> We are travelers on a journey.
> Fellow pilgrims on the road.
> We are here to help each other.
> Walk the mile and bear the load.
>
> —Richard Gillard, "The Servant Song"

I learned this song in seminary. I remember quite well the first time I sang it. It was during a chapel service my senior year at Southern Baptist Theological Seminary in Louisville, Kentucky. When the service ended, I sat in a pew following a chapel service and simply wept.

It was the beauty of the song. But it was also so much more. Seminary had been very challenging. I excelled in my classes. I learned and felt inspired in more ways than I can count or remember. Yet it is also true that my school was undergoing a dramatic upheaval. My denomination was in the most intense years of a rending split.

The board of trustees of our school was taken over by biblicists who wanted a new direction for the school and for the entire Southern Baptist Convention.[1] Our professors were leaving by the droves. In just my three and a half years in school, almost twenty professors departed. The sense of impending doom was palpable. Not only was my seminary changing the ground under my feet; my entire denomination was taking a new direction that did not include me.

That new direction included reversing the trend of the 1970s and '80s toward ordaining more women for pastoral ministry. Without ordination, ministry was impossible to imagine.

Where in my denomination could I possibly serve? The doors were closing, and in that moment, there were no windows in sight. I was not trapped so much as shut out of the house where I had grown up.

When we sang "The Servant Song," all the feelings of anger, disappointment, letdown, and sadness came tumbling out in the tears I was weeping.

After the service, I could not stop crying, grieving over a future that was being taken from me.

One of my friends slipped into the pew beside me. She sat quietly and listened compassionately as I poured out my frustrations and fears. *Why did I waste so much time in seminary when there are no jobs for me? Will I have to change denominations? What am I going to do? How will I live into this calling?*

Simply stated, I could not have gotten through the years of seminary without friends. We ate together. We laughed together. We hung out on the weekends and occasionally even studied together. We went to Sunday school and worshipped together in those days before we all had responsibilities to serve the church full time. I gathered with one group of women every two weeks, and we shared our stories fully with each other.

Following graduation, there was a long pause. Eventually most of my friends found jobs in the new and changing denominational world of Baptists. Most of us gravitated to the churches and ministries that were related to the progressive wing of Baptist life, where women's ordination was not debated but celebrated.

A church in North Georgia eventually called me. It took two years for me to get there. And when I did, I was pretty much the only young Baptist minister around for many miles in any direction. There were no other young Baptist clergywomen within an hour's drive of me. I decided that we just had to do something about that. I reached out to two friends. One lived about four hours away, and the other lived about five hours away. But they were people I trusted.

Beth and Amy and I started to get together as often as we could.[2] Sometimes we would meet around other denominational gatherings for a meal. Other times, we would plan a retreat and meet up in a place where we could spend dedicated time together. We would sit or swing or rock on a cabin porch for hours and talk and talk together. We would support each other in the work we were doing. We would listen to the doubts and fears and hopes and dreams that each one of us lived with.

In the times between, we would pray for each other, and call, and share our best ideas and our worst moments. I really cannot imagine getting through those times without those friends. When my time ended at the church five and a half years later, Beth and Amy were two of the people who walked with me through a painful departure and a life-giving transition to graduate school.

❧

The importance of supporting peers in ministry really can't be overstated. Several studies show that peer learning and support are essential for thriving in ministry. Those who meet regularly with peers are happier and more able to adapt to their situations than those who are isolated in ministry.

Supporting peers can get us through things. They walk us home and provide emotional and spiritual support. Friends know us and listen to us, and when we are struggling or reaching for a new kind of learning, they are sounding boards for our change. In fact, our peers in ministry offer us a kind of mirror in which we can see both how we change and grow over time and also how we are the same person with continuity across the years and decades of our work.

❧

The first and most important resource for going deeper on this significant part of your practice of ministry is indeed *your friends*. You can reach out to friends and get together with them through all kinds of media, from your phone to your computer, even during pandemic times. Perhaps it is time to reach out to a few of your peers in ministry and form a commitment and a dedication to be together and listen to one another on a regular basis.

The second resource is a book that reports the findings from several studies of peer groups in ministry. In the 2013 book *So Much Better: How Thousands of Pastors Help Each Other Thrive*, author and sociologist of religion Penny Long Marler and her colleagues note how adult learning differs from childhood learning.[3] Ministers, like other adult learners, "need to be convinced that a learning experience is really worth their time and effort."[4] In other words, sometimes we need a good excuse to get together with peers: engaging in a book study, planning sermons, strategizing for a protest, or writing youth curriculum. With a planned reason or structure for gathering, we also get the additional relational support that really makes a difference in our well-being.

The authors of *So Much Better* observe that for pastors, "commitment hinges on the promise of something more that really matters."[5] That something more is the benefit of being part of a circle of peers who can help you articulate what you need and want to learn. It is about learning from one another with improvisation.[6] Making a covenant to support one another can be an important part of helping peer support groups endure over time.[7] These practices of gathering and covenant keeping are key to growing in one's vocation and pastoral imagination.

🪶 QUESTIONS FOR REFLECTION AND CONVERSATION

Consider the following to guide your journaling or spark conversation with mentors and friends:

+ Are there friends in ministry whom I have not connected with in a while? Maybe I have a regular group of friends, and I need to reach out to them today.
+ Where are my supportive networks? Are they local or denominational or part of another kind of affinity group? How could I strengthen my bonds with peers who share my values and ways of living my vocation?

- ✦ What are the things I most long to share with close friends in ministry?
- ✦ What in me needs to be seen, heard, and validated by supporting peers?

🪶 THREE MINUTE MINISTRY MENTOR

Watch episode 6, "Supporting Peers," https://3mmm.us/Episode6

7

Ministry as Embodied

There is no simple answer for how one learns compassion. But it would be silly to try to teach care for those going into ministry without showing it, requiring students to witness it, and asking them to demonstrate it through their bodies.

—Bonnie J. Miller-McLemore, *Christian Practical Wisdom*

When we met Malinda, she was in her midtwenties, on the cusp of seminary graduation and interviewing for her first solo pastorate. Malinda identifies as white, and she grew up in Texas. She only began attending church with her father when she was in late elementary school. Church felt like a safe space for a young girl living through the grief and chaos of a family going through divorce. Through high school and college, Malinda experienced a sense of clarity and God's presence leading her to a vocation of ministry.

Following graduation from seminary, Malinda was called to her first solo pastorate. The church of fewer than one hundred members was in a small town in the southern United States. She was the only full-time staff person in a congregation that had employed a succession of pastors serving brief tenures.

We asked Malinda to think back on what she learned in seminary and what was helping her as a pastor. She said she couldn't think of a lot she learned in seminary, but there were a couple of things that stood out.

One of the things that stood out to her was her time in CPE. In one of the didactic sessions, Malinda heard a lecture by a pastor. Speaking from his experience, he said to the students, "If you're doing pastoral care in a hospital room and there is a baby, by all means, hold the baby." This really struck Malinda as important. She began to understand at that moment that being a minister was about more than thinking or talking. This pastor was telling her something about the *embodied* character of ministry.

He was conveying that the mercy and presence of God were known through the human touch and not simply by the words we say. This idea really stuck with Melinda. As she went forward into her pastoral call, she thought about the ways her ministry is not just something to think about; it is embodied in every way.

Another facet of her learning about how ministry is embodied came in the form of learning in CPE how ministry requires slowing down, focusing on the moment, and really being present with people. Malinda took these new understandings with her into the pulpit when she preached for her home congregation, the place she had first expressed her calling to ministry. Malinda recalls, "It all came together, and I preached a really good sermon, and afterward, people said, 'This is what you were meant to be doing.'"

☙❧

The embodied character of ministry impacts everything you do, from preaching and teaching to giving bedside care or leading through crisis, in the ways you bring your whole self to each situation. Mostly, our need and use of our bodies in ministry remain somehow beneath our notice. We do not think consciously about how we know, remember, communicate, and lead *by body*.

Think about this: You get into a car, start it up, and begin to drive, moving effortlessly onto the streets and through traffic, arriving at your destination. You park the car, extract the keys, and get out, having never really thought about what it means "to drive." Or if you are in a place where you use public transportation, similar steps are true: navigate to the subway station, pay, enter through the turnstile, hop the train, exit, find your way onto the street, and move to your destination. In either scenario, all the while you're thinking about many other things and making plans for what is next while your body performs these actions with little direct assistance or direction from your conscious, thinking brain.[1]

And yet performing these everyday tasks is also not the same for every *body*. Depending on your social location, one of the things you may be thinking while transporting yourself across town, or leading in ministry, is how your body is perceived or regulated by social conventions or people around you. For example, alertness may be a matter of embodied safety: the dangers of driving while Black are quantifiable.[2] The barriers of navigating public transportation when living with disability are frustrating. The judgments about your preaching if you are a woman of color are harsh. The dangers to your life if you are protesting while Black or Brown are proven realities.[3]

Both churches and public spaces continue to regulate and control which bodies can perform what actions. Historically, female bodies were outside the "office" or authority of ministry, and they continue to be disallowed or overly scrutinized in pulpits. However, the power of embodied presence to make change is also real. Protests from the Edmund Pettus Bridge to the streets of Ferguson changed the course of history. And homiletics professor and practical theologian Lisa Thompson observes, "In [Black women's] preaching we often witness fragments of equity and justice push through and sneak past the very structures that seek to render violence and injustice in their lives."[4]

In the work of ministry, you do things consistently like breaking bread, pouring juice or wine, stepping into a pulpit, gesturing while preaching, greeting people during coffee hour, offering a prayer at a meeting, or teaching a Bible study while perhaps writing on the marker board, making eye contact, moving about the room, and so much more. Your body performs so many actions during this work of ministry for which you need not receive direct assistance from your conscious, thinking brain.

Perhaps early on, when you learned to drive or take the subway, you needed to think carefully about each step of the process and had a heightened awareness about what you were doing and every action you took. Although the realities of your social location remain, now you are likely to perform a majority of these things as if "without thinking."

When you, like Melinda, began ministry, perhaps you needed to think about each step carefully, with heightened awareness about each action in the everyday rounds of ministry: making phone calls, organizing your study, writing notes for teaching and preaching, making visits, and much more. Yet as you integrate this kind of activity into your pastoral imagination, your embodied knowing, you can take many of these steps "without thinking."

To be clear, embodied knowing is not truly accomplished "without thinking" in the sense of mindlessness or lack of thought. Rather, we can conceive of this kind of knowing as an expanded and embedded kind of thinking and knowing of practical wisdom.[5] Over time, the knowing that we accumulate about how to do ministry becomes sedimented into our bodies. That embodied knowing, which we depend on unconsciously in many ways, helps us

- get out of our heads and more fully into our bodies and selves as active, emotionally attuned, and present, as if "holding the baby";
- remember what to do and how to do it without expending precious energy on thousands of small decisions; and
- communicate and convey ideas and feelings and spiritual connections through gesture and ritual presence.

This sedimented knowing becomes a basis for a growing intuition about how to be a minister and how to act with pastoral imagination. During the season of the coronavirus pandemic, we were largely isolated from other people in body. We were left to connect with one another by phone and by screen. This reality heightened our awareness about how we carry grief in our bodies, how the lack of informal and embodied communication leaves real gaps in how we convey to each other what we think, how we feel, and what we mean. It also left us longing to be in the physical presence of our friends, family, and spiritual communities. Our embodied connections are crucial to our well-being on so many levels.

Whether you are engaged in performing the various embodied actions of ministry for the first time or the 937th time, take notice today of just how much you *think, remember, and act by body* as you lift up bread, light the candles, don your clergy robe, process behind the choir, baptize a baby, protest in the streets, plan a virtual gathering, speak words of comfort at the bedside of someone before surgery, greet a grieving family, or pray.

To help you understand more deeply this embodied character of the practice of ministry, the resource to explore is *Christian Practical Wisdom*, a book by five practical theologians who bring their years of experience and wisdom into their collaborative writing.[6] Dorothy Bass, Kathleen Cahalan, Bonnie Miller-McLemore, James Nieman, and Chris Scharen dig deep into history and their own experiences to convey the significance of embodied knowing and practical wisdom. They both retrieve intellectual traditions and weave them with everyday living to show us how practical wisdom is crucial for our spiritual lives, our theological knowing, and our pastoral practice. The authors explore ways of knowing we have as disciples, as ministers, and as teachers of the faith that go beyond what we think about or even talk about.

QUESTIONS FOR REFLECTION AND CONVERSATION

Consider the following to guide your journaling or spark conversation with mentors and friends:

- How can I take a moment today and simply breathe and be present to what my body is communicating to me?
- What aspects of my embodiment and social location require me to employ heightened alertness or awareness for the sake of my well-being?
- How can I be fully present both to my body and to those around me in their embodied presence so that we might notice God's presence in and through this moment?
- When I slow down and think about how I enact and perform the work of ministry, what do I notice about how my embodied practice is changing over time?

THREE MINUTE MINISTRY MENTOR

Watch episode 7, "Ministry as Embodied," https://3mmm.us/Episode7

8

Equity in Ministry

If you aren't going to ordain women, why baptize them?

—Bumper sticker

When I took my first call to congregational ministry in 1994, I was delighted to find a place where I felt I could bring my full self and my full gifts. Yet even there, equity was still a challenge. I needed to educate people almost every week about why I hyphenated my name, how to introduce me, and why I might need ordination for my role. The pay was far from equal to that of other staff, and advocating for better pay was frowned upon by most of our congregation.

Certainly, my power and influence in that rural/suburban church was not on par with other ministers. And yet power and influence in ministry leadership are nothing to be grasped. Here's the reality I faced head-on: When men arrive in a new ministry setting, power and influence is assumed and unquestioned. Women—especially younger women—still have to earn almost every shred of recognition. These realities were not due solely to the fact that I was still under thirty and new to the work of full-time ministry. They were realities because women were still considered *new to ministry in general*. And no one was quite sure what to do with us, how to relate to us as leaders, or what to expect.

Fifteen years later, after a long season in the parish and a long season in graduate school earning a PhD, I began my work in theological ethnography, learning directly from ministers about how the practice of ministry unfolded over time. I was also delighted by the decision to interview as many women as men in the study.

When we began interviewing women for the LPI Project, we found many of them facing the very same struggles I faced years earlier. Even as I write this in 2020, women continue to graduate from seminary, wait disproportionately longer to receive a call, get paid less, and struggle to sustain a career within their calling. Far too many women are still wondering if access to or equity in the church will ever come.

❧❂❧

Perhaps you've never experienced a sense of inequality. Maybe you feel supported and reasonably well paid. And maybe you hold what feels like an acceptable amount of influence in decision-making in your organization. If this is the case for you, then perhaps you will look around at your situation and think about how your colleagues and peers are experiencing in/equality. Do a little research. To help with that task, knowing how one's particular setting affects the broader picture of equity in ministry can be enlightening.

Until 2018, a comprehensive set of data on the questions of equity in ministry had been missing for about twenty years. To remedy this problem, I set out with help from several research assistants, and we regathered data on women's leadership in US churches. We wanted to make current the findings from two earlier books. *A Time for Honor* (2001) by Delores Carpenter offered the first comprehensive look at women's leadership in historic Black churches. *Clergy Women: An Uphill Calling* (1998) by Barbara Brown Zikmund, Adair T. Lummis, and Patricia Mei Yin Chang drew together data and surveyed attitudes from predominantly white denominations.[1]

In 2018, I published a twenty-page resource to help readers understand the wider situation; find where their denomination, organization, or church fits into that picture; and see how equity in ministry is changing over time. What we learned is now available in *State of Clergywomen in the U.S.: A Statistical Update.*[2]

Although more historical studies and data on women's equity in the church is available, I was equally concerned about how clergy who identified as lesbian, gay, bisexual, trans, intersex, or queer found themselves faring in the church. Here are some of the key findings from the report:

+ In 1960, women made up 2.3 percent of US clergy. In 2016, women made up 20.7 percent of US clergy.
+ Since 2015, Roman Catholic lay ministers surpassed and continue to outnumber priests in the United States, and 80 percent of the lay ministers are women.
+ In most mainline denominations, the percentage of clergywomen has doubled or tripled since 1994.
+ Since 2003, the Episcopal Church, the UMC, and the Evangelical Lutheran Church in America have elected openly gay and/or lesbian ministers as bishops.
+ Unitarian Universalist and United Church of Christ clergywomen have reached numerical equity with clergymen.
+ In 2017, women made up less than 25 percent of seminary faculty and deans and only 11 percent of the presidents.

✦ Throughout the last decade, a growing number of women of color and a shrinking number of white-identified women are going to seminary to earn MDivs.

To be a church leader in our time requires not only a clear calling but also courage. Is it your hope and desire that your faith community be part of a change for justice and equality for people of all genders and social locations? Would you prefer the alternative as an institution defined as an obstacle to equality? You will need knowledge, commitment, and willingness to risk something big for the sake of something better for all people.

In many historic Black churches, the equity situation in the past, and to a lesser degree at present, looks like the nearly universal support of powerful male pastors counterbalanced by the unpaid labor of pastors' wives and church mothers who fill the pews on Sundays. These women staff the kitchens, classes, and benevolence ministries of the church. They also fill the offering plates to keep church life going, and women make up as much as 75 percent of the membership. To understand the first generation of Black women graduating from seminary, Carpenter gathered surveys in 1985, 1992, and 1999. One startling trend she learned is that 60 percent of these women went to work in predominantly white church jobs. More than 50 percent switched denominations during or after seminary. Their reasons included ordination, employment, and to a lesser degree, marriage. By 1999, the numbers were changing, and just 40 percent of the Black female MDiv graduates she surveyed were serving in white denominations. This signaled a growing acceptance of women's leadership in some historically Black denominations.[3]

The historic Black churches with the most dramatic growth in equity for women are part of the African Methodist Episcopal (AME) denomination. In 2017–18, the AME Commission on Women reported more than 4,400 clergywomen and nearly 1,200 women pastors in a denomination of seven thousand churches. Women serve at all levels of the AME, including as presiding elders, and four are elected bishops.[4]

Nevertheless, Debora Jackson observed in 2019 that the situation of inequality remains unchanged in many Black congregations. Women have accumulated power by filling leadership roles in all the functions of church life, including worship and preaching. Yet they have done so without pay and sometimes without even a title. Jackson says, "While women have assumed every leadership role in the black church, gender continues to function as a disqualifier for women's leadership by both African American women and men."[5]

No simple path to change is available. The complexity of how the systems of inequality are maintained is a part of their power. The hiddenness of these systems is a key to maintaining the status quo. How do we as Christian ministers and religious leaders stand a chance of making change? As my study and others reveal, measurable change has indeed happened in the last fifty years for women's leadership in American churches. And other gaps in equality have narrowed with regards to education, pay, and influence. Yet the gaps are still there, and we are up against inequalities, injustices, and the hidden biases in every part of society, including or especially in religious organizations.

A significant aspect of growing in the practice of ministry involves pushing ourselves out of our comfort zones and working for equity in ministry. We need a commitment to educate everyone consistently about the hidden power of bias. We need a commitment to share power and influence and in so doing reshape our organizations into more equitable ones.

QUESTIONS FOR REFLECTION AND CONVERSATION

Consider the following to guide your journaling or spark conversation with mentors and friends:

- When I assess my ministry setting for equity in roles, responsibility, pay, and decision-making power, what do I notice?
- What does equity for leaders look like when considering gender, sexual orientation, and race in my particular ministry setting?
- What would it look like for me to participate fully in working for equity in my context of ministry?

THREE MINUTE MINISTRY MENTOR

Watch episode 8: "Equity in Ministry" https://3mmm.us/Episode8

9

Ministry as Relational

I do not call you servants any longer . . . but I have called you friends.

—John 15:15

Trong grew up in church. His parents immigrated to the United States from Vietnam in the 1970s when he was a toddler. His family devoted themselves to the church, and the immigrant congregation was a tight-knit community. However, like many close communities, it was not absent conflict.

When we met Trong, he was in his thirties, and he had recently graduated from Fuller Seminary. In our initial interview, Trong told us about how central church was to his life and how important it was to be part of the faith community. When Trong graduated from college, he went to work managing a bookstore. He learned a lot about how to work with people and invest in relationships as a manager. But at the end of the day, what Trong really wanted to do was take more of a leadership role in his congregation. He began looking for ways to volunteer in the church's ministry with students.

The church was divided, however. A split in the congregation over location and leadership left the church with opposing groups. Trong began to see how the factions in the church were going to make his involvement in ministry, even as a volunteer, quite challenging. Some resistance to his leadership was coming from the paid ministry leaders. They did not want to include him in the ministry with youth. This felt very weird to Trong.

A number of paid youth ministers came and went. Then the church hired yet another new youth minister. And somehow Tam was different. He was the first youth minister to reach out to Trong. He invited him to lunch. They began to meet weekly, sitting down to talk over meals. They enjoyed just hanging out together.

As their friendship grew, Trong learned practical things from Tam, like how to put together a Bible study. He also learned how to build a relationship with someone who is a peer in ministry. Eventually, their friendship became a space in which Trong could explore his own call to ministry. It was through friendship, conversation, and shared ministry that Trong eventually embraced his own desire to go to seminary. Even though Tam was younger, he had become Trong's first ministry mentor.

Trong's story signals just how central relationships are to all that we do in the work of ministry. It sounds obvious to say *ministry is relational*. But ministry is not simply a job that trades on relationships. That view is too transactional. Ministry is relational in all the ways that our friends and families shape who we are, where we find acceptance and access to resources, and how we learn and grow.

As Trong experienced both being shut out of ministry and being welcomed into ministry, we can see how relationships were crucial at each point. When Trong tells us how he learned to put together and lead a Bible study from Tam, he is reminding us that so much learning for ministry is absorbed, like osmosis. The learning happens simply by being in relationship with people who show up and who give support while we figure things out. And as Trong's story highlights, relationships are also crucial for hearing and embracing one's sense of calling.

⬥⟐⬥

I am fortunate to be part of the community of faith that has been my spiritual home for more than twenty years now. In that place, I have experienced the joy of being in relationships over time that grow and change shape. Dozens of people at Glendale Baptist Church have walked with me and helped me survive graduate school and the long and sometimes sorrowful journey to parenthood. They celebrated with joy the birth of our daughter. They have seen me through many job changes and vocational shifts. I am a better person, parent, and minister for all the support and belonging they have lavished on me.

My life is also richer for the many ways I have been a part of their lives as well: the walking together and the praying, the welcoming new life and grieving lives ended, the cooking and caring, the navigation of conflict and change, the work of serving people who are hungry or need a place to rest or someone to stand with them in a crisis. As a community, we aspire to do justice and to (re) create life together. Through all these many processes my family has a place of belonging at Glendale. And together these relationships shape an authentic shared community.

In a mobile culture that offers so many ways to escape, hibernate, and isolate, I am delighted that week by week I get to stand in one sanctuary and share in worship. We sing in joy and lament together, watch children become adults over time, and bear witness to one another's lives.

During the season of the coronavirus pandemic in 2020, we faced a major loss of connection in which the relational and embodied aspects of ministry and life together were put on hold. We learned to worship, study, check in, and make decisions from our separate homes using digital modes of contact. Our sense of relational connection and community was challenged in every way, and yet with the Spirit's help we rose to the occasion.

Church remains one of the few social groups in a postmodern society where people can still be a vital part of a community over time from cradle to grave. At their best, churches offer genuine opportunities to see each other through all life stages, interact across generations, and walk together through all the seasons from birth through death with all the milestones and rites of passage in between.

To be sure, at their worst, churches can also do harm, fail to show up for each other in authentic ways, lose their purpose, and perpetuate all the worst features of the human condition. Churches are never perfect or without flaws. Lamentably, some churches do lasting harm relationally to their own members. And some churches participate in the privileges of the dominant white culture that continues to inflict personal and social harm on countless people.

Yet churches are also built on the ideas of God's good news of love, the possibility of forgiveness, and the manifestation of hope. And we can know none of these—love, forgiveness, or hope—without the beautiful and broken relationships of shared life together.

As you think about your practice of ministry, I hope you will take into consideration the significant ways that ministry is relational, how those relationships have shaped you, and what your call is to be in relationships in ways that embody God's love, forgiveness, justice, and hope.

The resource you need for going deeper into this facet of the practice of ministry is, of course, the relationships that already animate and fill your work in ministry.

✒ QUESTIONS FOR REFLECTION AND CONVERSATION

Consider the following to guide your journaling or spark conversation with mentors and friends:

- ✦ Who is shaping me relationally as a minister for good or for ill?
- ✦ How am I inviting others to think aloud with me about their life purpose and vocation?
- ✦ How could my relationships become a space in which my friends and I deepen our understanding of vocation as people called to ministry?

✒ THREE MINUTE MINISTRY MENTOR

Watch episode 9, "Ministry as Relational," https://3mmm.us/Episode9

10

Failing Creatively

What is the future of how we think about so-called failure, these dubious starts and unlikely transformations? We can answer it by finding ways to honor them, by not letting the path out of them stay hidden, by letting them be generative, even indispensable.

—Sarah Lewis, *The Rise*

Failure. It is one of those words that is big and scary, and we don't really want to think about it too much. Yet if you're going to do something complicated and challenging, like learning the practice of ministry, then you won't get it right all the time. Whether you call these shortcomings "flops, folds, wipeouts, or hiccups," as author and art curator Sarah Lewis calls them, failing is definitely part of the process.[1] There's no getting around it—so how can we think about failing *more* creatively?

I love working with new seminary students and ministers, chaplains, activists, and pastors in the first five years of their work. Everything is fresh. Everything is new. And the brain and body are still metabolizing all the new skills, information, and cues about how to do the work.

Do you remember your first internship? Perhaps you are in it now. For many people preparing for ministry, field education or internships are the first big moments of tasting what it's like to be in ministry. It can be like stepping into someone else's shoes to be the one who is responsible for praying, gathering people, leading, and offering care.

There are so many things to try to notice and pay attention to when you are stepping into ministry for the first time. Because so much is new, you can feel overwhelmed and become preoccupied with worry over not getting things just right or "failing" in the work of ministry.

While she was a seminary student, Kelly, a white woman in her forties, reflected on her internship in a way that really hit the nail on the head.[2] She said, "The truth is, I am really good at reading a book and summarizing the points and reading a paper and maybe even giving a speech, but ministry is so much more than that. So, when I am at my internship, I really need someone who is going to tell me when I mess things up and who is going to give me some feedback about how to do better. And most importantly, I need someone who is going to take a risk on me and give me a chance to try again."

This is crucial for the learning of ministry in all cases because learning something so complex as ministry can't be done simply by trying it once. You have to be able to try again and again and even fail along the way.

Failure doesn't have to be a sense of the end but a sense of *on the way*. In retrospect, some of my own early failures in ministry are rather hilarious. There was the time I nearly caught my clerical robe on fire while leading the church to gather around the communion table for the first time. There was the first time I performed a baptism without testing out the waders I was wearing in advance. As I was delivering sacred words from the baptismal pool, I felt the cool water seeping into my boots. I had to do the rest of the service wearing wet pantyhose. (Yes, I know, nobody even wears pantyhose anymore!)

How did I make my early moments of failure more creative? Well, I laughed at my foibles. I thought more about where my body is in space. And with more experience, I became less preoccupied with questions like *Am I doing this right?* And I became more present to questions like *Where am I now?* and *How am I responding to this situation?* As for the waders, I bought a new pair, and I tried yet again to put some emphasis on planning ahead.

To be sure, learning from failure presents a different and more complex problem for some people depending on social location. Certain kinds of failures can be hilarious, at least in retrospect, but in those early years, I was not really in an everyday posture of allowing myself to learn creatively from failure. Largely this was because I felt a pressure to perform so that I might defy those who expected me to fail or those who said women don't belong in ministry. Fortunately, my congregation was largely supportive and willing to take a risk on me and laugh with me.

This dynamic is quite complex for women, LGBTQIA folks, and people who society unfairly marginalizes simply because they identify as Black or Brown, Indigenous Peoples, or recently immigrated. (See chapter 19, "Brick Walls.") People who begin ministry from socially marginalized locations must cope with a double-binding situation when it comes to failure. Because they begin in a one-down or even two-down position, "failing" at anything can confirm stereotypes and biases rather than create opportunities to learn. To freely learn from mistakes and missteps, ministers need a wide and relatively safe space, courage to take a risk, and sturdy support from the communities they serve.

One of my favorite books of the last few years is *The Rise: Creativity, the Gift of Failure, and the Search for Mastery* by art critic and curator Sarah Lewis. She explores how failure is an essential way station on the path to discovery, invention, and mastery. She is especially interested in how failure is essential to mastery when it comes to sports, art, and other advanced skill-based practices.[3]

In *The Rise*, Lewis tells stories about archers mastering the shot, Edison failing ten thousand times before inventing the lightbulb, and how musicians and authors such as Duke Ellington and Tennessee Williams pushed past failure to create lasting works of art and literature. In these stories, as in ministry, failure is an essential component of mastery.[4] What exactly is mastery from Lewis's perspective?

Mastery is neither *perfectionism* nor *success*. Perfectionism, says Lewis, is "an inhuman aim motivated by a concern with how others view us."[5] Success, on the other hand, is "an event-based victory based on a peak point, a punctuated moment in time," she says.[6] Going beyond a single or even regular achievement, "mastery is not merely a commitment to a goal, but to a curved-line, constant pursuit."[7] This is her understanding of *the rise*. Thus "the pursuit of mastery is an ever onward almost."[8]

In other words, mastery is like a curved line that keeps reaching for a kind of expertise, keeps striving, keeps learning, and never truly "arrives." Lewis is reluctant to overuse the word *failure* because as soon as we use it, it slips away into becoming something else: "A learning experience, a trial, a reinvention."[9] Thus, like learning the complex practice of ministry, time and experience are required for mastery. Lewis sees the learning intertwined in the way we interpret what is happening: "There are all sorts of generative circumstances—flops, folds, wipeouts, and hiccups—yet the dynamism it inspires is internal, personal, and often invisible. . . . It is a cliché to say simply that we learn the most from failure. It is also not exactly true. Transformation comes from how we choose to speak about it in the context of story, whether self-stated or aloud."[10]

From our research in the LPI Project, we find that mastery as Lewis is exploring it comes close to *phronesis*, or practical, situated wisdom. We call this *pastoral imagination*, which integrates skill, knowledge, and know-how about situations and rituals of ministry, becoming habits and postures of wise pastoral practice.

This is where failure is absolutely unavoidable in the process of mastery. We cannot reach the far edges of knowing how to act, what knowledge is needed, or what new path is being created without tripping up along the way, without missing the point occasionally, and without honing our knowing in action. In this kind of learning, failure is not a one-time event but a way of taking continuous risk and responsibility for leading.

In ministry, the idea of failing creatively is also a matter of humility. We can never know all, see all, or master all. We must remain willing to ask "How could I be wrong?" and "Is there another way?" Thus even a willingness to fail is crucial to the posture of leading with wisdom and imagination.

Early on, this kind of posture feels intuitively wrong. We are trying to learn something new, and we want to achieve mastery faster than is possible. Beginning ministers can be quick to identify failures in a learning process as personal flaws or feel a sense of humiliation. This is why a ministry setting that supports learning through trying, patience, and support through missteps is crucial for new ministers.

As you're on your way to discovering what ministry is like, you need to give yourself permission to fail and find spaces where you can do that and be supported as you learn the complex practice of ministry. Can you seek out someone like Kelly found in her supervisor/mentor—someone who can see with you and help you embrace the creativity and paradox of failing?

🪶 QUESTIONS FOR REFLECTION AND CONVERSATION

Consider the following to guide your journaling or spark conversation with mentors and friends:

+ Is there a situation I have experienced recently when I thought of what I did as a *failure?* Maybe it was some small misstep, or maybe it was something more significant. When I think back over what happened and take time to consider it, what feelings arose for me? How am I locating that moment within my trajectory of learning?
+ Who has helped me along my pathway of learning by making space for me to try and to fail?
+ What changes are needed in my ministry setting to create more support and space for learning by women and people who are marginalized from the outset?
+ Rather than expecting *perfection* or merely *success,* how might I reframe failures in my learning as creative opportunities for discovery and change on the way to wise pastoral practice?

🪶 THREE MINUTE MINISTRY MENTOR

Watch episode 10, "Failing Creatively," https://3mmm.us/Episode10

11

Listening

We empower one another by hearing the other to speech.

—Nelle Morton, _The Journey Is Home_

I like to feel heard and understood. How about you? Yet finding people who really do that well and who have time to listen carefully can be a challenge. And then there is the trust. The best listening and understanding are steeped in trust. And trust takes time. Listening is crucial for ministry, and as a primary skill, it cannot be overestimated.

When Karynthia came to seminary, she brought with her a lot of experience in ministry, a full professional life in health care, and a bag full of dreams. I decided to match her up with Dr. Pat for one-on-one mentoring as Karynthia made her way through her master of divinity program.[1] Dr. Pat was a hospital chaplain wrapping up her doctor of ministry project when I recruited her to be a mentor. Both women were already well-established leaders in the Black church tradition.

When they began, Dr. Pat says, "We didn't have a clue where this was going to lead!" Over the next three years, a lot changed in their relationship.

The two women had a rocky start. I met with them and helped them reset expectations and clarify roles. Karynthia had never had a mentor she really trusted. She often felt like she ended up doing the mentoring in previous relationships where she was supposed to be the mentee.

What helped the two women really connect is that Dr. Pat is a good listener. And she would sit and wait and listen rather than interrupt a story that Karynthia was telling her. She would resist giving quick advice or suggesting a certain direction.

Dr. Pat would simply listen and wait and listen until a question formulated in her mind. And then Dr. Pat would pose that question to Karynthia. Then Karynthia would take the question and move deeper into her own self-understanding and her understanding of the particular ministry situation.

Karynthia describes the relationship this way: "These last three years were stepping-stones. They brought shape to what God is designing in my life. I could share the fragile parts of me that others don't see . . . the hurt, and also, we shared laughter. I need guidance on different things, and it has been wonderful to watch Pat listen to me, take a few notes, and come up with a question—instead of giving me answers."

Over time, that listening and conversation built tremendous trust between these two women. And each began to listen and be able to share with the other in a way that moved them beyond being simply a mentor and mentee. They developed what they call a "circle of sisterhood." Listening was at the very core of that sisterhood.

Dr. Pat says the mentoring time was like walking the Emmaus road together and becoming aware of the presence of the Holy Spirit in those moments. The Spirit was clearly in their circle of sisterhood.

Rev. Dr. Teresa Fry Brown is a professor of preaching at Emory University. One of her early books is *Can a Sistah Get a Little Help? Encouragement for Black Women in Ministry*. She observes, "Good mentors learn as well as instruct. They teach by precept and by example. They know when to speak and when to listen. They establish trust, keep confidences, and provide honest feedback. They encourage rather than demand."[2] Her words resonate and amplify the story that Dr. Pat and Karynthia shared with me about their experiences of growing trust through listening and showing up for one another.

In my Interpersonal Skills for Ministry class, I like to invite students into a particular exercise that helps them hone their listening skills. In this exercise, students sit together in groups of three. One person speaks. One person listens. And one person observes the interaction. Each speaker has eight full minutes.

I give guidance about the topic. And I remind students that they do not have to share anything they do not feel ready to share. They should take care with their choices of what to reveal. For example, I may ask *What would you share from your life that needs prayer right now?* or *Where have you noticed God's presence in your life this week?*

After each round, everyone takes a few notes on a sheet of paper addressing questions that I provide. Then everyone shifts roles. The exercises repeat until everyone has had a chance to be in each role.

This exercise not only produces insight about the skills of listening; it also often evokes in the participants a powerful experience of being heard. That experience can be both shocking and a little unnerving. It often makes students feel vulnerable. This highlights the reality that listening is not solely up to the listener. If one feels vulnerable or anxious, it is hard to speak up authentically.

The listening exercise can also be very empowering. For those who really take the question seriously and respond honestly, they can find themselves in a place of feeling deeply heard.

One of my favorite early feminist theologians, Nelle Morton, is best known for her idea of "hearing to speech." She writes about the power of listening deeply and hearing another person into speech in her book *The Journey Is Home*. In the book, Morton says the following:

> Hearing of this sort is equivalent to empowerment. We empower one another by hearing the other to speech. We empower the disinherited, the outsider, as we are able to hear them name in their own way their own oppression and suffering. In turn, we are empowered as we can put ourselves in a position to be heard by the disinherited (in this case other women) to speaking our own feeling of being caught and trapped. Hearing in this sense can break through political and social structures and image a new system. A great ear at the heart of the universe—at the heart of our common life—hearing human beings to speech—to our own speech.[3]

Both Teresa Fry Brown and Nelle Morton offer ways to go deeper into the profound experiences of listening and being heard. Listening is an important skill, and it is also a key theological understanding for how we bring the practice of ministry into life. Without it, we will suffer with less trust, empowerment, and the ability to effect change.

QUESTIONS FOR REFLECTION AND CONVERSATION

Consider the following to guide your journaling or spark conversation with mentors and friends:

- Where in my life do I feel fully heard, seen, and empowered to speak authentically?
- Where in my ministry do I need to listen more deeply? And when I am listening, how will I notice the presence of the Spirit, the "great ear," as well as the people with whom I am listening and speaking?
- How can I empower others by listening more carefully to their lives?

THREE MINUTE MINISTRY MENTOR

Watch episode 11, "Listening," https://3mmm.us/Episode11

12

Mentoring for Skill

A mentor is a trusted advisor. The basic mentoring relationship is friendship with someone who has more experience and acts as a guide to a less experienced person. This may be done in regards to a profession, job, career, or developmental stage. A mentor functions as a teacher who enhances a person's skills and intellectual development.

—Bishop Vashti Murphy McKenzie, *Strength in the Struggle*

Bob was born and raised in a churchgoing Southern Baptist home. He describes himself as growing up a "golden boy." In his late twenties, when we met him for the first time, Bob told us about his being active in his church youth group and how the youth pastor picked him out for leadership roles that led him to a call to ministry.

In college, Bob was student body president—respected and carrying with him a sense of idealism about church and the life of faith. He married his college sweetheart and, after graduating from college, took a ministry internship job in a large Baptist church in another state. His role was to start a new "next generation" service.

With little support and high expectations complicated by a disagreement over theology and mission with the senior pastor, Bob floundered. He recalls a low point in the pastor's office when the pastor discussed his expectations and disappointment in Bob. Also disappointed, Bob said, "When you hired me, you said you were going to be a mentor, and you were going to teach me things, and you haven't done crap."

The story doesn't end tragically, however. Bob quit the job but continued worshipping at the church. In a heart-to-heart with God, Bob heard a voice saying, "I didn't tell you to leave." It hit home for him that he didn't respect other leaders who quit when the going got tough. So he went back to the staff team to ask for his job back. Bob got a second chance.

Things healed, and he was able to see the pastor with respect, turning to him for advice. Yet he admits, "I kind of had to make a part of myself die in order to be there . . . I had to learn to support his system as opposed to doing my own thing." Bob says he learned a great deal from the experience about "reconciliation and forgiveness and my role in an organization."

After three years, Bob's desire for another level of authority and leadership led to his decision to attend seminary. After seminary, Bob became the lead pastor of a Baptist church in North Carolina. The relationship with his first supervising pastor has grown over time. Says Bob, "This pastor is now my first call when I have ministry questions, and his advice helped significantly in the first year of my transition into the pastoral role."

We often think of mentors as those people who are going to fill in a lot of gaps in our lives and give us everything we need. That can be a setup for misunderstood expectations and disappointment. Far more helpful is the approach of thinking about mentoring around skills of ministry. When you can focus together on the skills that you need to learn, then expectations are clearer, many more ways to go forward are available, and fewer opportunities arise for disappointment.

❧

I believe one of the easiest temptations when engaging in one-to-one mentoring is to carry our big relational needs and expectations into the work. I know in my first call out of seminary, I wanted a mentor so much. I wanted someone to rely on, confide in, be seen by, and trust implicitly. Who doesn't want those things?

Yet focusing so much on relational needs and expectations can put undue pressure on a mentoring relationship. Putting those needs and expectations on the front burner for mentoring can also lead to a serious missed opportunity to grow and learn in the practice of ministry.

What is the alternative? Mentoring and ministry are, after all, unavoidably relational! How can we avoid relational needs and expectations? We should not avoid them. There is, however, a helpful alternative: focus on mentoring for skill.

If a mentor and mentee or a mentoring peer group can put skills for mentoring on the front burner of the metaphorical mentoring stove, then something powerful can happen. By focusing first on skills, the relational support and trust will grow as it bubbles gently along on the back burner. This approach allows you to talk together about the relational aspects of ministry without expecting a mentor to be a rescuer, fixer, or problem solver.

Focusing on skill also allows you to have substantive focal points in your shared conversation rather than feeling stuck in wondering if the mentor will meet your expectations. Disappointments in mentoring relationships are inevitable, as Bob's story about his first mentor demonstrates! However, when the tasks of mentoring are clarified and skills, knowledge, and integration are front and center, then the disappointments can become opportunities for more learning rather than the end of the relationship.

❦

In the book *Deep Smarts: How to Cultivate and Transfer Enduring Business Wisdom*, professor of business administration Dorothy Leonard and professor of psychology Walter Swap assemble case studies and examples of how the wisdom of leadership is transferred through mentoring relationships in the world of business.[1] Leonard and Swap, a married couple, researched and wrote their book for and about entrepreneurs. Their work focuses on how wisdom, or "deep smarts," is critical for running start-up businesses. They say, "Deep smarts are a potent form of expertise based on first-hand life experiences, providing insights drawn from tacit knowledge, and shaped by beliefs and social forces. Deep smarts are as close as we get to wisdom."[2] They also frame the process of skill acquisition with the novice-to-expert model of skill acquisition. The *deep smarts* they are exploring take form in knowing, being, and doing and only grow with time and experience.[3]

The authors focus on two powerful modes of transferring knowledge and skill for the business world: mentoring and storytelling.[4] These are parallel and powerful modes for teaching and transferring the skills and knowledge to the practice of ministry.

For example, they show how business skills are built up in the "heads, hands and relationships" of entrepreneurs and business leaders.[5] Ministry skills are cultivated in a similar way. This capacity and growth of knowledge, skill, and wisdom can be thought of in terms of learning pastoral imagination. How does a new minister receive the wisdom needed for her work? Certainly with experience and time, and the support of mentors and stories is also needed to expand the process of growth in a new minister's hands, head, and relationships.

Mentoring for pastoral wisdom or imagination is important and complex work. It may look simple on the surface, but as Bob learned, it is complicated and can easily end in disappointment. Yet focusing on skills and knowledge related to ministry with a mentor who takes care and time, insight, and awareness can be a solid pathway to growth. As Bishop Vashti Murphy McKenzie advises, it is the work of a beginning minister to seek a mentor who has skills and a willingness to show the way.

✺　QUESTIONS FOR REFLECTION AND CONVERSATION

Consider the following to guide your journaling or spark conversation with mentors and friends:

- What qualities should I look for when recruiting a mentor?

◆ What "deep smarts" do I want to understand better for my practice of ministry?

◆ How could I make the most of my potential mentoring relationships by focusing on skills and asking for stories?

🌿 THREE MINUTE MINISTRY MENTOR

Watch episode 12, "Mentoring for Skill," https://3mmm.us/Episode12

13

Stakes of Ministry

It seems to me that when you ask, *what is pastoral imagination?*
It is somehow the intersection of what's at stake with what is
good.

—Charles Foster

The call came late in the day on a Friday. I was the only minister on a staff of
four who was still working in the office that afternoon. When the phone rang,
it was a church member looking for the pastor—the senior pastor, Jim.[1]

A church member was dead. Gary had simply dropped dead at work. Literally. Dead before he hit the ground. Gary was forty. He was married to Julie
and was the father of four children ages three to eleven. People were going to
Julie's house. Where was our pastor Jim? He was needed.

This was before everyone carried a smartphone. I tried calling Jim's house. I
tried his wife's work number. I left messages everywhere. I called Gary's deacon,
and I checked in with church members again to tell them I could not find Jim.

I was supposed to meet my husband for dinner. I couldn't figure out what
else to do. I felt uneasy. I was in shock. Gary was only a few years older than me.
His children were young. His wife was one of my favorite moms to work with
on church projects. I relayed the news in disbelief to my husband, wringing my
hands as we drove to the restaurant.

I was missing the urgency of the situation and looking for someone else
who would respond. Even my body told me I was wrong. The sinking feeling in
my stomach kept me from eating much of my dinner. I kept trying to reach Jim
from my husband's cell phone.

The call was for me, but I kept thinking it was for someone else. The pastor. My imagination failed. My ability to see myself fully as the pastor who took
the call and needed to go and be with the family was beyond my grasp in that
moment of crisis. I missed what was really at stake.

By Saturday morning, I awoke with a great sense of failure. I was beginning to see where I went wrong, and I hurried to make up for my mistake. I

went to Julie's house, and when I found her, we cried together. That moment was a beginning point for a long walk through grief.

In ministry, the life-and-death urgency of our work is not always completely evident, especially to a beginner. Yet advocating for clean water, educating about domestic violence, responding to the threat of suicide—these are frontline moments of ministry that have a clear sense of urgency about them. The stakes are high, and these moments matter because life and death are on the line.

In the spring of 2020, many ministers came face-to-face with a new level of high stakes in the world of ministry. As a worldwide pandemic erupted in early March, pastors, chaplains, and ministry staff found themselves facing life-and-death circumstances every day. The big irony was trying to walk the line between staying physically distant and canceling in-person gatherings while also contemplating care for those who were sick and dying of COVID-19 and all the usual diseases and chronic illnesses without being able to interact safely in person.

Christian educator and early advisor to the LPI Project Charles Foster said in one of our first advisory meetings in 2009 that it is precisely where "what is good" meets "what is at stake," or the urgent, at that exact spot, that we will find "pastoral imagination" coming to life. Seeing and acting on those high stakes is key.

⌘

How do we cultivate a pastoral imagination that can rise to the highest stakes in the work of ministry?

A resource that helps us think about the high stakes of any situation and how to respond to it in the best possible way is the book *Blink: The Power of Thinking by Not Thinking* by Malcolm Gladwell. Although the book is not about ministry per se, Gladwell does help us think about cultivating expertise, what Sarah Lewis might call *mastery* (see chapter 10, "Failing Creatively"), and what we call *pastoral imagination*. It is a capacity that sees a situation clearly and responds to the high stakes of the moment in the most fitting way. It is often done in a nanosecond, the blink of an eye.

In the moment when Gary died, I missed what was at stake when someone called for a pastor. I was looking for someone else, but the phone call came *for me*. Fortunately, that failure to see what was obvious led to other learning when I began to see my misunderstanding.

It was a beginner mistake. And although I felt embarrassed and chagrined when I realized my missteps, it was also a powerful growing moment. It really felt like a big failure that I did not go directly to Julie's house when the call came. Yet my recovery resulted in some lasting changes to my self-understanding and my capacities as a pastor. And my colleagues took time to process with me what happened and included me in leading Gary's funeral service. I also took an intentional and active role in supporting Julie in the year that followed that fateful day.

One of the big takeaways for me in these missteps and recovery was a permanent adjustment in my self-understanding as a pastor. As I regained my footing, I was able to do some creative and compassionate pastoral work with Julie and with the community as a whole. The other big takeaway came when I saw what kind of deep listening was needed amid such a shocking loss. I took a new risk in the way I reached out to support Julie in that year that followed her spouse's death.

So the stakes were high. I stumbled. And yet with the help of a few others and a willingness on my part to start again, I reengaged and recovered. Julie struggled with her loss, of course, but she never lost the grace of being herself and letting me and others into her life during her grief. She taught me a great deal about what was at stake in a loss so profound.

After that loss, I do not believe that I again hesitated or faltered when I heard about a crisis or sudden loss. I gained significant clarity about what is at stake, and I came to understand more fully how to respond.

QUESTIONS FOR REFLECTION AND CONVERSATION

Consider the following to guide your journaling or spark conversation with mentors and friends:

+ What is at stake in the ministry to which I am called? How am I prepared to respond?
+ Has there been a point in my ministry thus far when I came face-to-face with my identity as a pastor, priest, chaplain, activist, or minister in a new or urgent way? If so, how did I respond to this new understanding?
+ Within my practice of ministry, how am I hearing the calls that come in just for me?

THREE MINUTE MINISTRY MENTOR

Watch episode 13, "Stakes of Ministry," https://3mmm.us/Episode13

14

Contemplative Prayer

Contemplative prayer is not so much the absence of thoughts as detachment from them. It is the opening of the mind and heart, body and emotions—our whole being—to God, the Ultimate Mystery, beyond words, thoughts and emotions.

—Thomas Keating, *Open Mind, Open Heart*

In my fifth year of ministry in my first call to a congregation in North Georgia, the atmosphere was thick with conflict. The church was in its twelfth year, and looking back a couple of decades later, I know it was in an organizational life cycle of modest decline that needed renewal. I could not see any of that at the time. I don't think anyone else could either. All we could see was disagreement and anxiety.

As the youth and education minister and as an ordained woman, I felt the brunt of a great deal of that anxiety, and open conflicts focused on me. It was the worst kind of congregational behavior, with unkind speech, secret meetings, and political maneuvers. Most of it escalated around the time of retirement and departure of another staff member.

The conflict was less about what it appeared to be on the surface and more a symptom that signaled a significant need for intentional change. It takes more experience, perspective, and wisdom than most new ministers can muster to see these congregational life-cycle issues. Often the focus of the conflict is on staff and leadership, and our situation was no exception.

Thus I was under a lot of personal stress and feeling like a target of one group of members who wanted me to resign while receiving positive messages from another group who hoped I would become their next pastor. In this season, I felt like I simply ran out of words. All the words I used to pray publicly and privately felt empty and vain. I was not eating or resting well. I was losing weight, and at times, I could not even find my voice. Literally. I got laryngitis.

As a journal keeper, I reached for my pen and notebook and used my writing as an outlet to process the overwhelming situation. I found myself writing over and over in my journal, *I need to get centered.*

Then one Sunday afternoon in September, I headed into the church to prepare for youth ministry in the evening. I stopped by the office to make copies. And there on top of the copier was a brochure. The brochure was titled "Centering Prayer." I had never heard of it, but it sounded like something I needed.

I quickly dropped the brochure into the copier and made a two-sided copy. Then I left the brochure right where I found it.

The next morning when I awoke, I reached for the instructions on centering prayer, which I had placed on my nightstand. And thus I began a daily twenty-minute practice of praying in silence without words or images that lasted for more than thirteen years. That prayer supported me through the ending of that ministry position, in which I felt daily like I was standing in the eye of a hurricane. The practice of contemplative prayer helped me survive the conflict intact. The practice also nourished me through the years of doctoral study, becoming a parent, dissertation writing, and finding my first academic job.

The practice of contemplative prayer was a godsend in every way.

The practice is simple. Sit still and quiet in a place where you can be fully alert and also fully relaxed. Choose a sacred word or phrase to guide you back into silence whenever your mind strays. And it will. The word—such as *Spirit* or *Jesus, Father, Mother, Stillness, Peace*—is not a mantra; rather, it is a sacred word to guide you and help you return to the silence. The silence is not empty. Silence is the language of God, and silence is full of an abundance of God's presence. The prayer invites you to simply be in that sacred presence.

The practice of contemplative prayer is now anchored in my whole being and available to me at any time. I have taught it to many people at retreats and in my seminary classes. I find that students and people of faith are hungry for deep rest and the solitude and quiet of silence.

What is the connection between the practice of prayer and the practice of ministry?

The connections we make between prayer and ministry depend on how we understand each practice. I grew up in a noisy, talkative tradition, where *prayer* was mostly words and communication with God—in the power of the Spirit and in the name of Jesus. If we were not talking, we were supposed to be listening for a word from God. In that same tradition, ministry was something done by white men called by God. How they prayed outside of public worship was mostly hidden and unclear to me.

I teach prayer in my seminary classes because I think there is a profound connection between one's spiritual practice and one's energy and focus for ministry. Praying is not just charging your batteries up so you can keep going like the Energizer ministry bunny. Spiritual practice and ministry practice are intimately related. Prayer is a source and grounding for one's identity and purpose of tending to faith communities, sacred rituals, and the work of justice; the stewardship of mercy; and the tremendous need for pastoral imagination.

The silence of centering prayer can also be a bit frightening when thoughts come up that perhaps you had been pushing away or hoping to avoid. This and other complications of centering prayer need guidance from the people and communities who prayed and then wrote about their experiences over the centuries.

An important and now classic text for understanding contemplative prayer, one that guided me, is by Fr. Thomas Keating. In his book *Open Mind, Open Heart* and on his organization's website, Fr. Keating anticipates nearly every question that can arise while learning the practice of contemplative prayer.[1]

New seasons of the year, new seasons of life, and times of challenge and conflict like the one I experienced at the end of my time serving the North Georgia church are times ripe for new practices of prayer and meditation. If you are facing a transition, perhaps exploring a new spiritual practice would be a way to ground yourself during the change and upheaval around you.

I wrote the following poem about the experience of practicing centering prayer while still being aware of the physical sounds and mental images that tugged at my mind and senses.

rain

after days on end of mercury topping the charts
it is sweet relief waking to soft drumming rain
on leaves outside my window
low clouds churn and roil and my daughter says to the
    thunder
that's the sound of my belly growling, I'm so hungry
in the next room her giggle rises
while I return to my prayer word and sit still as a droplet
    waiting to fall
I let her words, the sounds from outside my head and
    inside my heart pass by
all so much weather
like moods that rise up and crash around the house
like sauna conditions when the sun finally pushes through
    clouds
like the thrum of desire, the bitterness of resentment, the
    savoring of flattery,
look it in the eye, don't flinch, and watch it go
all just so much weather

what remains is stillness, like marrow, like sap, like down-
    filled nests,
like the center of a rain drop
holding on
plummeting back to earth
in the moment everything falls away
and at once, I am a singular drop, the whole universe,
the sacred in the moment
giving way to words and feelings that will never see the
    light of day
nor the deep of night,
giving way to awareness itself,
giving over everything
to the echo chamber of silence,
in every particle, every hope, every tick of the clock, every
    hummingbird feather,
every droplet waiting to fall
is the sound of God waiting to catch me.[2]

The best support will come from a community of practice—people who will pray with you at a designated time each day, week, or month. Keating's book and website and many other classic and contemporary texts can also accompany you as you explore the practice of contemplative prayer.

QUESTIONS FOR REFLECTION AND CONVERSATION

Consider the following to guide your journaling or spark conversation with mentors and friends:

- What spiritual practice is calling to me now? And what prevents me from beginning?
- What connections do I notice in my life between the practice of prayer and the practice of ministry?
- How has prayer reshaped my mind and body over time?

THREE MINUTE MINISTRY MENTOR

Watch episode 14, "Contemplative Prayer," https://3mmm.us/Episode14

15

Emotional Intelligence

In my own experience, a great transformation begins when we look at our minds with curiosity and respect rather than fear and avoidance. Inviting our thoughts and feelings into awareness allows us to learn from them rather than be driven by them. We can calm them without ignoring them; we can hear their wisdom without being terrified by their screaming voices.

—Daniel Siegel, *Mindsight:*
The New Science of Personal Transformation

Eleven-year-old Riley is having a crisis. Inside her brain, Joy and Sadness have gone missing. They're wandering around lost in the nether regions of her long-term memory. They are trying to get back to headquarters. Along the way, they bump into Riley's old imaginary friend Bing Bong. He's part elephant, part cat, and part dolphin—but mostly cotton candy. The three of them set out to return to headquarters (the executive-function section of Riley's brain).[1]

As a tween, Riley is going through the early stages of remodeling her adolescent brain. Feelings are out of kilter, and connections to family, hobbies, memories, and identity are shaky. Both inside and outside, Riley is in a crisis.

Psychologist Daniel Siegel would say that Riley is going through a two-part process of adolescent brain remodeling: pruning (reducing unused brain material) and myelination (strengthening important brain pathways).[2] In other words, she's getting rid of memories: graham-cracker castle, sparkle pony mountain, and the stuffed animal hall of fame are all coming down. Stories and memories she no longer needs are crumbling. On the other hand, new and important parts of her identity are gradually making stronger pathways in her brain.

Meanwhile, Sadness and Joy are still on a quest to return to headquarters. However, Bing Bong has found the imaginary, song-powered wagon he and Riley created. He still has plans for that rocket-wagon. He and Riley were going to the moon!

Suddenly it is being pushed toward a giant cliff. Bing Bong cannot reach the wagon in time. He sees it swept into the place of lost memories. He sits down sadly at the edge of a cliff, looking like he might cry.

Joy comes over and tries to cheer Bing Bong up. She tries to reassure and then fix the situation. She makes silly faces, tries a guessing game, and tugs on him to get him moving. She even tries the tickle game. But nothing works because Bing Bong is sad. Joy is in a big hurry to get back to headquarters. She is eager to shortcut any other feelings that distract her from her purpose. In exasperation, she walks away. But then Sadness comes to sit down beside Bing Bong.

Sadness immediately begins to connect with Bing Bong, acknowledging his feelings of sadness over his loss. She gets Bing Bong to tell a story. She doesn't try to change his mind about how he feels. Soon he is pouring everything out to her, and he even cries. The curious thing about Bing Bong is that when he cries, candy pops out of his eyes instead of teardrops. ("Try a caramel one, it's delicious!") After he's had a good cry, he gets up and says, "I'm okay now. Come on! The train station is this way."

Joy is shocked and amazed. How did Sadness do that? Her approach of acknowledging feelings instead of trying to avoid them worked, and it resulted in something happening. Learning to listen and learning how complex emotions work together are two of the big takeaways of the movie *Inside Out*.

༼ঌয়ৄঔ

Understanding the complexity and interplay of emotions like joy and sadness, fear and anger, surprise and disgust is crucial if we are to care well for others in our congregations, small groups, ministry settings, and/or activist movements. Recognizing emotions in ourselves and others, expressing and managing feelings—these are the work of emotional intelligence. Without this kind of intelligence, we can find ourselves stuck and unable to connect with others or move our plans or lives forward.

The emotional intelligence we receive from families and have cultivated by our communities is not the end of the story. Brains are ever changing, and not just during the period of adolescent remodeling like Riley was going through. Social psychology and brain science help us understand how emotional intelligence can continue to grow, change, and expand over time. Even mature adults can expand their skills and perceptions related to emotional intelligence at every stage of life.[3]

What exactly makes up one's emotional intelligence? There are lots of academic and popular accounts of what is included in an emotional intelligence quotient (EQ). Here is a quick summary of some key features:

1. Being able to recognize and identify emotions in your own body and mind and discern what information they are offering about yourself and the world around you

2. Being able to observe, honor, and experience a full range of emotions and not becoming overwhelmed or paralyzed by them
3. Recognizing complex and sometimes rapidly changing emotions in others without flipping your lid or running away[4]
4. Knowing how to respond to the emotional tone and communication of others through mirroring and empathy
5. Utilizing emotion for motivation and self-regulation in work, family, and friendship

Emotional intelligence is a tremendous gift for the relational and embodied practice of ministry. Every day we will be called on to interpret the complex emotions of people in our communities and to respond with empathy and understanding. These are important building blocks of meaningful relationships. To lead well and with pastoral imagination, we need to cultivate our emotional intelligence.

Consider watching for your learning and enjoyment the movie *Inside Out*. Riley's story of adolescent change may resonate or bring to life the various ways you navigated change at earlier points in your life. Perhaps there is someone you care about who will watch the movie with you—just ask them.

QUESTIONS FOR REFLECTION AND CONVERSATION

Consider the following to guide your journaling or spark conversation with mentors and friends:

+ What feelings in my life need acknowledgment, expression, or honoring?
+ How will emotional awareness enhance my practice of ministry?
+ How can I relate with empathy to people in my orbit who are struggling either with managing strong feelings or with getting in touch with any emotions at all?

THREE MINUTE MINISTRY MENTOR

Watch episode 15, "Emotional Intelligence," https://3mmm.us/Episode15

16

Engaging Ritual

> Through the ritualized telling of the story of salvation,
> grounded in the context of the assembled people, the moral
> character and identity of the Christian community is formed,
> informed and shaped.
>
> —Mark Allman, "Eucharist, Ritual, and Narrative"

"My leadership was put on a firing squad"—this is how Pastor Ginger described the worst month of her ministry.

Ginger is a white Lutheran pastor with more than twenty-five years of ministry experience. When we interviewed her, Ginger had been leading her current congregation for four years. She shared this story while we were gathered with a group of seasoned pastors for a daylong conversation hosted by the LPI Project. She called her story a "kind of failure/success thing."

First Lutheran Church was in a time of both budget stress and personnel crisis. In January, the congregation held its annual meeting, a Lutheran practice of looking back to assess the previous year with reports and narratives and an opportunity to look ahead at the coming year. Pastor Ginger and the leadership team of the congregation spoke to their crisis and presented the financial and ministry plan for the coming year. They suggested one solution that might include a staff restructuring. No particular plans were announced concerning which jobs might be impacted.

With only this modest information in hand and no advance notice about particular staff changes, First Lutheran's longtime choir director felt the announced changes were directed at her. The day after the annual meeting, the choir director called a staff meeting. Agitated while she spoke, the choir director took out her frustrations on Ginger, and then she resigned on the spot.

The congregation holds deep commitments to liturgy, sacraments, and music. The choir director was highly skilled and well liked, especially by the ninety-member choir. Ginger intuitively knew this could be very bad for her own leadership. She felt "pretty stunned," but she refused the choir director's resignation, insisting on more time to talk. That evening at choir rehearsal, the director handed out a letter of resignation. By that night, Ginger had hundreds of angry people at her throat on email, phone, and text messages. The actions had set off a firestorm.

Over the next month—her worst in ministry—Pastor Ginger found her situation so physically nerve-wracking that she says she only survived by downing "gallons of antacid!" Pastor Ginger's first response was a long email to the choir, but that only fanned the flames. The council advised her to accept the resignation publicly and let the director go.

That approach, however, did not sit right with Ginger. She said, "As a businessperson, that would've been the right thing to do, [but] I believed that in the church we could somehow act differently." She also knew she "was out on a limb alone."

So Pastor Ginger pulled together some key choir members, a pastoral colleague, and a local seminary professor to help her sort through her next steps. Although she was acting against the advice of the church council, she felt the lay leaders' support and appreciated the freedom they gave her to lead.

After a few weeks, Pastor Ginger tentatively approached the choir director. She proposed sharing in the opening prayer before choir rehearsal and serving communion together to the choir. It was a risk, but she knew the power of worship and sacraments to convey the grace and mercy of God. She said, "It took the power off of either of us because the sacrament carried the power. I think what made it work, obviously, is that we all kind of admitted our own brokenness in the whole mess."

The full choir accepted the gesture, participating and even weeping. While the ritual engagement did not resolve everything, it allowed for a new agreement. The choir director continued in a half-time position, and they had another year of good ministry before the choir director departed First Lutheran on good terms.

Additionally, it was a turning point for trust in Ginger's pastoral leadership with the staff and with the congregation as a whole. She concluded her story by saying, "In many ways, God's grace has shaped all of us through that." She says her prayer was "Oh, thank you! Help me learn!"

❧

Ritual can be a significant aspect of public activism and a powerful statement of values that go beyond words. Rituals can bear witness to both profound harms and powerful conversion. Ritual leadership can be misleading or abusive, and it is not simply good because it is a ritual.

Recently I took some of my seminary students to a "Beating Guns" event in Nashville, where author Shane Claiborne and pastor Michael Martin led us in a passionate liturgy filled with statistics and singing, rap music and stories, Scripture and poetry, digital images and fire. One of the central aims of the worship event is to transcend the gun debate in America. They projected these ideas on a screen for worshippers to see and contemplate. One slide says, "Guns are the problem, and we must reduce the number of weapons," and next to it, "Humans are the problem, and we just need to change hearts."

We gathered in the nearly two-hundred-year-old Christ Church Cathedral in downtown Nashville. The church is not only the oldest Episcopal church in the city; it is also the cathedral parish of the Episcopal Diocese of Tennessee. The V. Rev. Timothy Kimbrough welcomed us, and he reminded us that the first building of the church, located several blocks away at Sixth and Spring Streets, was built with the physical and unpaid labors of enslaved people in the 1830s.

The rise of guns and the rise of white supremacy came at the same time in the United States. To hold a service of rituals at this house of worship actually did spiritual and theological work on several levels.

At the opening of the service, Pastor Michael showed us an automated weapon, designed to kill as many people as possible as quickly as possible. He held it up in the sanctuary of the cathedral. This weapon was already severed in half. It was no longer usable as a killing machine. In the ninety minutes it took to complete our worship service, Pastor Michael and others from the Nashville community turned that exact weapon from an instrument of death into an implement of life.

On the tour, each service is punctuated by turning a gun into a garden tool. Each tool retains the serial number of the disarmed gun so that the transformed history can be traced into a new future. The call of the prophets to turn swords into plowshares echoes through the Hebrew Scriptures:

> [The Lord] shall judge between many peoples,
> and shall arbitrate between strong nations far away;
>
> they shall beat their swords into plowshares,
> and their spears into pruning hooks;
> nation shall not lift up sword against nation,
> neither shall they learn war any more;
> but they shall all sit under their own vines
> and under their own fig trees,
> and no one shall make them afraid;
> for the mouth of the Lord of hosts has spoken.
>   (Micah 4:3–4)

Why do these rituals matter now? The statistics on gun violence are staggering. And just one day before the Nashville event, the world witnessed yet another mass shooting in a horrific event where fifty Muslim worshippers were killed in Christchurch, New Zealand. Another three dozen people were hospitalized in the country's second largest city.

The United States has 5 percent of the world's population and 50 percent of the world's guns. Speaking to worshippers, Claiborne made his point clear: "We need God to change our hearts, but we need to get off our butts to change some laws."

For me, the real power of the ritual and the presence of something holy came in the transformation that we witnessed in the service: Change was ritualized right before our eyes. All the guns in these worship services are donated. Each gun is cut down and reforged in a portable furnace that reaches temperatures in excess of 2,100 degrees. In the glowing white-hot heat, we see the literal refashioning of a gun into a garden tool—a trowel or spade.

That night in Nashville was so cold that we sat inside Christ Church for most of the liturgy. At one point in the service, we were invited to take small pieces of paper and write down the hostilities we wanted to eradicate from our own hearts. Soon we trekked outside where the portable forge was set up. Additional flames flickered in small portable gas stoves around the parking lot. Everyone was invited to release their own grudges and hostilities by dropping them into the flames.

Anyone in attendance who had experienced the violence of guns—through suicide, homicide, or accident—was invited to take part in the physical transformation of the gunmetal. They could literally transfer the energy of their grief, pain, trauma, anger, and other emotional residue from their losses into the gun, reshaping it into an implement for good. From their bodies, the energy of anger and grief became part of a newly reshaped instrument. A disarmed gun became a tool for cultivating growing things. They invested and released their lived experience and emotions into the glowing hot metal, transforming it from an instrument of death to an implement of life.

I felt the power of the ritual as I witnessed the transformation. Children, mothers, fathers, and siblings took turns pounding the glowing metal. The alchemy of their trauma and grief found release and new life in a plowshare. A garden trowel carried in its shape the transferred energies of people who had been harmed by the former instrument of death and destruction.

The power of ritual is hard to overstate. When pastoral imagination comes to life in a ritual such as communion shared by people who have been estranged or in a hammer and forge that turn trauma and grief into an instrument of life, we are participating in the mystery and the power of God's love and justice in the world.

You have access to the beauty and power of the rituals in your own tradition: baptism, singing, anointing, communion, prayer, and so on. I also recommend the book *Beating Guns* by Shane Claiborne and Michael Martin.[1]

QUESTIONS FOR REFLECTION AND CONVERSATION

Consider the following to guide your journaling or spark conversation with mentors and friends:

- How will I engage the rituals of my tradition as I lead in ministry?
- Where do I need to open myself up to the powers of imagining ways that ritual might transform communal life?
- What traumas, grief, or broken relationships in my community need the power of ritual?

THREE MINUTE MINISTRY MENTOR

Watch episode 16, "Engaging Ritual," https://3mmm.us/Episode16

17

Aha Moments

What no eye has seen, nor ear heard, nor the human heart conceived, what God has prepared for those who love [God].

—1 Corinthians 2:9

"In our church, we had a stained-glass window of a triangle with the eye of God, and that eye was always following me." Monica, now in her late fifties, recalls growing up fearful in her Roman Catholic parish. She was born into a white family of dairy farmers in the upper Midwest. She says she even felt God watching her when she pretended to be a priest, using Necco candy wafers to "play communion."[1]

Monica is a participant in the LPI Project. She told us that as a girl, she imagined becoming a nun or maybe a teacher. When she grew older, she studied accounting, and she married her high school sweetheart. They began a decades-long commitment to running both a construction company and a farm together.

Soon the local priest recruited Monica—over her many protests—to become a director of religious education. After resisting the early requests, Monica eventually embraced the work wholeheartedly. When two of Monica's family members died, she found herself drawn to becoming a volunteer for hospice care.

One afternoon at a hospice volunteer training session, a chaplain told a story about her own mother's death. Monica recalls, "I don't even know what she said, but all of a sudden it was like my heart was burning. I've never had that feeling before, and I thought, 'Oh my God, I'm supposed to be a chaplain!'"

Previously, Monica relied on her husband and family to talk her out of rash decisions when her impassioned yearnings to serve God were idealistic and impractical. But that day she went to the Catholic Education Ministries Office in her parish, and she asked, "What do I need to become a chaplain?"

One thing she needed was more formal education, and things fell quickly into place for her to begin her studies at a Roman Catholic graduate school. As

Monica began her coursework, she felt unsure about how to embrace a ministerial identity or gain official endorsement for chaplaincy. What she discovered quickly, however, were gifts, calling, and confirmation from her community that she had a vocation of lay ministry.

One semester she enrolled in a pastoral theology class, and she was assigned to a hospice care ministry to conduct listening exercises with patients. Only three patients were in care at the time, and none was able to carry on a conversation, so the chaplain himself volunteered to do the assignment with Monica.

It began rather superficially, but after a few weeks, the chaplain casually mentioned he was dying. As Monica kept listening, she learned that he was suffering from a terminal cancer. At that point, the conversation turned and deepened.

The chaplain and his wife began meeting with Monica weekly to talk about his impending death and the accompanying fears and regrets they had otherwise been avoiding discussing. The three of them grew very close, and Monica was becoming their minister. She could see what she was doing was helpful. Each week, she thanked the chaplain for helping her with her assignment. He always turned the thanks around, offering validation for her calling.

Monica found the experience very affirming. The time she spent listening to a dying chaplain and his wife confirmed gifts that others also recognized and named in Monica, such as her strong sense of "compassion" and ability to be a "healing presence." By spending those weeks listening and caring for the chaplain, Monica discovered, "This is ministry. This is who I am. This is what I'm called to do, and it was not lights and bells, but it was an *aha moment*!"

"God," said Monica, "has called me to this healing ministry."

⁂

"Aha!" So many kinds of moments deserve this word! Over the last ten years, we have conducted interviews with fifty seminarians-turned-ministers and twenty-five seasoned pastors and priests. We asked each of them to tell us about "aha moments" of their learning in ministry. Thus the LPI study is filled with wonderful, surprising, and profound moments of learning in practice.

In a few rare instances, we heard stories of classroom learning. What we heard most often were stories about CPE, seminary internships, field education, camp experiences, and other moments when people were deeply immersed in the practice of ministry itself.

Monica's story really has two "aha moments." The first one came at a moment when she felt a burning in her heart and an urgency to follow that sense of calling. She encountered the work of ministry and responded to the story that the hospice chaplain shared about her mother's death. In that embodied response—the sense that her heart was burning—was the first wisdom of her body pointing her to a calling that may have been hovering at the edges of her awareness for many years, perhaps since she played priest as a child and served communion with Necco wafers.

The second "aha moment" came in the surprising reversal of roles with her chaplain supervisor. In the stories we have collected from many ministers, we notice that a certain kind of surprise often meets a deep knowing that has been growing over time. We often call these "holy cow" moments, a phrase we borrow from Eve (see chapter 2, "Seeing Holy Depths").

To be sure, much learning for ministry comes slowly and gradually, but when there is a realization that dawns on us, we do well to capture it and seal it into our being. As Monica says, such moments are not always accompanied by lights and bells, but they are profound nonetheless. They can become for some a kind of fountain of purpose for one's practice of ministry. Monica recognized that hers was a calling to a ministry of healing. For a decade now, Monica has been living into that calling and serving people who are ill and recovering and people who are dying. She serves now as a Catholic chaplain in a regional hospital and a clinical pastoral educator.

⤝⥈⤞

In the second letter to the Corinthians, the author writes about "God's wisdom, secret and hidden" (1 Cor 2:7). It is a wisdom that is timeless and yet misunderstood by leaders with authority, the empire of the present age. Sometimes our own lives can remain hidden from us. Only God sees what is fully there. Yet on some occasions we step out into a new place, and the fullness of knowing is ours in a glimpse. In a moment, we have clarity that brings together what has previously been hidden.

In her beautiful, vulnerable, and sometimes hilarious book *Everything Happens for a Reason: And Other Lies I've Loved*, author and historian Kate Bowler describes an aha moment that came to her buried in an avalanche of letters.[2] At the age of thirty-five, Bowler was diagnosed with stage-four colon cancer. Up until the very moment of her diagnosis, she was deep in a study of prosperity gospel communities in the United States. One of the strange and unsettling results of these relationships was that hundreds of the people she had met felt compelled to write to her when she became ill.

Bowler describes three especially harsh, no matter how well intended, letters, emails, and messages she received. "These are the three life lessons people try to teach me that, frankly, sometimes feel worse than cancer itself," she says. The "Minimizers" want her to learn the lesson from her illness that she "shouldn't be so upset, because the significance of death is relative." The "Teachers" want to offer a different lesson, emphasizing that "this experience is supposed to be an education in mind, body, and spirit." The "Solutions People" want Bowler to save herself. "Keep smiling!" they say. And be faithful.[3]

None of these lessons nor their writers helped or comforted Bowler. She says the only ones who helped were the ones who could write honestly—not about the purpose of dying or suffering but about "who was there" when they faced death. Then she shares her own aha moment as "something that happened to me, something that I felt uncomfortable telling anyone." Bowler says, "It seemed too odd and too simplistic to say what I knew to be true—that when I was sure I was going to die, I didn't feel angry. I felt loved."[4]

Aha moments come in many shapes, forms, and sizes. They are often in unexpected places. These holy cow moments may seize you dramatically, or they may sneak up quietly beside you. When they grasp your imagination and shift your life, hang on. They may become the touchstones that give you strength and courage for life or even for death.

QUESTIONS FOR REFLECTION AND CONVERSATION

Consider the following to guide your journaling or spark conversation with mentors and friends:

- When I look back to my moment(s) of calling to ministry, what seeds are there that continue to grow in my practice now?
- What "aha moment"—large or small—have I experienced lately in my practice of ministry?
- How am I giving the moments that surprise me in ministry time to reveal the deeper questions or learning that they offer?

THREE MINUTE MINISTRY MENTOR

Watch episode 17, "Aha Moments," https://3mmm.us/Episode17

Preaching Jesus

"It is no use walking anywhere to preach unless our walking is
our preaching."

—Saint Francis of Assisi

When the spring term started in February of my second year in seminary, I
was still a complete novice at both preaching and pastoral care. I only had two
full-time classes that term: homiletics and CPE. Being in both learning environments at the same time turned out to be a gift.

Dr. Chuck Bugg was my homiletics professor. The hospital where I was
learning to be a chaplain was only a few miles from the seminary. This was great
except for the few times when I took the wrong turn and ended up at the seminary or the hospital on the wrong day, making myself late to the right location!

Interestingly, some of my best learning about ministry in CPE was about
preaching. Although hospital CPE usually focuses on patient care, in my
particular program, we were also expected to lead worship in the hospital on
Sundays.

As part of the weekly didactic (or teaching) portion of my learning at
the hospital, we were treated to occasional visiting teachers. To prepare us
for preaching, the CPE staff called on a local minister—my very own pastor,
Rev. Jim England—to give us some guidance before we stepped into the hospital pulpit. In that session, Jim helped me begin rethinking how to preach the
stories of Jesus.

I already knew Jim as a reliable and inspiring preacher and a kind and
generous pastor. He shared with me and my cohort of novice chaplains how
he prepared each week for his preaching task. He talked about the significance
of entering into the biblical story completely. He invited us to enter into the
gospel stories with our whole selves—body, mind, five senses, emotions, intentions, and even aspects of ourselves we don't particularly care to think about.

When Jim invited us more fully into the text, he was teaching us something important about the risk of preaching Jesus. In my limited experience,

perhaps like other seminarians and novice preachers, I had a tendency to enter into the text in preparation for preaching or teaching by basically hiding behind Jesus.

I would look over the shoulder of Jesus or peek out from behind his robes. Jesus was the central character in most of the gospel stories. So when I began to read a text, I identified with him as the protagonist. Then I looked at the rest of the story from the vantage point of Jesus's protection. I filtered what was happening in the story through the perspective of Jesus, where he was standing and seeing the world.

Jim England put the brakes on that approach. He said, in effect, "When you are preparing to preach, come out from hiding behind Jesus. Stop looking over his shoulder. Stop judging everyone he was talking to. Step out in front of Jesus and hear the words that he says. See the actions that he takes and open yourself to his message. Be on the receiving end of a parable, a beatitude, a commandment."

Suddenly I became the antagonist in the story. The words of Jesus were aimed at me. I was the one who had a log in her eye, couldn't get along with my neighbor, came crawling back to my parents, or felt the sting of seeing my younger brother treated better than me. This perspective was completely upending my tendency to be the champion and channel of the words of Jesus.

᭢᭢

On the days I was in class at the seminary, I was learning that preaching is a topic about which hundreds and probably thousands of books are already written. We read a few of them, yet we were also learning in the laboratory of preaching about the embodied, emotional, and relational aspects of preaching.

Dr. Bugg introduced us to the art of preaching by giving us images to guide us as we grew into being more mature preachers. For example, he taught us a powerful lesson about preaching that I could take in intellectually, but I could not understand it fully for several more years. He said, in effect, "When you're preaching, you need to be able to see clearly with your inner eye what it is you are saying. You can't simply be saying the words that are on the page or sharing good ideas. You need to visualize the message and then describe it to your listeners in ways they can follow you."

He liked to say that preaching was like getting people on the bus with you. And as you move through your sermon, you need to keep them on the bus with you. In other words, preaching is an event that tries to take people somewhere new. It takes a particular kind of effort to get them to come with you and stay with you.

Whether taking a walk and getting out in front of the words of Jesus or getting people on a bus with you to follow your ideas through a sermon, preaching is a fully embodied and dynamic practice. I practiced my preaching in the classroom. But the real test of what I was learning came at the hospital.

I preached my first sermon outside of class standing at the front of the tiny hospital chapel. It was Easter morning, and I preached about Mary Magdalene from the Gospel of John. Rev. England invited me to step into the story and identify with characters and emotions in the story. I did. Dr. Bugg invited me to see the sermon and get people on the bus with me. I tried.

Immediately after the worship service was over and patients were wheeled back to their rooms, I sat down with my peers and supervisors for a critique of my sermon and worship leading. It was unnerving. What I remember about that circle is that I feared the criticism, yet what I heard was affirmation. It turned out that I loved it so much that I volunteered to preach again . . . on Mother's Day.

That was my first time preaching Jesus from a pulpit, but it certainly wasn't my last.

"Preach at all times and use words when necessary." Have you heard this saying? I have heard it many times and used it myself, attributing it to Saint Francis of Assisi. After a little digging, however, it turns out those might not have been the words that Saint Francis said. What scholars can affirm is that Saint Francis said something similar, something closer in English to "It is no use walking anywhere to preach unless our walking is our preaching."[1]

As your practice of ministry changes, grows, and matures, so should your preaching and public speaking. Even if you are not a regular pulpit minister, your life, your walking, your talking, and your public presentation have an obligation to embody the grace and teachings of Jesus. This obligation is not solely because you are a minister but more importantly because you are a disciple of Jesus.

One of the most challenging aspects of understanding Jesus is the long history of misunderstanding the Jewishness of Jesus. When I reread my first sermon preached on that Easter Sunday morning so long ago, I don't see overt blaming of Jewish leaders, and I recall learning in seminary how important it is not to disparage "the Jews" in any way, giving special care when it comes to the passion story of Jesus. But I also can see hints in that sermon that I didn't understand enough about the realities of Jesus's Jewishness.

For going deeper in that understanding, I highly recommend the 2006 book *The Misunderstood Jew: The Church and the Scandal of the Jewish Jesus* by Dr. Amy-Jill Levine.[2] This is a book that helps Christians reduce their misunderstandings of Jesus, who was in every respect a first-century Jewish rabbi. The book also works to build understanding between Christians and Jews through careful analysis and breaking open stereotypes that keep animosity and misunderstanding in place.

Preeminent scholar of the New Testament and champion of Jewish-Christian dialogue, Levine says, "Today Jesus's words are too familiar, too domesticated, too stripped of their initial edginess and urgency. Only when heard through first-century Jewish ears can their original edginess and urgency be recovered."[3] She invites readers to see how profoundly important it is for Christians and preachers to see the Jewishness of Jesus, a first-century rabbi. She also wants us to "see Jesus as firmly within Judaism rather than as standing apart from it, and it is essential that the picture of Judaism not be distorted through the filter of centuries of Christian stereotypes; a distorted picture of first-century Judaism inevitably leads to a distorted picture of Jesus."[4]

It takes a whole community of pastors, preachers, scholars, and saints to help us preach Jesus well. Preaching on all subjects remains an embodied, relational, and emotionally fraught task. It is political and personal. It requires us to dig deep in the scholarship of the Bible and history and also to learn through embodied experience and feedback. The next time you take on the task of preaching Jesus, I hope you will pause and consider the risks and responsibilities of that work.

✒ QUESTIONS FOR REFLECTION AND CONVERSATION

Consider the following to guide your journaling or spark conversation with mentors and friends:

- ✦ What have I learned about preaching Jesus? Are there ways I hide from him? Misunderstand him? Overlook his Jewishness? Or oversimplify Jesus or his teachings?
- ✦ The next time I am preparing to preach a Gospel text, how will I step out from behind Jesus to see and hear the words and intentions *for myself* more clearly?
- ✦ What risks are there in deciding to preach Jesus in the current historical and cultural moment? How will I keep my listeners moving along with the message?

✒ THREE MINUTE MINISTRY MENTOR

Watch episode 18, "Preaching Jesus," https://3mmm.us/Episode18

Brick Walls

> Really it wasn't that useful for me personally to be beating my
> head against that brick wall.
>
> —Pastor Debbie

What kind of brick walls have you run up against in ministry? They take
many forms. A refusal by a denominational body to recognize your call? An
unwillingness on the church's part to make much-needed change? A lack of
imagination to see possibilities for transformation? Some of the brick walls
of injustice—like sexism, racism, and heterosexism—are nearly invisible until
we run headlong into them.

As we gathered to hear stories from participants in the LPI Project a few
years ago, we asked the ministers to bring us up to date on their lives. Theresa,
a white woman in her early thirties, jumped in to tell her story. She recalled
that the last time we gathered with her cohort in this circle, she was desperately
searching for a second call because her two-year pastoral residency was coming
to an end.

In that search process, she found herself for the first time in an otherwise privileged life experiencing oppression completely beyond her control. As
a woman in a committed partnership with another woman, she found herself
trying to convince churches of her worth as a minister, and it felt like she was
"banging her head against a brick wall."

Just a week after her residency ended, however, Theresa found herself
interviewing for a chaplain's job with a midwestern college that was surprisingly ready for her gifts. She learned from prior experiences interviewing with
churches how to educate a committee from the outset about her marriage
rather than apologize for her inability to meet their expectations.

She gave a dynamic interview, and the school hired her. She says, "It was
like the brick wall had not gone away, but it is as if I walked around it. I'm aware
it is still there, but I'm not banging my head on it anymore, although I still have
some bruises, maybe a black eye and some scars."

The college where Theresa went to work as a chaplain and adjunct professor was in the midst of many financial challenges and a lot of anxiety, but as she says with recognition and determination, "I serve the church. And I love, love, love everything I do." After two years of ministry as a college chaplain, Theresa says she feels, in the words of the apostle Paul, "grounded and rooted in love" for her family and her work (Eph 3:17).

Despite the real limits of her situation (the brick walls have not gone away), Theresa reimagined her own place and gifts for ministry moving beyond apology to educating others, claiming her gifts, and making the most of the possibilities within her reach.

Although some of the walls Theresa ran into were surely visible, other aspects of what she coped with came in the form of silence and invisibility, failing to acknowledge or honor her experience as a queer person. These are the walls that Cody Sanders and Angela Yarber call "microaggressions in ministry."[1]

❧

Brick walls come in many shapes and sizes. They stand in the way of ministry with sometimes hidden force. Often what feels like a brick wall is a deep and abiding social injustice or traumatic loss.

Debbie is a single white Lutheran pastor. When she was in her late twenties, she served a small rural church in the economically depressed Iron Range of northern Minnesota. She shared with us her frustrations over the stubborn challenge of helping folks in her congregation of ten to twelve understand how to welcome visitors. The profound economic and personal losses, the social isolation of the community, and the emotional stoicism of the church members left Debbie feeling like any attempt to introduce change was "like talking to a brick wall."

She recalls, "Families would come to church, and when you only have ten people in a congregation, you know who the visitors are. It's pretty obvious. I would watch this church not shake hands with them during the passing of the peace, not introduce themselves, not welcome them, not hand them a bulletin, not show them where we were in the book. Then they would say with straight faces, 'Why haven't any of them come back?'"

"It was heartbreaking," said Debbie, "because they wanted the church to be there for people living in the Iron Range. A story of a lot of their lives has been one of loss or of marginalization, and this is just a constant experiencing of that. Yet they were just doing it to themselves, and they couldn't see that or accept it."

The "overwhelming sense of loss" was a drain on Debbie's pastoral energies. She observed, "The absences on a Sunday morning, I think, were felt more strongly than the presence of anyone that was there. I think they would sit in that church building that was mostly empty on Sunday morning and would kind of feel the weight of all of that emptiness in the pews." Lillian Daniel calls this dynamic having "ghost families" in the church, which haunt and influence through their absence.[2] To a new pastor, it feels like banging one's head into an invisible brick wall.

In her one-year internship, Pastor Debbie struggled to find her way past or around the brick walls of the congregation. "Really," said Debbie, "it wasn't that useful for me personally to be beating my head against that brick wall."

With every interview we conducted across ten years, we heard inspired stories of the ways that many of the people in our study worked their way around the brick walls that rose up to block their lives and ministry pathways. How do ministers, especially those new to the practice, notice, confront, and work their way around various brick walls?

In their book *Microaggressions in Ministry: Confronting the Hidden Violence of Everyday Church*, authors Cody Sanders and Angela Yarber commend ways to see and challenge, move around, or take down brick walls. Both authors are theologians and pastors, and they have firsthand experience in assessing and confronting the small, sometimes hidden injustices that can frustrate, invalidate, and do lasting harm to the people of God.[3]

As self-identified queer clergy, Sanders and Yarber have each faced bias like the ones Theresa experienced in her search and call process. Their book provides numerous examples of brick walls built out of cisgender privilege, white privilege, male privilege, and multilayered privileges that mutually reinforce one another and make microaggressions nearly impossible to detect. However, when you occupy a social location that has been marginalized, the violence and harm of the microaggressions can be felt even before they are seen or heard overtly.[4]

Yarber and Sanders offer practical and clear approaches for ministers and anyone facing microaggressions in a church setting. Here is a summary of recommendations for confronting or preventing harms to LGBTQIA folks in the church, including pastors and ministry leaders:[5]

What the microaggression looks/sounds like	How to counteract the microaggression
♦ silence; systemic erasure; absence of naming of sexual orientation or gender identity or identity markers that are important to hearers	♦ using language publicly and privately that names experiences and identities: gay, lesbian, bisexual, transgender, intersex, queer, asexual

◆ continued use of gender binary language; intentional lack of acknowledging fluid and changing identities, orientations, and interpretations; lack of acknowledgment about all binaries	◆ asking for and using each person's pronouns; intentional and ongoing conversation to expand and complexify biblical interpretations with lived experience; expanding theological imagination about the multiplicity and fluidity of identities

In Debbie's congregation, she consistently felt ignored and disregarded, in part due to her gender and status as a single person. The members of the congregation also perpetrated many microaggressions by refusing to see, acknowledge, or respond to Pastor Debbie. They also refused to welcome visitors. These aggressions were rooted in grief and pain.

Yarber and Sanders offer four recommendations for confronting gender bias against women in particular. The widespread inequities for women clearly affected Pastor Debbie, and Theresa felt it as she was seeking a new ministry position. These suggestions are aimed toward ongoing commitments to change one of the most recalcitrant sources of microaggressions in the church. Yarber and Sanders recommend these changes for organizations that wish to reduce their harms of women:

1. individual: educate individuals about gender bias;
2. organizational: create and revise value statements (mission and vision statements, covenants, etc.) to be explicitly affirming of people of all genders;
3. theological: cultivate, construct, and revise theological materials for worship, study, and proclamations by including, affirming, and valuing women; and
4. social/political: "galvanize your community, your church, and your denomination to work for . . . change."[6]

❦

Even when ministers love their work and strive to expand and cultivate the practice of ministry, brick walls have a way of rising up to impede the way, especially for ministers who are part of marginalized social groups. The work to make this change is not simply the responsibility of the marginalized person or group. It is shared, communal, and covenantal work. It is the work of the dominant groups with power to make a place of ministry that is more welcoming and affirming of everyone, including the ministers (see chapter 8, "Equity in Ministry").

☙ QUESTIONS FOR REFLECTION AND CONVERSATION

Consider the following to guide your journaling or spark conversation with mentors and friends:

+ What are the obvious and hidden brick walls in my situation where I sometimes bang my head?
+ What are some of the losses, griefs, and systemic injustices that keep the walls in place?
+ How might I step back from these brick walls in my ministry and imagine a different path around them?
+ In what ways can I empower and galvanize my organization or community to do the work of ending microaggressions and bringing down the walls?

☙ THREE MINUTE MINISTRY MENTOR

Watch episode 19, "Brick Walls," https://3mmm.us/Episode19

20

Identity and Place

Somewhere between biology and culture, a personal space opens up for morally responsible action.

—Shaun Gallagher, *Action and Inaction*

Let us consider how *identity* and *place* mutually inform the practice of ministry. Where we were called from and where we serve make a huge impact on the kind of pastor, activist, chaplain, or minister we understand ourselves to be. Our places, past and present, give not only context but also meaning to the work we do.

Fr. Stephen is in his forties and a convert to Orthodox faith as an adult. He grew up on the move as the child of a military family. He was raised as an evangelical Christian, and he discovered the "smells and bells" of Episcopal Church worship as a college student. His military service as a young adult led him to pursue a calling to ministry as a US Army chaplain. He came to seminary with three years of ministry experience already behind him. He felt impatient to finish his studies and return to chaplaincy. The real challenges were just beginning at that point.

In the army, Fr. Stephen says his ministry "is peppered with unique challenges because of the environment." The challenges include sharing worship space with other Christian traditions and other religious groups and trying to maintain the sacredness of many worship objects among military personnel who have no sense of the value or significance of those objects.

Other challenges for Fr. Stephen include moving often, being deployed to war zones, trying to serve communion from the bumper of a Humvee, and attending with care to soldiers who are not Orthodox or even Christian. Yet they come to him for advice, counsel, and comfort.

All these many challenges make Fr. Stephen go "back and forth, day to day." One day he feels "a sense of purpose and meaning and a drive to continue" in his calling. Other days he feels like he's on "the brink of despair and asking, *Is this even worth my time, energy, and effort?*"

Because of his military deployments, he says his "body has been all over the place, from Texas to Afghanistan to northern Washington . . . and all those places and all those spaces have their own unique demand on me as a chaplain and priest, and it's always shifting."

Fr. Stephen says, "Nailing down a sense of identity as a pastor has been very challenging" because he finds himself "standing in different situations all the time." While these challenges are not unique to his situation, he says they "create a great deal of difficulty for me sometimes just figuring out who I am supposed to be."

He asks, "How do I do Orthodox prayers and ministry when there's nobody else around and I'm the only Orthodox priest and there are no other Orthodox soldiers? Yet there are people standing there who need somebody to tell them about the presence of God, the love of Jesus Christ, and the power of the Holy Spirit." Fr. Stephen asks a key question: "And how do I do that in a way that honors my tradition and also invites them in?"

Perhaps you are trying to figure out how to be a pastor in a hospital or how to lead a movement of protesters. Maybe you are forging your pastoral identity with those who are dying in hospice or in a center for people struggling with homelessness. Wherever you are, that place *makes a difference* to who you are and who you are becoming.

❧✕❧

Place matters. In so many ways, it matters. Where you were born. Where you go home at night. Where you were raised. Where you work and live and play. Each of these places matter, and they shape who you are.

The places to which we return day upon day and year upon year mold and meld a deeper sense of identity and give contours to the kind of people we become. Among the many things that can be said about how place impacts our identity in ministry are these, which are also key aspects of learning the practice of ministry:

1. **Social Location.** Where we live and work give shape to our social location, which includes identity markers like gender, class, sexual orientation, gender identity, and racialized identities. Defined places like a military deployment in Afghanistan, a two-hundred-year-old church in Boston, and a hospital in rural Tennessee maintain particular ways of understanding who people are and what they should do. Narratives of race and gender and social structures live not just in books or our imaginations but in the very places where we live, play, and work. In the postmodern world, identities are more and more overtly gendered, racialized, sexualized, and ethnicized. The narratives that circulate about the

meaning of social location take on a different significance when they are named or told in new geographical locations.

Fr. Stephen is a priest, a chaplain, a father, an American, a military officer, and much more. When he shows up in the desert or on the military base, in an Orthodox church or in a restaurant with his family, different narratives of his identity come to the forefront. It is not that he is not each of these identities, but their prominence and meanings shift with the place. His social location as a white heterosexual American male in his midforties also impacts the way his other roles are understood by the people around him and perhaps even by himself. He must consistently negotiate his identity and place with the questions he is asking.

2. **Relationality.** Place has an impact on the communities we can create and in which we can participate. Places shape our imagination and impact the immediacy of our relationships as well as their value and durability. And relationships themselves, especially the ones forged in family bonds and with deep friendships, stay with us and shape us as human beings. Fr. Stephen's relationships with family, the military, and fellow Orthodox priests and community are not static but constantly changing as he moves from war zone to stateside and even from base to base.

3. **Place Knowing.** We actually take cues from our environment about what we know, how to act, *where* to take action, and even what our actions mean. For example, when I am in my car, I know how to drive almost without thinking about it, and my surroundings give me many clues about how to respond to traffic and other obstacles. The place I'm in even helps me know how to get where I am going. Outside that car, I am hard pressed to tell you all the steps and concerns that go into driving. The story from Fr. Stephen helps us see that when he is in an Orthodox sanctuary, he knows how to set up a service, serve the elements, and move through the rituals of worship. When he's in the field, he is challenged to imagine serving Eucharist from the bumper of a Humvee. Place shapes our knowledge, our skills for acting, and our understanding about the immediate world and ourselves.

Philosopher of cognition (the science of *how we know*) Shaun Gallagher writes extensively about embedded and embodied knowing—that is to say, our knowing is always situated, not universal or easily translatable to other contexts. He says, "If autonomous agents are already limited in their autonomy by biological factors, they are also embedded in physical environments and social interaction contexts that can either further limit or expand their autonomy.

Somewhere between biology and culture, a personal space opens up for morally responsible action."[1]

Let's translate that into a ministry context. Already we have been exploring how ministry as a practice is embodied: sedimented in our flesh and bones so we know the tasks of our work as if without thinking and building up a kind of knowing that becomes intuitive. We have said less about how the practice of ministry is embedded. Fr. Stephen's observations raise questions that help us think about how our practice and identity as ministers are profoundly shaped by our environment, our circumstances, our social location, and physical context. Each setting also calls on us to use our pastoral imagination to bring the ministry to life. Fr. Stephen has to stretch his thinking to serve communion from the bumper of a Humvee. He has to move within the relational field of military rules and rituals and find ways to share worship space with many other groups, some of whom have competing values.

How is he a minister, chaplain, priest, and military officer in each circumstance and situation? How does he act on his moral and spiritual values in each setting? Certainly, the variety creates some powerful dissonance in Fr. Stephen's thinking and action. Over time, these multiple places also give indelible shape to his identity. He now carries a vast array of circumstances and settings—stories in which he enacted liturgy, took note of the holy, and prayed, preached, and cared for people in need. These multiple situations and narratives become part of his pastoral imagination and expand his capacity for improvising in new situations.

QUESTIONS FOR REFLECTION AND CONVERSATION

Consider the following to guide your journaling or spark conversation with mentors and friends:

- How are the places I am from and the places where I serve impacting who I am and how I live my call?
- How has my identity as a minister been changed by the place I am currently serving?
- How am I learning to improvise my pastoral imagination and identity as a minister in each new place I encounter?

THREE MINUTE MINISTRY MENTOR

Watch episode 20, "Identity and Place," https://3mmm.us/Episode20

21

Practicing Resurrection

> Ask the questions that have no answers.
> Invest in the millennium. Plant sequoias.
> Say that your main crop is the forest
> that you did not plant,
> that you will not live to harvest . . .
> Practice resurrection.
>
> —Wendell Berry, "Manifesto: Mad Farmer Liberation Front"

The story of Jesus's resurrection is central to Christian theology and faith. Yet the concept of resurrection in our time remains troubled and stands in need of renewed life and holy imagination. Scholars, ministers, and churches that I know are engaged in such reimagination of what resurrection means for our time.

I believe it is part of our ongoing work to wrestle with the idea of resurrection and consider ways we might notice when it shows up in the world around us.

What is the problem, exactly?

To start, believing resurrection literally is incompatible with our scientific view of the world. Spiritualizing it leaves the idea hollow and useless. Yet we are surrounded by violence, death, and dying. And the world seems desperate for new life and renewed spirit. The big idea I am inviting you to consider is how *practicing resurrection* could be the most compelling way to move inside this big concept of Christian theology and faith.

What might it mean to practice resurrection?

And if ministry is a *practice* that can be learned, a complex and multifaceted, professional, and spiritual practice, then what exactly is resurrection *as a practice*? Certainly, it must be complex and multifaceted. But can it be learned? Is it embodied or relational? Can it be a matter of profession? Is it indeed a spiritual practice, or is it just a pie-in-the-sky idea, some leftover mystery from our religious past?

I first came across the idea of *practicing resurrection* in the writings of farmer, poet, and novelist Wendell Berry. He published "Manifesto: Mad

Farmer Liberation Front" in 1973, but I was a small child then. I did not hear the piece until at least twenty years later, when I was in seminary.

Just a few years ago, I stumbled into an opportunity to hear Berry speak in Nashville, and I got to ask him about practicing resurrection. The conference was about food and faith. I was in my car and on my way to hot yoga when I heard on the radio that Wendell Berry was speaking that very morning at a church between my house and the yoga studio. I turned my car around, and I drove to Saint George's Episcopal Church.

My turnaround became one of those serendipitous moments for which I will remain grateful.

༄༅

See . . . I grew up in a low-church tradition: no robes, liturgical seasons, lectionary Scriptures, or seasonal colors in the sanctuary. Just red carpet, blond maple pews, and concrete block walls with abstract stained glass in the high, half-circle windows. The worship order was the same nearly every week of the year: three or four hymns, two prayers, one sermon, passing the offering plate, invitation, benediction. Lunch!

We thought our pastor was really shaking things up when we started observing four weeks of Advent leading up to Christmas. I had heard of Lent as a child but thought it was something Catholic like rosary beads or fish on Fridays. I had no problem with any of that; it simply wasn't my tradition. So I never practiced Lent until I was in college. Even then, I approached Lent in its popularized form, thinking that giving something up for forty days might help me lose weight, or pray more often, or break my addiction to diet soft drinks.

As for me in my low-church Baptist ways, I thought Easter was just one day of the year—the day to celebrate the resurrection of Jesus, that impossible, magic-sounding part of the Jesus story.

When I moved to Louisville, Kentucky, for seminary, I joined a progressive Baptist church, and I began to get a better education about the church calendar and the seasons of the year that follow the life of Jesus. My church and the seminary experience together helped me understand that Easter is more than a day; it is a full season. And resurrection is not really magic. But it is spiritually profound to think about the impossible happening in one's life. My first sermon was about resurrection (see chapter 18, "Preaching Jesus").

My time in Louisville was also my introduction to Wendell Berry, who lives just a short drive away in the hills of Kentucky, near the Ohio state line. I first read his novels and then some of his poetry. By the time I left Kentucky for Georgia, Berry's writings were a staple on my reading list.

༄༅

In Nashville, I sat rapt, listening to the conversation among Wendell Berry, his longtime collaborator and student Norman Wirzba, and Hebrew Bible scholar

Ellen Davis. They talked about food, earth care, faith, and how they are all interconnected. When the presentations were over, I was still holding my yellow index card with a question. I visited with a few friends who also attended the gathering. Then I stood in line to talk with Wendell Berry.

He was seated by the time I reached him, so I got on one knee to get closer to eye level. (One should almost never ask elders to look up while talking.) We chatted for a few minutes. And then I asked him my question: "What have you learned in the last forty years about practicing resurrection?"

"Oh, I don't even know how I could answer that," he replied with a self-deprecating chuckle. "It seemed like a good idea when I wrote it," he added, smiling.

"Well, that's fair," I replied, chuckling with him. "I'm also wondering what you think that idea might have to say about food and faith? Is there a connection to the conversation today?"

"Well now . . . I think about getting my farm ready. You know, doing all that needs doing and keeping the fences tight. I make sure everything is done whenever I leave, for my family. In case anything happens. Then I come back home . . . and it's like resurrection."

Totally practical. Totally honest about the fragility of life and the possibility of death. Completely accountable to those he loves. And with good humor. That's how Wendell Berry practices resurrection.

Perhaps I have made it too hard in my life. Perhaps I needed to take yet another lesson from Wendell Berry. Practicing resurrection isn't perfection or magic. It's an honest practicality about how brief and how vulnerable our lives are. In so many ways, we are already the walking dead. To live with joy and abundance and humor is to practice resurrection. To look after our relationships and the things in this life that we must steward and care for and to resist the narratives that would reduce us to something less than human—to do these things is to practice resurrection.

How will you practice resurrection?

Returning to the question of the connection between ministry as a practice and resurrection as a practice, I think we should turn the question around: What can practicing resurrection teach us about the practice of ministry? About honesty, vulnerability, humor, and irreducibility? Read the "Mad Farmer Liberation Front" again. How might your practice of ministry, your pastoral imagination, look different if you allowed Berry's vision and the stories of Jesus to be in conversation in your everyday work?

❧ QUESTIONS FOR REFLECTION AND CONVERSATION

Consider the following to guide your journaling or spark conversation with mentors and friends:

- What does the Jesus story of resurrection have to offer my practice of ministry?
- How am I practicing resurrection today? This week? This season?
- What is the embodied and relational character of resurrection in my life?

❧ THREE MINUTE MINISTRY MENTOR

Watch episode 21, "Practicing Resurrection," https://3mmm.us/Episode21

22

Transforming Injustice

Racial reconciliation is a social and spiritual movement in which our identities, our relationships, our social structures, and indeed our world are to be transformed.

—Chanequa Walker-Barnes, *I Bring the Voices of My People*

As a second-career seminarian, James had already put in thirteen years as a pastor of an AME church in the South when we met him during an LPI interview day. When we asked what in his life shaped his ministry, James told us stories of being bussed to all-white schools. He told us about basketball teams that would forfeit a game rather than play any team with even one Black player. He was that one player. He told us about being on those teams and the pain, anger, and grief he felt.

James also told us how his mom could not always come to his games, but she always said to him, "Treat people the way you want to be treated," and how hard it was for him to reconcile what she said to him with what he was experiencing in his classes and on the court.

James dreamed of being a professional baseball player, but a "racial fight occurred" in his high school, and the baseball team was disbanded. James told us about his mother coming to him in tears, saying she could not afford to send him to college. Still he persisted and won a college scholarship in basketball. However, when James reached college, he was carrying with him a lifetime of loss and hurt. He could not stay in school. James told us, "I dropped out because I really couldn't process all of this anger and bitterness." The oppression and harms of personal and institutional racism took their toll on his spiritual and emotional health. He stayed angry for many years.

But anger was not the end of the story. James put it this way: "Somewhere along the way, having been raised in the church, God convinced me that I had to let it go (it wasn't something I wanted to let go), or it was going to destroy me. So then I began to really listen. I heard God clearly. What God said to me is 'I want you to take the experiences that you had and make sure it doesn't happen to anybody else.' So my life has been one of trying to share with people the things that shaped me along the way."

Now, as an inner-city AME pastor, James has turned this vision from his mother and the clear word from God toward physical, mental, and spiritual healing and uplift in the neighborhood. While in seminary, he wrote an exegetical paper about the wedding feast in Luke 14. Through the assignment, James said, "God spoke it clear in my spirit: 'You have become the very people you are writing this paper about.'" His middle-class, professional congregation was located right next to a very poor neighborhood, most of them commuting in to attend church from the suburbs. And as James put it, "There wasn't a single poor person in that church."

Over the years, this epiphany led him to guide his congregation to confront their own class biases. They responded by launching free meal programs and offering job counseling. They also created an innovative revolving loan program to fight oppressive payday loan businesses that prey on the poor and especially people of color. James says about the taunting, fighting, and injustice he experienced as a young person, "It set me back as a child, but it cast me forward as an adult."

❧❦❧

Injustice is a powerful and pervasive reality in our world. In the United States and most Western countries, both white supremacy and heteropatriarchy define the rules of every game we play. Injustices that are interwoven, upheld, and perpetuated by white supremacy and heteropatriarchy impact our work of ministry and our identities as ministers unavoidably. These structures shape how we learn pastoral practice no matter our specific calling—as pastor, organizer, chaplain, nonprofit executive, minister, or missionary. Injustices take many forms, are often rooted in long histories, and do great harm to the well-being of hearts, minds, and economic stability.

These structures shaped the experiences James had as a young child and as a teenager when the country set out to "integrate" schools and sports teams. The accumulation of harms from many generations and through years of his life were at fault in James's loss of education and potential income when he could not sustain the energy to stay in college. The structures do multiple deep harms, and they made for injustices throughout James's life.

In her 2019 book I *Bring the Voices of My People: A Womanist Vision for Racial Reconciliation*, author, pastoral theologian, and clinical psychologist Dr. Chanequa Walker-Barnes sums up the problems clearly.[1] She says, "Race is intertwined with gender and other categories of identity, just as racism is intertwined with sexism and other forms of systemic oppression. Racism is about a matrix of power and domination that is designed to support and maintain white supremacy. It is not merely about relationship. Indeed, racism structures relationships in such a way that even when separatism is overcome, power imbalances remain."[2]

Walker-Barnes spells out the implications of understanding the matrix of race and racism: "This understanding of racism obliterates the conventional Christian notion that reconciliation can be achieved simply through a focus on interpersonal friendships between people of different races."[3] Walker-Barnes is dismantling widespread Christian beliefs. The problems of race and racism cannot be eliminated by *just getting along* or *just making friends* or *just switching choirs and preachers one Sunday a year.*

While reconciliation may not be achieved through personal relationships alone, neither is it achievable only by economic means. Walker-Barnes says, "Reconciliation cannot be reduced to simple economic reparations. Racial justice must certainly include financial reparations to mitigate the multigenerational impact of displacement, stolen labor and land, inadequate education, and discrimination in employment, housing, environmental policy, healthcare, and the criminal justice system. This, however, is the entry point into reconciliation, not its *telos.*"[4]

One of the most important aspects of the story James told us is how he is leading his community to make an impact that is multifaceted in the neighborhood around his church. Class structures in his city and in this country are built on white supremacy, and those structures work to keep impoverished people in poverty. James and his congregation found creative ways to dismantle that system through microlending, community gardening, and neighborhood building initiatives. Infusing funds and relational capital into the neighborhood around the church put James and his congregation into a partnership with the holy in an initiative of healing and reconciliation for his city.

Notice that there are no white characters visible in this drama. In too many cities, white churches continue to sidestep their responsibilities in working for justice in impoverished neighborhoods that white supremacy created.

⌀⌀⌀

The central argument that Walker-Barnes makes in her book is that we need to move the voices and experiences of women of color from the margins to the center of conversations and actions that aim to heal, restore, and reconcile the wounds of racism. She says, "As focusing on the narratives of women of color demonstrates, the wounds of race extend far beyond external disparities. Thus, reconciliation must also include explicit efforts to redress the psychological, physical, spiritual, and relational impact of white supremacy upon all peoples."[5]

In the story James shared with us about his life, the centerpiece is a vision given to him by his mother. She struggled, and her pain was deep, yet she held out a vision to James "to treat others the way you want to be treated" (Matt

7:12). James found it difficult to reconcile what his mom advised him to do. And if he had only taken her advice relationally, then it would not be adequate to take root or transform injustices in James or help him lead his church to engage and transform the injustices of the neighborhood.

Instead, the vision grew in the light of a powerful and motivating word from God to "let go of anger," which helped James in his own experience of healing, and it also helped him answer a call to ministry. He entered seminary looking for an education to make him the best pastor he could be. Then came an assignment where he was confronted by a Scripture passage that illuminated the impact of evil and harmful structures of race, class, and gender. When James wrote his paper on Luke 14, he experienced conviction and epiphany. It inspired him and brought many powerful moments to life in partnership with his congregation. Together they are building a movement for healing and justice in an otherwise bleak part of his city.

What I hope white readers will see in this story is that the work of transforming injustice is a long game. It is about more than making friends with people who are not white. It is about centering the vision of people who have suffered, prioritizing the experiences of Black women and women of color, and letting their vision lead and guide us into transformative activity, economics, and relationships. It is about letting go of our need as people of privilege to be heroes and saviors, our need to be right and be in control. For those of us who identify as white and as ministers, we face the challenge of reshaping our pastoral imaginations away from always centering our own ideas and leadership. Church and society condition us to center ourselves uncritically, and we now must resist that impulse and "stop choosing seats of honor" and "making excuses" when invited to the banquet (Luke 14:8, 18). We have a calling to count the cost of our discipleship (see "Appendix: Questions for Redemptive Change").

As Walker-Barnes sums up our obligation, "To be Christian, then, is to be committed to God's mission of reconciliation. This means that racial reconciliation is neither a solely interpersonal nor a solely economic interaction. It is our responsiveness to God's offer of new life in Christ. We cannot opt out of it. We are either working toward justice and reconciliation, or we are not Christian—period."[6]

✒ QUESTIONS FOR REFLECTION AND CONVERSATION

Consider the following to guide your journaling or spark conversation with mentors and friends:

+ What is my social location? Have I taken time to own my experiences of privilege and of oppression? How do they impact my calling and practice of ministry?

- How am I facing injustices in my ministry?
- What is the possibility of transforming racial injustice? What is our obligation as people of faith and ministers of the gospel to participate, follow, and/or lead in such change?
- What is my organization doing to transform injustices named by Walker-Barnes (education, employment, housing, environmental policy, health care, or criminal justice)?

🪶 THREE MINUTE MINISTRY MENTOR

Watch episode 22, "Transforming Injustice," https://3mmm.us/Episode22

23

Sabbath

Sabbath challenges us to resist the ways that other people and things control our time.

—J. Dana Trent, *For Sabbath's Sake*

In recent years, Sabbath has been reclaimed by many Christians in an attempt to push back against the twenty-four-hour news cycle, constant noise and movement, entertainment, and the total availability of everything one could imagine simply by tapping a few keys on the computer. In such an urgent, immediate, and unrelenting world, to practice Sabbath is extremely countercultural. It is also a way to reclaim space and time for spiritual attentions. For ministers, it is a pathway to nourish vocation.

Marcus is a white pastor in his thirties and a participant in the LPI Project. When we interviewed him at about five years postseminary, he told us about how he came to a greater cultivation of Sabbath in his practice of ministry.

One summer while Marcus was serving as an associate pastor at a Presbyterian church in a western state, the congregation received a grant that allowed the senior pastor to take a much-needed sabbatical. The grant also allowed the church to focus on cultivating leadership during the sabbatical time.

Marcus was given the assignment of leading worship, preaching weekly sermons, giving pastoral care, and addressing a few other areas of ministry while the senior minister was away. There were other staff at the church, so Marcus did not do all of these tasks solo. He chose to preach a series of sermons about leadership.

As a minister with many responsibilities on Sunday, Marcus chose Monday as his day to practice Sabbath rest. He did as little as possible on Mondays. Because he lived in a small town, he tried to walk to only the store, the park, or the library on his day of rest. With a toddler and an infant in the house, there was no sleeping late, but he could make choices that restored his well-being. He liked to pile the children into a stroller and take a walk through his neighborhood. Marcus also liked riding his bike or reading just for the joy of reading. He usually cooked dinner for his family on Mondays, a pleasure his busy weekdays did not often allow.

When people in his congregation offered appreciations for the summer preaching series, he would tell them about what he was learning about his new spiritual practice of Sabbath. To be effective as a leader, he would say, he needed to practice the rhythms of rest and renewal.

In her 2017 book *For Sabbath's Sake: Embracing Your Need for Rest, Worship, and Community*, author J. Dana Trent recounts her own story of living a life besot by busyness, teaching, work as a chaplain, overloads of stress, and chronic migraines.[1] In the book, she explores facets of Sabbath, including calling, rest, worship, and community.

Trent's own journey to clarity about the need for Sabbath took a turn when she experienced major side effects from her migraine treatments. The experience, she says, "made me realize I was trying to fight physical decline and depression with avoidance and busyness instead of self-care." Trent knew those strategies "weren't holistic solutions" and that alongside medical treatment, she needed a "spiritual elixir." To change, she says, "instead of forcing myself into a Wonder Woman suit, I needed to make time for rest."[2]

❧

My striving to practice weekly Sabbath intentionally took hold in the year before my daughter was born. Before that season, I tried in fits and starts to take time off and practice Sabbath rest in the years I served the church full time, but I would say those efforts only met with minimal success. Graduate school also had a way of sneaking into every corner of my mind and life and making genuine time of intentional wandering or puttering a bit too challenging for me. Even now, after many years of both more attention and more intention, Sabbath remains an aspirational piece of my spiritual life.

Somehow, making plans to expand our family and bring a tiny human into the world brought the practice of Sabbath more concretely into my life about fifteen years ago. Finding time for rest and renewal that included worship and community suddenly became more urgent. I'm grateful that my friend Rachel Gunter Shappard invited me to lead a women's retreat specifically about Sabbath practices during a literal and metaphorical pregnant moment in my life. A deep study of the history and significance of spiritual rest and renewal convinced me to embrace the practice more fully.

A few years earlier, David and Colleen Burroughs asked me to write the curriculum for Passport youth camps several times, including a year when the theme was *Katundu* ("baggage, junk, stuff" in Chichewa). Campers spent the summer exploring how to be less tied to their stuff and how to lean deeper into silence, solitude, and simplicity—all gifts of Sabbath practice.

Each time I've taught and written about rituals and practices of Sabbath, I find myself more drawn into Sabbath-keeping.

There are many books exploring the rituals and practices of Sabbath in the Jewish and Christian traditions. Here are a few things I have learned over the last fifteen years of aspirational Sabbath practice. First, the practice of *Sabbath has many dimensions*, but key among them are stopping the work, effort, spending and consuming, creating, and all attempts to shape the outcomes of life.

On the positive side, the invitation is to rest, play, worship, revel in my closest relationships, and wander without purpose. The theological grounding comes in the stories of creation, when God rested, thousands of years of wisdom in which Jewish people practiced Sabbath-keeping, and the renewal of the practice in the teachings of Jesus. Additional spiritual and theological roots of the practice include embracing the beliefs that we neither run nor control the world, that our lives are finite, and that our trust belongs in the sacred and holy presence that created and renews all things.

Following from this first set of convictions, it will sound somewhat obvious to say that *Sabbath is countercultural*. So to practice Sabbath with any consistency, one needs a community of practice or a sense of calling to keep the practice alive. Perhaps it is most helpful when both calling and community are available to support weekly Sabbath-keeping.

Third, Jewish and Christian religious practices, and remnants of Sabbath laws and cultural traditions, make *certain times of the week more amenable to Sabbath practice*. The five-day workweek, Jewish and Christian worship that happens most often between Friday and Sunday, and even the remaining consumer patterns of store closings and the rhythms of business and education each week offer some basic structure to lean on when beginning a practice of Sabbath.

There is an underbelly to these weekly patterns: many people who labor on these days will have to find other times to rest and practice Sabbath. They are working so that more of the world can rest. Included in this group are people whom we've come to call "essential workers" during the pandemic of 2020. They are the people who work in health care, food service, and infrastructure operations; postal and delivery workers; bankers; and first responders, to name a few. Many of these laborers in the United States are also people who identify as Black and as people of color, meaning their need for rest is likely greater, while their ability to take time off from laboring may be significantly less flexible. Thus Sabbath breaks open the need for more labor justice (keep reading for more on that topic).

Most ministers, pastors, and priests also must find another day and time of the week for rest. It is possible to take your Sabbath from Thursday night to Friday morning or from Monday morning to Tuesday afternoon if it works for you, in spite of the fact that all the signals and situations around you will be sending different messages and making rest and renewal a bit more challenging. These choices also mean the communal aspect of Sabbath may feel more challenged. However, if that is the time you have, then by all means, give it a try. My intention has been to take Saturday evening through Sunday supper time, as best as I can, away from technology, shopping, consuming, creating, cleaning, making, and doing. Instead, I lean into space and time for worship, exercise, puttering around, and being with my family and friends.

Fourth, *we need Sabbath practice more than ever in human history.* Everything I said in the last point is being undermined on a daily basis with the never-ending news cycle, the mobility of our communications with small computers in our pockets, and the inconceivably endless amount of new ideas, music, research findings, work opportunities, and social engagements coming at us from every direction every day. The demands we place on the earth's resources are fast depleting those sustaining gifts also. The earth itself needs rest from human extractions. During the early months of 2020, the global coronavirus pandemic slowed down many businesses and transportation modes, meaning the earth received a major, yet brief, drop of 17 percent in greenhouse gas emissions.[3] This fact makes the call for reducing output sound much more possible. Could we practice global Sabbath intentionally and periodically (without a pandemic)?

Fifth, *Sabbath is a confrontation with injustice.* Most of these descriptions of Sabbath thus far come from a managerial-class, white-identified take on how to make space and time for rest and renewal. This privilege is not something everyone can access or enjoy. Not only the news cycle and internet offerings but more and more demands for twenty-four-hour shopping, consuming, and services of all kinds mean more people must be at work for more hours of the day. When approached thoughtfully and intentionally, Sabbath can be a call for righting injustice, for greater fairness and more dignity for all workers, as well as for resistance to the gods of consumption.

Finally, *I do not practice Sabbath so that I can be more productive.* Yet this is one of the great temptations because it is one of the side effects of practicing Sabbath. Instead, Sabbath rest is an end in itself. Having time to be bored, play, sleep, or be lost in worship without a concern for the ending time so as to engage fully in the community's sense of the holy, to revel in and enjoy those closest to me—the people who have my back—all of these are the gifts of Sabbath. Period. These are gifts that keep on giving. They make space to contain anxieties of life. Sabbath practice is built around the spiritual work of attending, loving, and listening. Thus devoting a significant part of one day each week to Sabbath deepens these human skills and leads to richer relationships and potentially to more profound wisdom. Although Sabbath does not exist to make us more productive, it does renew our energies when we practice it. That renewed energy is crucial for us to do the work of love and justice to which we are called.

While learning the practice of ministry, you need clear pathways of renewal and care for your soul. Sabbath is a tried and true way to renew your spirit. In all honesty, Sabbath also remains a complex issue when it comes to accessing time and resources for making space.

QUESTIONS FOR REFLECTION AND CONVERSATION

Consider the following to guide your journaling or spark conversation with mentors and friends:

- When am I taking time to rest deeply? What practices of Sabbath are nourishing my ministry? My soul?
- What justice issues related to Sabbath practice concern me?
- How could I practice Sabbath more consistently? What have I found helpful for the practice?

THREE MINUTE MINISTRY MENTOR

Watch episode 23, "Sabbath," https://3mmm.us/Episode23

24

Vocational Discernment

Vocation does not mean a goal that I pursue. It means a calling
that I hear. Before I can tell my life what I want to do with it, I
must listen to my life telling me who I am.

—Parker Palmer, *Let Your Life Speak*

When we met Asha in one of the first LPI Project interviews, she was twenty-
six and just about to graduate from divinity school. She was discerning what
direction her call would take her next.

Asha grew up in the South and was baptized as an older child in a traditional Black Missionary Baptist church. Her family attended regularly, and her
parents were very involved in church; however, Asha did not feel a strong personal connection to the church as a child. Asha believed that her divinity school
preparation held both gift and promise. When we interviewed Asha, she was
attending a Christian Methodist Episcopal (CME) church with her spouse. He
was on the CME ordination track, but he was not in formal theological training.

After sharing with us about growing up, Asha told us about a significant
turning point in her life. She was shocked when her parents announced they
were divorcing during her sophomore year in college. She was reeling and left
to feel adrift and grieving. Looking back, she says the utter lack of pastoral care
for her or her family at the time made the breakup of her childhood family even
more devastating. One of the ways she coped with the loss was to spend her
junior year abroad studying and skip the midyear return trips home.

While living and taking courses in Spain, she became involved with a multicultural Bible study and worship community. The leadership was egalitarian,
and the Bible study sessions were structured with a "freedom to question," giving Asha a new opportunity to "talk about Scripture in a different way." For the
first time, Asha was thinking outside the hierarchical structures of her childhood church. And for the first time, she was seeing women lead in a congregation. She remembers thinking at that point, "I really haven't *seen* women in
leadership in ministry before in my life."

In the new church, she not only saw women leading; she became one of the Bible study coleaders. She also looked around the multicultural worship gathering and thought in a new way about "the vastness of the kingdom of God." Even with these changes in her imagination, Asha was still thinking "ministry" equaled "pastoring," and she was wrestling with her childhood church's conviction that "women could not be pastors." This kind of thinking nearly cost her a significant opportunity. At the last moment, however, Asha changed her mind and applied for a Lilly Endowment fellowship to explore vocation.

Thus, in her senior year of college, the fellowship opened a door for Asha to spend time in a local congregation. She ended up in a Black Presbyterian church with a white female pastor. In that congregation, Asha got her first taste of praying publicly and leading liturgy in worship. She says, "It was a really amazing experience."

Following college, Asha spent two years doing Young Adult Service Corps, where a consistent portion of her time was devoted to vocational discernment with her peers. She found herself increasingly drawn into social justice concerns and work. Asha struggled over which divinity school or seminary to attend, and even when she settled on one, she constantly felt a nagging sense of doubt. Part of her concern was wanting to spend less time with books and papers and more time helping her community.

Although she struggled with feelings of ambivalence throughout divinity schools, she found a solid community of friends, and she stayed the course. On the eve of her graduation, she told us that she had learned a great deal:

> I think divinity school has really given me the tools to think about my faith critically, like in a loving way . . . and to share some of those things with different people, especially the people in the church that I'm going to right now [CME]. But the funny thing is, I feel like I have all these things to share, but I don't necessarily have an outlet or a clear pathway to do that. The tension is sort of a frustrating thing for me. I have these ideas about church and God and all these other theological things that I really don't have the position or authority to share.

When we asked her to characterize the piece that's lacking, Asha began to talk of balancing leadership and facilitation:

> I have such a fear—because I grew up in such a hierarchical tradition and the ones that I'm most familiar with are also very hierarchical—I do not want to take that place of authority, to perpetuate the system. But I also see a need to be on the inside so you can change and empower people, that you can't just [be] on the outside complaining about what's wrong if you're not willing to get in there and take some responsibility

and work toward fixing it. But I don't know where that might be most fruitful in the Christian Methodist Episcopal church or in the Presbyterian church. I mean, who knows? And so I feel very disjointed in that way.

꧁꧂

Hearing some of the tensions and gifts in Asha's story may help you identify some of the tensions and gifts in your own work of vocational discernment. Unpacking one's purpose for life is no small thing. For many people, it takes most of a lifetime to say fully what they believe their purposes to be. And for others, purpose changes over time and through the seasons of life.

Quaker author Parker Palmer in his 2000 classic, *Let Your Life Speak*, says, "Vocation does not mean a goal that I pursue. It means a calling that I hear. Before I can tell my life what I want to do with it, I must listen to my life telling me who I am."[1] He is commending to all of us a deep listening and honesty with ourselves. He tells a story from his childhood in which he spent a great deal of time making small books about the wonders of flight, drawing airplane wings, and typing captions on a manual typewriter. Although it may sound and look as if he was circling around a love of aviation, he found a more telling reality when as an adult he came across some of these "literary artifacts." It was not piloting but rather making books that intrigued him.[2]

Clues for our sense of vocation are everywhere in our lives, says Palmer, yet we can easily get caught up in the "oughts" of life and get misdirected. The better way? Palmer says, "The deepest vocational question is not 'What ought I to do with my life?' It is the more elemental and demanding 'Who am I? What is my nature?'"[3]

For me, a sense of purpose in life emerged early, but the pathways of work and family that became available to me for that purpose were complicated. I felt a call to ministry, yes. But in fact, there was a deeper sense of calling about what kind of life I wanted to live that was hard to articulate.

Two years of searching for a ministry job, five and a half years in that work, and the abrupt end of congregational ministry all led me to a deeper realization. What I discovered upon being forced out of my ministry job was something significant about the shape of vocational purpose in my life—being with people in a particular way and making space, creating conditions, to see and be seen in a genuine way—this is the deeper life purpose that was and continues to be emerging for me. Taking on the training (seminary) and the work of congregational ministry was the best and probably only path I could take at that point in my life when I did it. And that path was difficult for sure as a woman. I tried to consider other jobs, but I always returned to ministry in my twenties and early thirties.

I have no regrets about taking that path. It was, however, when that first congregational call to ministry was over that I really began to see my purpose as so much deeper than working in the church. It was about a particular way to be human and be with other humans and with the world itself. A growing stream of clarity about that purpose continues as I take new tributaries and turns in each new season of my life.

Hearing stories from many people in many stages and seasons of life and how they discern the purpose, their calling, their work, and their families can be a great encouragement. It can also be incredibly clarifying. As one therapist I know likes to say, we need contrast to reach greater consciousness.

Each of our stories is its own unique conglomeration of ideas and circumstances, power dynamics and family legacies, social privileges and injustices. How we work this out, and if we are willing to share it with others, is itself a tremendous gift. To bear witness to one's own story and the story of others is both powerful and inspiring.

QUESTIONS FOR REFLECTION AND CONVERSATION

Consider the following to guide your journaling or spark conversation with mentors and friends:

- ◆ What turning points or shifts in my imagination have been significant for my sense of vocation and calling?
- ◆ When I listen to my life, what tensions, promises, and gifts are shaping my present vocational discernment?
- ◆ What purposes are mine that go deeper than my job(s), goals, or even the roles I am currently filling?

THREE MINUTE MINISTRY MENTOR

Watch episode 24, "Vocational Discernment," https://3mmm.us/Episode24

25

Examen

I call it consolation when an interior movement is aroused in the soul, by which it is inflamed with love of its Creator and Lord . . . every increase of faith, hope, and love, and all interior joy.

—Ignatius of Loyola, *The Spiritual Exercises*

One of the joys in my work with Central Seminary in recent years has been matching individual students with experienced mentors as they prepare for ministry. These are long-term relationships between each student and mentor. Each team of two meets monthly as a minimum. They make time for their relationship to grow, and in the process, feedback and support become more meaningful.

Each month when students and mentors meet, they complete and send to me a very brief "five-minute report." This is more than a checklist, although it can be done that way. Taking a few minutes to answer the questions acknowledges more formally the informal conversation topics they considered in their meeting. It honors the importance of their time and learning together.

The monthly report asks mentors and mentees to briefly name the themes they discussed, to celebrate successes, to note concerns, and to ask for resources they need. Altogether, the questions make space for a regular, shared practice of spiritual examen.

Examen is a form of spiritual practice that utilizes questions for attending to one's life. Examen is a way of discernment. It allows us to look back to times and events of our everyday lives or particular circumstances or moments. Examen helps us ask questions that allow us to notice the presence and guidance of God's spirit. Examen can also help us look to the future and ask what might bring consolation or desolation. This approach can help us see a way forward, one that honors our experience and seeks God's wisdom.

At the end of the formal relationship of mentoring for Central students, which lasts approximately three years, I have the delight of meeting with each student/mentor pair and asking them questions. The three of us spend time in shared examen.

One of the questions I ask is "What were some of the high points or take-aways from your mentoring relationship?" I learn a great deal about how the mentoring relationship has grown when I take in the responses to this and other questions.

When I interviewed one graduate, Margaret, and her mentor, Janet, Margaret shared her appreciation for Janet.[1] She said, "I think what I really appreciated was the intimacy that developed, the spiritual intimacy, because I really felt my mentor's genuine . . . love for me. The compassion was palpable, and it wasn't a squishy love; it called me to be my best self. A don't-forget-you-said-this-seven-times-before kind of love. Which I really needed; I needed her strength and her direct style."

Questions of examen give mentors and mentees an opportunity to pay attention to the ways they are changing and growing spiritually and vocationally over time. It helps them name the ways God is present in their lives (see chapter 11, "Listening").

⟋⟍⟋

Countless books and websites are available to help you learn the spiritual practice of examen. Like all spiritual practices, examen is best learned in community and with accountability. One resource that has been especially helpful as I lead students deeper into the work of examen is Daniel Wolpert's book *Creating a Life with God*.[2] In the book, Wolpert does a beautiful job of introducing the Ignatian practice of examen and eleven other spiritual practices that can enrich your life and leadership as a chaplain, activist, pastor, or priest.

Examen is like a gateway to a variety of spiritual explorations or paths. For example, vocational discernment is a challenge that takes time and many questions (see chapter 24, "Vocational Discernment"). The questions of examen are fitting and valuable for the big questions of life, including vocational discernment. What should I do? Where should I turn? How do I know which way to go at this point in pursuing my call? Where is God leading?

Examen also invites us to test our experiences from the past as well as our plans and visions for the future of our practice of ministry. In each examination, we can ask how the past or future situation brings consolation or desolation, giving us hints about how to move forward. Examen is also useful, as it was to Margaret and Janet, as a spiritual approach to exploring the value and meaning of mentoring relationships.

Where did the practice of examen originate? More than five hundred years ago, a young man named Ignatius (1491–1556) was born into a wealthy noble family in Spain. Ignatius of Loyola became a knight and in 1521 was sent off to war. Ignatius was injured by a cannonball, and he had to return home to the Basque region of Spain to recover.

As he recuperated in the months that followed, he had little else to do (no Facebook, Twitter, or Netflix), so he read. The Bible and books about Christian saints filled most of his time. He began to wonder seriously, *What is my life all about?*

As Ignatius grew more physically well, he ventured out and devoted himself to a vocation of prayer and discernment. After seeing a vision of Mary and Jesus in 1522, he began to pray and write intensely, and in 1523, he wrote the foundation of what became a classic text, *The Spiritual Exercises.*[3]

This book continues to shape the spirituality of priests, religious leaders, and laypeople particularly through the exercise of examen. After theological study in Spain and France, Ignatius of Loyola founded the Society of Jesus in 1539. The Jesuits continue to lead, teach, and hold tremendous influence in church and society in many places around the world.

Over the centuries, examen became a tried and proven pathway for discernment. This form of *spiritual review* allows us to look back to times and events in our everyday lives and ask questions that help us notice the presence and guidance of God's Spirit. Knowing what brings consolation or desolation helps us see a way forward that honors our learning and God's wisdom.

Ignatius describes consolation and desolation this way:

Spiritual Consolation. I call it consolation when an interior movement is aroused in the soul, by which it is inflamed with love of its Creator and Lord . . . every increase of faith, hope, and love, and all interior joy that invites and attracts to what is heavenly and to the salvation of one's soul by filling it with peace and quiet in its Creator and Lord.[4]

Spiritual Desolation. I call desolation . . . turmoil of spirit, inclination to what is low and earthly, restlessness rising from many disturbances and temptations which lead to want of faith, want of hope, want of love. The soul is wholly slothful, tepid, sad, and separated, as it were, from its Creator and Lord.[5]

Drawing on the questions posed by Ignatius and the interpretation of the practice by Daniel Wolpert, here are steps you might take to explore the practice of examen for yourself and in conversation with trusted people in your life.

1. Choose that which needs discernment. For example, a passage of Scripture, an event or specific time period from your past, a decision you need to make. State your need for discernment as a question (i.e., Is this path right for me? What did I learn from that situation?)
2. Become indifferent to the outcome of what you want to discern in the process; spiritual detachment allows you to see the situation more clearly rather than deciding ahead of time what the outcome is or should be.

3. Ask questions of consolation and desolation:
   A. What surprises me about this matter of discernment?
   B. What feels muddy, unclear, or confusing about this matter of discernment?
   C. When I hold this matter of discernment close to my heart, do I feel a sense of "hope faith, and charity, and all interior joy" (Ignatius)?[6]
   D. When I hold this matter of discernment close to my heart, do I feel "turmoil of spirit . . . restlessness rising from many disturbances and temptations which lead to want of faith, want of hope, want of love" (Ignatius)?[7]
4. Pray and rest in the responses you have heard in this process of questioning. Ask God's guidance and allow time for the Spirit to lead you to more clarity.

Examen for the practice of ministry takes many forms. There are innumerable questions that rise up as one learns and grows in practice. Discernment is needed for the big decisions. There are also the questions of the daily minutia of ministry that may be worthy and deserving of our careful and prayerful attentions. Practicing the examen and considering what brings consolation and desolation can become a spiritual habit that informs your leadership in ministry and assists you in questions large and small.

QUESTIONS FOR REFLECTION AND CONVERSATION

Consider the following to guide your journaling or spark conversation with mentors and friends:

- How might I use examen to pay attention to the spiritual contours of my ministry?
- What questions of discernment are most pressing at this moment? How can I use examen to explore them?
- Is there some way that examen might be useful for leading my community through an important decision or appreciating God's presence in our work together?

THREE MINUTE MINISTRY MENTOR

Watch episode 25, "Examen," https://3mmm.us/Episode25

26

Future Stories

These *future stories* make a significant contribution to the fabric of our core narratives, the tapestry from which our ultimate identity is woven. We not only are a self, we are becoming a self, and we give shape to the not-yet-conscious self through the future stories we create.

—Andrew Lester, *Hope in Pastoral Care and Counseling*

When I studied psychology, culture, and religion at Vanderbilt, I took a deep dive into books, ideas, and thinkers who prepared me to think about the past. I learned to look with careful attention to ways the past experiences, events, and lived stories from family and childhood bring shape to our lives.

Years of study in psychology, theology, and history taught me to consider how our personal stories of the past bring form and content to our identity. I also learned to look at stories embedded in religious texts like the Bible and rituals like communion. And I learned to read cultural legends like nursery rhymes and fairy tales and socially shared narratives, such as Betsy Ross sewing a flag or the Pilgrims' first Thanksgiving, to see how many kinds of past stories hold power to affect our self-understandings and life meanings. A great deal of what I read taught me to deconstruct the multiple meanings embedded in these pasts. Sometimes the family and community stories from our pasts are hidden from us, yet they also have a way of bringing contour and texture to our identities.

As I approached the end of my doctoral program, I found myself stuck when it came to finishing my dissertation and completing my degree. In that difficult time, I realized that stories of achievement from my past, my family history, were contributing to my feelings of stuckness. However, I also had several stories about my own future that were at odds with each other. One future story said I would be like family members of my past, and I would stall out on this degree. Other future stories I was telling myself gave me an imagination for finishing, teaching, and contributing to the lives of ministers. Some days I did not know which future story would win.

Stories from the past are not the only ones that powerfully shape our identities. We are also shaped by stories we tell about the future. Sometimes we know we are telling them, and sometimes they are hidden to us. But future stories also do important work in our lives and our self-understandings.

⚜

When we met Carly, a white woman in her forties, as part of the LPI Project, she was serving as the missions pastor of a reformed church in the northwestern part of the United States. In that role, she often traveled the world helping her wealthy, highly skilled, and privileged congregation make connections with mission partners around the globe. Carly says she felt a big challenge when it came to helping her congregation see possibilities for ministry in the same way that local pastors and leaders presented them to her.

Yet over time, and through her experience of living and working outside the United States, Carly developed a knack for helping people see future possibilities for global partnerships. She told us about her meeting with a group of pastors and leaders in Zambia who were thinking about taking their ministry in a new direction.

The Zambian pastors told Carly, "You know, we're mostly doing funerals these days because there is so much HIV and AIDS in our community, and we are so burdened for all these children. Could you help us with this?"

The Zambian pastors spoke to Carly about US missionaries. They said, "Teaching us to preach and teaching us about the Bible and all that traditional stuff is really good, but we're telling you the problem in our community is these kids, and we've taken in as many as we possibly can and there are more . . . to come."

The local pastors described their idea—one they believed came from God. They said, "We would start this farm and we would have homes and we would do our best to make community. [We think] it is a way that the church can live out the gospel. We think it will work. Could you imagine your church partnering with us?"

Carly listened to the future story of the pastors. She said to them, "You know your context, and you know what can work. I think we'd love to walk down that path with you."

In that particular moment, Carly says she learned that "the pastoral role is, in part, carrying your people in your heart in a way that you know them and how it is that God might draw out their skills and talents and resources to make this work." Carly told us, "To watch God work has been amazing, and scary at first. And awesome to see."

Pastor Carly listens carefully to the future stories of the Zambian pastors. They help her see their situation more clearly. They also imagine a future for the children who lost their family connections through the HIV/AIDS crisis. This future builds on their pastoral wisdom and opens up a more meaningful and hopeful future for the children.

Carly was helping the Zambian pastors convey their future stories to her congregation at home, and she was helping her US congregation embrace a future story about itself and its role with a farm that did not yet exist. She was brokering future stories that brought new possibility and healing to a broken yet beautiful situation.

❦

The idea of future stories was developed by pastoral theologian Andrew Lester (1939–2010) in his book *Hope in Pastoral Care and Counseling*.[1] Lester said that human identities are shaped not only by the stories we tell ourselves and others about our *past* but also by the stories we tell to ourselves and to others about our various possible *futures*. "We construct our sense of identity out of stories," says Lester, "conscious stories and those we suppress."[2] Lester helps us see how the future stories we tell nourish hope and possibility. With stories we narrate both our past experiences and the future hopes, plans, and dreams we live into every day.

In terms of the practice of ministry, this way of thinking about future stories is valuable in many ways. Here are a few that I find especially helpful:

1. Future stories allow us to give better care to people when we can see how they are impacted not just by what happened to them last week, last year, or in their childhood or infancy. We can explore with them how their future stories—about health, family transitions, job changes, and so on—are shaping their identities right now.
2. Future stories help us as we lean into learning the practice of ministry. They give us a way to imagine our future learning rather than thinking we must know everything now.
3. Acknowledging our future stories and seeing multiple possibilities for our future(s) expands the hopefulness we can embrace in the current moment.[3]
4. When we listen to one another's future stories, our possibilities for partnership and empathy grow.

During the 2020 coronavirus pandemic, people felt losses of many kinds, including the untimely deaths of loved ones. Perhaps among the most difficult to name and acknowledge were the losses of many different future stories. We see it in the ways that plans were thwarted, jobs and economic situations were destabilized, life events were put on hold, and schedules were in constant flux. Each of these realities point to the ways that future stories matter deeply to us and give form to our identities and present moments. A host of new future possibilities also emerged in this same time period. The everyday practice of ministry will be marked by the realities of the pandemic, and perhaps it will open up new ways of bringing the practice to life.

QUESTIONS FOR REFLECTION AND CONVERSATION

Consider the following to guide your journaling or spark conversation with mentors and friends:

- How does the notion of "future stories" help me think about my practice of ministry?
- How are the future stories I am telling myself and others impacting the here and now of my life and my identity?
- What future stories do I need to broker in order to bring together new possibilities for the healing and transformation of the world?

THREE MINUTE MINISTRY MENTOR

Watch episode 26, "Future Stories," https://3mmm.us/Episode26

27

Preaching and Prayer

We express our yearning to be in the center of God's plan for
healing our souls and healing the world in our music and in
our prayers. We create artistic holy spaces for listening to what
God requires of us in scripture and in the preached word.

—Rev. Jacqui Lewis, senior minister, Middle Collegiate Church

When we met Rev. Benita, she was leading an outreach ministry to feed and
care for people around her neighborhood. Each year with her husband and children and other volunteers, she organized a large ingathering of food and school
supplies for the much wider, impoverished area of Little Rock. Rev. Benita is
African American, in her midforties, and retired from the military. She was set
to graduate from seminary within a few months when we interviewed her the
first time as part of the LPI Project.

In our third interview with Rev. Benita, she was five years out of seminary
and pastoring a new multicultural congregation in Atlanta. Rev. Benita shared
with us how she learned to preach in different styles and about the importance
of knowing the Scriptures not just for information but for her own spiritual
growth.

Rev. Benita told us that her early training in ministry—before attending
seminary—came through her work in a nondenominational church, where she
was assigned responsibilities that taught her a lot about prayer, evangelism, and
pastoral care. However, the learning about sermon preparation was minimal,
and she was only asked to submit one written sermon a month. From that early
training, she says she began to see her need to rely on the Holy Spirit to lead
her in developing sermons.

Eventually, Rev. Benita was ordained for ministry. Along the way and
with help from her seminary professors, Rev. Benita says she shifted from
being a topical preacher (starting with a topic and moving to a text) to diving
deeper into the resources available for the study of Scripture. Eventually, she
became more of an expository preacher (working through a text carefully and

systematically). She also respects the lectionary approach to preaching, which follows a set of Scriptures usually in a three-year rotation of New Testament and Hebrew Scriptures and covers a large portion of the Christian Bible. What she has learned from the lectionary approach is the value of daily reading from a wide number of Scripture texts.

Now when Rev. Benita prepares to preach, she follows a pattern like this: She says about reading daily, "So I'm already in the Word and I'm already praying and worshiping the Lord daily." She asks the Lord in prayer, "What is it you would have for me to do?" She says, "I study a little bit each day." The sermon comes along—"hopefully, prayerfully written"—through the week. Rev. Benita says she still likes to "write out the sermon . . . I'm old-fashioned. I take a paper sermon to the pulpit along with my Bible."

She says, "What I've learned is each day that I spend with the Lord, it really helps build upon what it is the Lord would have me to say to the people because, first of all, my daily devotion is what is crucial. That is my spiritual growth. That is my own excitement about what the Lord speaks to me through the Word concerning my growth. And it keeps me excited about what God is saying to the people."

Whether you are a lectionary preacher, a topical preacher, an expository preacher, a series preacher, or a narrative preacher, your relationship to the Scriptures needs to be more than study, knowledge, and information. Your own immersion in the texts and the stories of Scripture are an important part of the spiritual practice of ministry and preaching. Study and prayer are not separate things entirely, but they are distinct facets of a whole practice.

⚜

What is the role of prayer and meditation in the practice of ministry? Rev. Benita has given us one clear and meaningful response to the connection between prayer and preaching.

I have worked on that question for many years, primarily through my teaching and also in my research and writing. The question became a point of focus around the time I finished my doctoral studies. Fortunately, when I was coming toward the end of my dissertation writing and thinking about academic jobs, my friend and fellow pastoral theologian Mary Moschella urged me to plan the courses I really wanted to teach rather than wait for some better or more ideal time to create them. That led me to create a course called simply "Prayer and Pastoral Care."

As often as I can, I introduce seminary students to the significance of contemplative practice, silence, meditation, and other forms of prayer as a grounding source for their vocational aspirations. And by *aspirations*, I don't simply mean climbing some ministry ladder to achieve more status in your denomination or church or nonprofit agency. I mean the aspiration of becoming the kind of pastor or minister or activist you believe God is calling you to be.

Prayer comes into every aspect of the ministry life. In our second interview with Naomi, a white woman in her late twenties, she shared a story about a congregational moment when she needed to step in and lead with both preaching and prayer.

Naomi was an assistant minister in a welcoming and affirming United Church of Christ congregation where she worked with youth and young adults, and she led worship. During her nine months in the congregation, Naomi had preached on Sundays when the senior minister, Kathy, was away, and Naomi regularly led worship. On a Saturday night in June, Kathy's eighteen-year-old son was in a skateboard accident, and although he was wearing a helmet, he sustained a severe brain injury.

Some church members rushed to the hospital. Naomi decided she better focus on how to organize the worship service the next morning. She spent a little time conferring with her wife, who is also a minister and was serving a different church across town.

A lay leader was scheduled to preach the next morning, but given the circumstances, Naomi decided it was best if she took the lead in the service. Many people would be learning for the first time about the critical injury of their beloved pastor's son, who had grown up and been nurtured by the congregation and who had just graduated from high school.

Naomi decided to start the service with a clear announcement of the news and a time of prayer. She drew on the leadership of four women, all lay leaders in the church and each one close to the pastor's family. Naomi invited each woman to offer an update from Pastor Kathy during times of prayer interspersed throughout the service.

At the end of the service, Naomi "invited people to come forward for a circle of prayer after worship instead of coffee hour." She says about forty people joined her in the circle at the front of the sanctuary. Although Naomi felt unsure about what to say "in the midst of an epic tragedy," she reached for her *Anabaptist Prayer Book* and took the model of praying with a collective response, and she wrote new lines of prayer, inviting the circle to respond "In your mercy, Lord, hear our prayer" and hold silence.

Naomi also drew on her learning from the seminary field education model of "doing and being and thinking in ministry." She says, "I took the doing and the being components, and I said, 'We all want to do something. We want to rage at this tragedy. We want to fix things for Kathy and her son, but our challenge and our call at this time is just to be.' That really connected with the people because no one knew what to do."

Naomi was still a beginning minister just out of seminary when she was flung into this situation. She turned to the resources she knew, and she leaned heavily into prayer. She took the risk of stepping in and making decisions for the good of the congregation. Naomi made her message one of care and acknowledgment without trying to fix a tragic situation. Preaching and prayer were deeply intertwined in that morning and over the next six weeks as Naomi stepped into the role of interim senior minister.

A resource that attends to preaching preparation is WorkingPreacher.org. Whatever your style of preaching, and whatever the circumstances of your congregation or community, you will find resources that support your spiritual life and your study there. Whether you are preaching on a video platform or live feed on social media, leading worship that is recorded in advance, or preaching live and in person, this resource can support you as you prepare to deliver words of good news, comfort, hope, and challenge to the people in your care.

QUESTIONS FOR REFLECTION AND CONVERSATION

Consider the following to guide your journaling or spark conversation with mentors and friends:

- In what ways are my spiritual life and my preaching preparation related?
- What helps me in my preparation for preaching? Where am I struggling and/or thriving with spiritual engagement?
- In a crisis, where do I turn to find help to prepare me for preaching and care?

THREE MINUTE MINISTRY MENTOR

Watch episode 27, "Preaching and Prayer," https://3mmm.us/Episode27

28

Thinking Theologically

There is something about the hope-activating life of God, that makes you put yourself in the life of another and you see the world through their lives. . . . The truth is that life has a way of evoking unspoken and spoken feelings, thoughts, declarations and questions about hope.

—Anne Streaty Wimberly, *The Courage to Hope*

I wrote the following story at age 25 while in my second year of seminary. It grew from my early attempts to cultivate my own capacity and skill for thinking theologically from life. It is an intense family story about pregnancy loss.

Before I was born, my parents were living in Norway, where my dad was stationed with the US Air Force. They discovered in the fall of 1964 that they were expecting their first child. And they were excited, having looked forward to welcoming a baby.

Unfortunately, things did not go as planned. On a very cold and snowy January night, my mother began to hemorrhage. The base doctor was nowhere to be found, so a Norwegian doctor finally was summoned. When he arrived, the only thing he said, after one look at my mother was "The baby is dead."

At the hospital, the nurses spoke no English other than "Oh, you'll have more babies."

The story has been no family secret. It has been told often at my home, and every year on January 16, my mother used to cry all day long . . . until two years ago. My mom and dad decided that to help alleviate my mom's never-ending grief, they would name the child who died twenty-five years earlier.

So they made up a certificate and put the baby's name on it: David Campbell. When they shared this with me, I became overwhelmed with emotion and grief. This was a real person, my brother, whom I would never know. As I reflected, I realized that if he had gone to full-term and been born a healthy child, I may not have been born.

I found in David a unique image of God for me: an image of God who gives up life in order that I might live. This is the meaning I found in my own personal reflection; it is not a meaning all miscarriages or stillbirths will have.

⬥

In seminary I took a pastoral care course, which introduced me to the idea of thinking theologically by starting with life. My classmates and I were assigned a number of books in which theological reflection on life and ministry were the focus. The three-week intensive class was designed to anchor this capacity into my pastoral leadership. Every day, we brought stories to class, and we tried to build our intellectual muscles of thinking theologically about those stories.

I confess that in the beginning, I found it very challenging to simply write a story. I wanted to move right away to the moral or the meaning of the story. I'm glad I had the chance to try repeatedly to simply tell a story. Each day for three weeks, I would sit with a small circle of fellow students, and we would share what we had written.

Eventually with practice, I stopped assigning the meaning or the moral of the story, and I got better just telling it. Hearing a story in its fullness, spoken in community, is a good first step toward thinking theologically. If we move too fast toward meaning or making judgments—whether ethical, relational, or otherwise—we can miss the important details and subtlety that will finally make theological reflection richer.

After hearing a story with others in community, we would take the steps of making connections between our stories and stories from the Bible, church history, and other faithful people past and present. Multiple possible meanings, insights and wisdom emerged. Sometimes we found no particular meaning at all.

This exercise gave me a good foundation for the ongoing practice of telling stories and constructing theological meaning(s) in community. Story sharing in community became a basis for theological reflection for my sermon preparation, curriculum writing, teaching adults, and leading children and youth. I was able to say when I interviewed for congregational jobs that I could bring to the work a capacity for thinking theologically and leading others to do the same.

Thinking theologically is not simply a mental exercise. It is communal and based in our shared stories, and it informs the way we act and live. For instance, I was not simply trying to get teenagers at my church to analyze a situation using theological terms. I wanted them to know theology in action. So we got to know other teens living in the local children's shelter. We practiced love in action. Then we practiced sharing our stories of love in action. We tried to connect those stories with the older and wider stories of Christian faith and practice.

Action, reflection, stories, and frameworks of meaning come into a full circle of rich theological imagination that goes beyond just thinking. For me, it has become an ever-expanding, theologically informed way of being in the world and embodying the practice of ministry.

⟋ᴥ⟍

The story about my family and the loss of an infant whom my parents named David has a single moment of theological reflection at the end. That story became part of the first sermon I ever preached (see chapter 18, "Preaching Jesus"). Getting the story down without any meaning was my first step. Paying attention to the details and telling it in a way that honored all of the people who are part of the story was my task ahead of assigning any theological meaning.

Only months later did the story find its way into my first sermon, with permission from my parents. Here's the additional reflection I preached so long ago:

> David bore the image of God, like all persons do. His image of God clearly showed the image of God as one who suffers. It was out of the silence of a baby who would never cry, out of the darkness of my parents' broken dreams that I saw an image of God's sacrificing love.
>
> It took all the years of my life for me to see any meaning out of this tragic event, but somehow in naming David, much of it became clear, just as Jesus speaking Mary's name brought clarity to her. For me it took looking back to see that God was there with David and yes, *in* David, showing us what God is like.

The words I chose for that novice sermon were surely won out of intense spiritual and theological labor. Our short lives on this earth are a series of births and deaths. We assign them all kinds of meanings. The meanings that I designated at the midpoint of my journey through seminary were an accumulation of classroom learning, therapy, CPE, and countless books and conversations. I don't know the impact of those words on anyone else, although I found one note in my CPE notebook about thanks from a woman in a wheelchair whom I pushed back to her room following my first sermon. And I have fuzzy memories of sitting in the circle of my peers and supervisors and receiving not the criticism I thought might come but words of affirmation.

School makes us think that everything we do in life is for a grade. But the stories of our lives, sermons over which we labor, and theological reflections—these are not made to be graded. These are made to enrich and deepen our lives. They are made by and for love.

Now, so many years later, I add more nuance; I give more care to my (potential) listeners. I move with caution, and I resist assigning meaning too early or too definitively. Thinking theologically from life is a complex, ever-changing, and ever-growing process. It is a bit like stepping into a river and navigating the best we can in the rapid current of life moving all around us; it is like grabbing onto whatever we can for the sake of meaning and keeping our purpose in life afloat. It is like reaching for hope wherever it will buoy us up.

In her book *Soul Stories: African American Christian Education,* professor Anne Streaty Wimberly develops the idea of "story linking."[1] The linking creates moments of theological connection and shapes theological purposes toward liberation. Wimberly, who studies youth lives and resiliency, says, "Story-linking is a process whereby we connect parts of our everyday stories with the Christian faith story in the Bible and the lives of exemplars of the Christian faith outside the Bible. In this process, we link with Bible stories by using them as mirrors through which we reflect critically on the liberation we have already found or are still seeking, as well as glean wisdom that guides our ongoing liberation efforts."[2]

Wimberly's book offers a rich exploration to expand your thinking theologically from life by connecting stories across time and situation and eventually coming to a place of deeper understandings and meanings. The power of identifying and linking stories will provide a good foundation for you and your community as you construct theological meaning together.

QUESTIONS FOR REFLECTION AND CONVERSATION

Consider the following to guide your journaling or spark conversation with mentors and friends:

- What stories do I need to honor in my life by bringing them to voice, paper, or screen?
- In what ways can I pay attention with care to the details of stories unfolding in my life and in the lives of those in my care?
- What links and connections can I make between the story (or stories) of my life and the ancient and contemporary stories of people of faith?
- How am I thinking theologically in each area of my practice of ministry?

THREE MINUTE MINISTRY MENTOR

Watch episode 28, "Thinking Theologically," https://3mmm.us/Episode28

29

Apprenticeship

Patience!

—Yoda

"I was born and raised in Harlem and right now I live [on that corner] and I'm in the New Harlem that's being transformed." When Wanda, an African American minister in her forties, walks around Harlem pointing out the landmarks, she's more than a tour guide. She knows the churches on each corner and every subway stop. She knows the back-alley shortcuts, the best street vendors, and who's on the way to an Alcoholics Anonymous (AA) meeting. She grew up on these streets, and she carries a full map of the neighborhood, its buildings, and its people in her mind and heart.

Wanda sees her practice of ministry as one of drawing the longtime residents out of their pain and anger and bringing them into the newness offered by her seminary and church. She says her calling is "to go knock on the doors to get the people out to be a part of the community. And the only reason that I'm a part of the community is because of Christ, and because when I walk past buildings, I want to know what is in my neighborhood and I want to know what's going on. But people in the neighborhood don't do that. They walk right past."

Wanda does not walk past. She has apprenticed herself to the community. She sees that her "duty" is "not to condemn people . . . for what they do" but "to show love" and to walk with people as they experience healing and restoration in Christ.

When we met Wanda for the first time, we interviewed her and her cohort of recent seminary graduates in a storefront art gallery in Harlem. She knows so many people in the neighborhood, they literally waved to her throughout the interview day as they walked past the large street-level windows of the gallery.

Wanda's apprenticeship to her *situation of ministry* is relational and embodied, and it has grown over years of life and now more than a decade of ministry. It is an apprenticeship in how to love.

Apprenticeship has a long history in many professions. It is a kind of learning in which a novice or a newbie comes alongside the more experienced practitioner. Becoming an apprentice to a *person* is an important way to learn a trade or profession such as carpentry or medicine or falconry.

In the Star Wars movie *The Empire Strikes Back*, Luke Skywalker arrives on the stormy, swampy planet Dagobah in search of Yoda. From the outset of his apprenticeship, Luke is impatient. In fact, he has no patience at all. He does not know what or who he is seeing. Instead, he exudes overconfidence, frustration, and darting attentions.

You can watch Luke thrash around in his new situation and see how he tries to rush the next steps of his training. Does it seem familiar?

I can certainly say I've been there and done that.

When it comes to new situations and new learning, patience is not my strong suit. And when I was at the beginning of my training as a minister in practice, this was even more true.

Luke had a master teacher in Yoda. The enigmatic and ever-present wise teacher of Jedi knights makes us long for mentors and teachers who will take us on patiently and guide us into self-understanding and greater mastery of our practice.

Not many learning situations work out like they did for Luke, however. Most of the time, we are plunged into strange and incomprehensible places with dynamics that mystify and frustrate. Like Luke at the opening time of his training with Yoda, we can find ourselves thrashing around. We try to decipher the swamp and figure out where to go and what to listen to. We have no idea what is really important.

While some ministry situations still allow for apprenticeship to a person, more often the apprenticeship is to the situation of ministry itself, with many teachers and opportunities to learn from around every corner.

For the last hundred years, seminaries and divinity schools have largely separated ministers in training from actual contexts and practitioners of ministry, but some church traditions still put a high value on apprenticeship. And young ministers, especially in some Black church traditions, become apprenticed to a senior minister for a period of training. Only after they are found ready do they step out to lead on their own.

In the apprenticeship to a *situation*, new ministers experience the gift of an extended time of being immersed in a place, its people, its organizations, and its power dynamics. The apprenticeship allows them an opportunity to know all of this deeply and in a firsthand way.

Fr. Isaac took his first full-time call as a priest at Saint Peter's Orthodox Church, located in a small town in the southern United States. His wife is a medical doctor, and through the network of Orthodox families and friends, she simultaneously started a new hospital residency in a nearby city. The couple is in their thirties. They identify as white, and they are raising two young children.

Saint Peter's was newly organized, and they lacked a building. Fr. Isaac found himself completely swept up in a multimillion-dollar land and building project immediately upon arriving. The construction crews worked six days a week. He led worship on the seventh day. He doesn't truly remember how many weeks he worked without a full day off. His apprenticeship at the church was one of construction, blueprints, meetings over coffee, worship, and pastoral care to people still stinging from previous priestly lapses and harms.

The newly formed community was at once thrilling and exhausting. Fr. Isaac needed to figure out how to take care of himself and renew his soul. He decided to take up falconry. The last time we interviewed Fr. Isaac, he told us, "I'm a licensed apprentice falconer. This is my last year being an apprentice."

Everywhere he goes in his small town, Fr. Isaac is a known figure. He cannot go to the grocery store, the library, or his favorite coffee shop without being recognized and possibly cornered to have a talk about the Trinity, or someone's faltering marriage, or the building project over at Saint Peter's.

To get a little time to himself away from the public eye, Fr. Isaac says, "One of the things that I did was create a 'life list.' The only thing that needs to happen to put something on the life list is I have to think it's cool and it has to be doable. I think summiting K2 would be cool, but it's not doable. Summiting K2 is not on the life list."

Catching and training red-tailed hawks, however, is on the life list. How does this apprenticeship help him? "Well, you have to take this hawk out and you have to hunt with it, and you have to do it about three or four days a week. Maybe it's only for an hour, but it has to be done." This gives Fr. Isaac brief blocks of time alone without interruption or even his cell phone. It refreshes his soul.

When we interview Fr. Isaac, he walks us through the complicated steps of training a red-tailed hawk, from catching and feeding it to hooding it and teaching it to fly, hunt, and return. According to Fr. Isaac, there is more than one sanctioned way to train a hawk. The newer and more experimental way is simpler; it builds trust with the bird quicker and is noncoercive.

Fr. Isaac has learned a great deal about ministry from his falconry apprenticeship. It offers him a detailed analogy for "how we make things more difficult sometimes by taking too many steps." He notices that "by removing ourselves a little bit and having a little bit of faith, things will play out naturally." It helped him realize, "I am actually doing something counterproductive in ministry by trying to insert myself all the time."

He takes the analogy further: "With hawks, they know you are the source of food, and they will come to you with no force. With people, if they know you love them, they will come to you just fine, like a hawk."

He says he has also learned about how to be a better pastor from how he approaches friendship. He does not treat parishioners as his personal friends, but he has learned from friendship that first, "people just want to be loved," and second, "you're not actually going to fix anything, and that's okay." Although Saint Peter's is a growing congregation, Fr. Isaac says, much like his friend Fr. Lucas, "I have to be okay with shutting the doors; otherwise, I am ministering out of a place of fear. I can be okay with the worst-case scenario and learn to love the thing I wish would not happen" (see chapter 35, "Overcoming Isolation," for Fr. Lucas's story).

In falconry and in friendship, Fr. Isaac is learning from an apprenticeship to love, which helps him in every case do ministry in a more loving and faithful way, by not being overinvolved or trying to insert himself and fix things. With patience, Fr. Isaac is deepening his work of bringing ministry to life.

In her beautiful book *Breathing Space: A Spiritual Journey in the South Bronx*, Lutheran pastor Heidi Neumark tells her story of ministry apprenticeship to a neighborhood and church in another borough in New York.[1] It is also a story of apprenticeship to love, patience, and friendship and a slow transfiguration of pastor and church. The learning from that apprenticeship is not always easy. And patience is not always abundant. Says Neumark, "Sometimes when I'm short of patience, I focus on the little things, which I find myself doing more and more. Today, this teenager is going to college, the first in her family to graduate from high school—'I can't decide whether I want to be a teacher or a psychiatrist or a pediatrician!' Today, this woman is speaking up for justice—'I sat at the table of history today, Pastor, instead of just reading about it!' Today, this man is experiencing forgiveness. Today, this child feels cherished in the house of God."[2] An apprenticeship to a beloved community is truly the most amazing teacher.

🪶 QUESTIONS FOR REFLECTION AND CONVERSATION

Consider the following to guide your journaling or spark conversation with mentors and friends:

- How might I apprentice myself more intentionally to the situation of my ministry?

- What of my apprenticeship in ministry is challenging my patience? Who and what are my teachers, mentors, and friends in this situation?
- Where am I apprenticing myself to love?

🪶 THREE MINUTE MINISTRY MENTOR

Watch episode 29, "Apprenticeship," https://3mmm.us/Episode29

30

Learning Goals

HARNESSING FRUSTRATION

By describing what they can't stand, people unintentionally divulge what they stand for.

—Tony Schwartz and Catherine McCarthy,
"Manage Your Energy, Not Your Time"

What is your current learning goal for ministry? If you are still in seminary or perhaps participating in a peer learning group, then someone may ask you to set a learning goal for your ministry practice. This can be challenging. How does one figure out what makes for a good ministry learning goal?

Maybe you need more competence in preaching, teaching, organizing, or pastoral care. Maybe you need a goal to help you move beyond the edges of your competence. How exactly will you improve your practice?

I want to share very briefly with you how I help my students do this when they are setting goals for field education or internship classes. I also use this process with new pastors and ministers. First of all, I ask them to dream expansively and set what I like to call "a big, squishy goal." Something that will take years of practice before you say with confidence, _I am reaching my goal._

Here are a couple of examples: I want to be an effective and inspiring prophetic preacher. I want to come alongside people who are suffering and bear witness to God's presence in the situation. I want to organize and activate people of faith to take action for justice.

These are the kind of goals that cannot be accomplished in a single term of seminary or maybe even in the ever-elusive ten thousand hours.[1] But they are motivating and inspiring in themselves. They help students and growing ministers reach for more learning. To give these kinds of goals some legs and move them forward, we need a few other steps.

What comes next usually surprises students. I ask them to take a moment and think about what really ticks them off when they see another minister messing up in this area of ministry.

Pause and ask yourself, *Can I name something that makes me angry when I see a minister act in a certain way?* Hold it there in your hand.

Here is an example. One of the things that really infuriates me is to see a minister condescending to, or looking down on, or speaking down to another person.

Now I want you to turn that thing you've identified around slowly in your hand, and I want you to imagine the other side and ask yourself: *What positive value in my life and ministry does this thing violate for me?*

When I hold that condescension up in my hand, I can feel my frustration about it. And I can also turn it around and see that it makes me mad *because* it violates my own positive values of human dignity and respect, grounded in the love of God and neighbor. Such love and respect belong to every person. Of course, I struggle with maintaining this posture of love at all times, so my frustration is not just at other ministers but also at myself for not always living up to my own values in a way I desire.

Identifying what frustrates me when I see it in others helps me identify what I care about deeply and value most highly. Backing into this understanding about myself gives me a strong sense of motivation for setting and reaching my own learning goals for ministry.

❧

Harnessing frustration for good in our lives is big work. Anger and frustration as emotions have multiple purposes in our psyches and sense of well-being. In college, I took a full one-hour course called "Anger." Up to that point in my life, the emotion of anger was mostly something I feared, dreaded, and certainly never expressed openly. Nice Baptist girls didn't get angry. This became increasingly problematic as my clarity about injustices and my commitment to feminist values and liberation grew.

One of the most important things my professor Bill Blevins taught us in the class is that *anger is a sign that something needs to change.* I began to see anger not as something to avoid but as something to learn from. But even when I put it in perspective as a sign for change, knowing what to do with anger was still challenging. Do we express it or channel it into other activities? Does change need to happen *out there?* Or is the change needed *in here?* These questions were a good starting point for me. They helped me value anger in my life. They also helped me make friends with it a little rather than pushing it away.

Knowing *that* there needs to be change and knowing *what* change needs to happen are two different things. It was a very gradual learning process in my adult life, and it is ongoing. Yet finding ways to harness the power of anger and frustration is liberating.

One of the ways that I worked with this dynamic last year was to make a Lenten ritual and practice of attending to my anger. Throughout the season of Lent, each time I felt anger or frustration arise at someone or some situation,

I did my best to pause and examine that anger. I would take time to hold it up and also to turn it around and ask myself, *Which of my own positive values is being violated?*

This three-part ritual of *noticing, turning,* and *asking* was powerful for me. The effect of this daily spiritual work for seven weeks was to defang and declaw my feelings and put me in touch with a greater sense of my values and purpose. The ritual helped me increasingly replace my anger with compassion and my frustration with appreciation for myself and for others. Compassion and appreciation hold the power to renew my energy. They also cultivate dignity, trust, and respect between and among people.

⁂

A terrific resource for going deeper with the work of harnessing frustration is a *Harvard Business Review* article entitled "Manage Your Energy, Not Your Time" by Tony Schwartz and Catherine McCarthy.[2] In their study of business leaders, Schwartz and McCarthy noted that good leaders need rituals to help them give energy to the things they say they value. They also note that there is often a "divide between what people say is important and what they actually do."[3]

In order to help leaders close the gap, they recommend a process that harnesses frustration as a pathway to uncover deeply held values. Schwartz and McCarthy use the question "What are the qualities that you find most off-putting when you see them in others?" In a hypothetical example, if Pastor Juan is put off by rudeness, then the frustration he feels can be a pathway to uncovering his core values of respect and dignity. To infuse more respect and dignity into everyday work habits, Juan can cultivate rituals that elevate his practices of respect and dignity for himself and for people in his church and community.

When it comes to setting goals for ministry, starting with "our values" in a simple, straightforward way may lead us to goals that are not very inspiring. Taking the pathway of identifying and turning around frustration, however, can help us reach clarity about what really matters deeply to us. With that clarity, we can imagine how to get more of those values into our work and lives.

❧ QUESTIONS FOR REFLECTION AND CONVERSATION

Consider the following to guide your journaling or spark conversation with mentors and friends:

+ What is my big, squishy ministry learning goal?
+ How can I set goals for my practice of ministry that will really be aspirational and will help me flourish in ministry? Which goals will matter to me and to those with whom I serve?

+ What frustrates me or puts me off in the behavior or character of other ministers? What does that tell me about my own deeply held positive values?

🦜 THREE MINUTE MINISTRY MENTOR

Watch episode 30, "Learning Goals: Harnessing Frustration," https://3mmm.us/Episode30

For more ideas about setting ministry learning goals, see the next two chapters, which explore redirecting fear and seeking accountability in your goal-setting process.

31

Learning Goals

REDIRECTING FEAR

The complete identification with the story going on in our heads about fear distorts self-knowledge and increases the obsessive thinking that makes us prisoners.

—Martin Laird, *Into the Silent Land*

When I work with students to plan their field education, we spend a lot of time, long before stepping foot onsite, on setting goals. In fact, I will work with them to set goals that will lead them to context rather than deciding on goals after they pick a ministry site.

Whether you are a seminarian or a beginning minister or even someone with years of ministry experience, learning goals for ministry can help you deepen your practice. And they can also be challenging to set. Initially, I ask students to embrace a *big, squishy learning goal*. Here's how I break it down:

- *big* . . . because it is aspirational and more than you are currently able to embody or enact
- *squishy* . . . because it has lots of room for growth; it might include more than one skill set
- *learning* . . . because it is more than an achievement; it is cultivating and nurturing your thinking, being, and doing
- *goal* . . . because it should move you toward a more effective practice of ministry

One of my former students likes to call it a "big, scary goal." Jessica is on to something. Often there is some dynamic of fear in pressing out into the unknown.

Here are some examples of big, squishy learning goals: I want to teach and inspire young people to embrace the vocations that God is awakening in them. I want to lead people of faith to work for racial justice in our city. I want to support caregivers spiritually and emotionally as they accompany their loved ones toward death.

As described in chapter 30, "Learning Goals: Harnessing Frustration," I often help students harness anger and frustration to help them uncover deeply held values that motivate learning. Usually this works really well. However, at other times, it is fear rather than anger that we need to redirect in order to find the right motivation for learning.

If students have trouble getting fired up about the ways people can mess up ministry or if they have trouble getting in touch with frustration, then I ask them, "What are you afraid of when it comes to reaching for a big ministry goal?"

Pause and consider, What is the thing that makes you feel afraid, like you'll never be able to accomplish your goal? Hold on to that for a moment.

One of my fears is that I will not get the help I need. This is a lifelong, maladaptive belief that has plagued me. I think of it as a blueprint kind of belief (see more about this in chapter 42, "Blueprint Stories"). It is my spiritual and emotional work to loosen that fear's grip on my life and stop trying to do everything myself.

When I hold up my fear to the light of day rather than harboring it in a back corner of my heart and mind, I can see how irrational and unfounded that fear is. For instance, a simple look around my life gives me evidence that I often have exactly the help I need. And when I *trust* that help is coming, it almost always shows up. I see how I've been imprisoned by fear that is based on an unfounded story.

With fear, the trick is not so much to turn it around as it is to lift it up. Fear is not motivational in the same ways anger is; rather, fear as an emotion may be real, but the stories we tell ourselves about that fear can be completely unfounded. When we lift fear up and look at it honestly, we can see what needs attention. Then we can cultivate trust and ask for support. Trust and support make possible the risk of learning that is not ensnared by fear.

Now return to that fear you were holding a moment ago. What stories are you telling yourself about that fear when it comes to ministry?

⊷❧⊶

Pastor Trong moved with his wife and children from the northwestern United States to Texas when he was called as associate pastor at a Vietnamese Evangelical Church (VEC). Soon he found himself running into various fears that made goal setting for ministry very difficult (see chapter 9 for more about Trong's early call to ministry). Now in his forties and having immigrated from Vietnam to the United States as a toddler, Pastor Trong was caught between generations in his ethnically Vietnamese congregation and ministry colleagues.

In a daylong interview of Fuller Seminary graduates, Trong shared with us about the struggles of the congregation. He noticed "a lot of fear in what's going to happen" arising from the first-generation members. He said there is an "odd kind of dynamic in Vietnamese churches started by first-generation people" who immigrated to the United States in the 1970s and '80s. On one hand, they "want something for their children, but they just don't know what that something is. And they are also fearful." They are fearful of changes as well as what they might lose.

He is familiar with several similar immigrant congregations and says the churches are like "time capsules" of culture, language, foodways, and social patterns. In worship and other aspects of church, says Trong, "they just got locked into that mode of doing church and worship services that do not deviate" from the way it worked in earlier times. Familiar patterns are hard to let go of. People feel fear over the potential losses.

As the second, third, and fourth generations of children and grandchildren become more accustomed to American ways of speaking, relating, eating, and worshipping, the elders see they should address those needs, but when they do so, they feel new layers of fear: "Are we going to be relegated to the minority within our own church?"

When the traditional, first-generation pastor left the VEC, Trong's colleague Chinh was moved from associate to senior pastor. Pastor Chinh harbored a vision for the church in which the second and third generations would take the helm of leadership for the congregation. However, Pastor Chinh also felt some fear about how the vision might be received, so he did not share it widely. He only discussed it with staff and a handful of lay leaders.

Pastor Trong says his own ability to set goals or give direction to his areas of ministry in the church felt completely hampered by the layers of fear and avoidance. He decided to resign from the church, and he took a self-imposed sabbatical rather than continue in a ministry setting with so little direction.

The day we interviewed Trong, he was still without a call, although he started in a new position some months later. That day, he said, "There should be some kind of reality check in seminary" about situations like the one he found himself in.

Looking back to seminary, he wishes "some professor had just gotten up and said, 'I know you all are superhyped about working in churches, but this is what it could be like . . . sometimes.'" He wishes someone would have warned him about the fears he would run into and given him some idea about "what to do when there's disappointment. What do you do when things don't pan out the way you had hoped? And what do you do when you're stuck in a tough position like that? Who do you go to?"

⚘

To redirect fear is really to displace it with love and trust. Even in dire circumstances, love and trust are available. A sacred and holy presence is with you, ready to accompany you. Redirecting learning goals—and sometimes entire vocational pursuits, as Trong did—away from fear and into love and trust is itself a big, squishy learning goal. It takes a risk to let go of fear.

Fr. Martin Laird, in his book *Into the Silent Land*, further clarifies the point: fear as an emotion is not the real problem.[1] Remember, emotions have their own value (see chapter 15, "Emotional Intelligence"). Rather, "letting go of the story" we tell ourselves *about fear* is the bigger work. As Laird summarizes, "The complete identification with the story going on in our heads about fear distorts self-knowledge and increases the obsessive thinking that makes us prisoners."[2]

Trong knew he could not stay in a ministry situation so riddled with fear and avoidance. He took a risk, changed his story, and resigned without a clear calling to another place. He was unwilling to let fear direct his path. With courage, he reached out to people in a different location who could help him find a new place of ministry.

Learning to face, confront, and redirect fear, and the stories we tell ourselves about that feeling, makes a practical pathway forward. But to be clear, the path is not easy. Laird lays out the process of redirecting the power of fear in our lives through the practice of contemplative prayer. He sums up the moves this way: "This skill of observation and discernment, which the ancients call 'vigilance,' has three elements. First turn around and meet the afflictive emotion with stillness. Without dedicated practice this won't be possible. Second, allow fear to be present. Third, let go of the commentary on the fear. This third element is the most challenging."[3]

Laird is commending these steps as part of a committed practice of contemplative prayer (see chapter 14). Setting big, squishy ministry goals can bring us face-to-face with some of our deepest fears and the stories that grow up around them. Taking the risk of looking those fears in the eye and letting go of the stories can prepare us for better learning in the short term and a more sustained practice of ministry in the long term.

QUESTIONS FOR REFLECTION AND CONVERSATION

Consider the following to guide your journaling or spark conversation with mentors and friends:

- What is the thing that makes me feel afraid, like I might never be able to accomplish my goal?
- How can I uncover fears so as to infuse love and trust into my learning goals for ministry?

◆   What stories rush into my mind when I feel fear and how do they prevent me from taking the necessary risks for learning?

🪶 THREE MINUTE MINISTRY MENTOR

Watch episode 31, "Learning Goals: Redirecting Fear," https://3mmm.us/Episode31

32

Learning Goals

SEEKING ACCOUNTABILITY

As students in collaboration with their partners set goals, craft
plans, implement those plans, and reflect on their accomplishments, they set a lifelong pattern for learning.

—Sarah Drummond, "Assessment
and Theological Field Education"

"I often feel like a fish out of water when it comes to pastoral care. I am an
introvert who can be socially awkward from time to time, which can prove to
hinder moments of pastoral care," said Margo in her final reflection paper for
her first internship.[1]

When starting her third year of seminary, Margo also stepped onto the
path of congregational ministry for her first of three internships. She was a
new mother, new to the internship process, and recently relocated to her home
state of Alabama. These and other life challenges made the internship both the
"most difficult . . . and the most rewarding" term of seminary to that point for
Margo.

Months earlier, to get Margo and her classmates ready for launching into
field education, I asked them to explore and set *big, squishy learning goals* for
their ministry internships (see chapters 30 and 31 for more about learning
goals). The purpose was not to set goals so they could check the boxes or jump
through hoops for the program. The aim was to set learning goals for ministry
that might make a real difference in their practice of congregational pastoring, hospice chaplaincy, launching a pop culture and theology podcast, building
church websites, reenvisioning worship, or working in a community health care
clinic.

I ask field education students to read Sarah Drummond's chapter called
"Assessment and Theological Education" to get started.[2] To help students
begin crafting goals, Drummond suggests that they enter into a conversation

with friends, family, and mentors to seek accountability for their learning from the outset. She prompts the students to ask the following three questions:

1. What am I already good at, to the point that I do not need to spend a lot of time on it in field education?
2. Where are the biggest gaps in my abilities?
3. I do not know what I do not know: What blind spots about my own ministerial effectiveness and the nature of ministry can another point out to me?[3]

These are excellent questions no matter your age or position in your work as a chaplain, pastor, priest, community organizer, pastoral musician, or youth leader. Setting goals for the sake of learning is not merely the sign of a beginner. It is also the sign of a mature learner willing to keep expanding one's pastoral imagination and deepening one's practice.

After my students have set a basic framework for goals out of the conversations with each other and me, I move them toward the questions about harnessing anger and redirecting fear (see chapters 30 and 31). This stage of turning around and redirecting motivations and feelings takes some time, one-on-one exploration, and support. The process results in much more honest and meaningful learning goals.

Once students have a clear sense of their learning goals, I urge them toward finding a field education site where they can work on learning that is most important to them. Not every program operates in this way, and field education students in other programs are often matched with the setting first. Then they take time to think about goals with their new supervisors.

In either case, the next step of planning is also one that seeks accountability to the ministry context. After Margo considered her abilities, gaps in learning, what she felt most motivated to learn, and the needs of the small church where she would serve, she settled on two ministry learning goals: (1) to practice effective preparation and presentation of sermons and (2) to provide intentional pastoral care. She also set a third self-care and spiritual formation goal.

With learning goals set and a ministry context established, bringing the learning to life requires some additional planning. Again, Drummond provides an excellent framework for this "action plan." For each big, squishy goal, students need to define objectives, tasks, and resources to support their learning and move them along through their time.[4]

Objectives are the concrete, measurable steps that help you work toward a big, squishy learning goal. For example, Margo's goal of practicing effective preparation and presentation of sermons was big and squishy for her because she had not preached before. She needed very concrete and realistic objectives about preparation, delivery, and assessment of her sermons. For a novice preacher, setting a goal of preaching two times during a field education term was concrete, realistic, and measurable. As a newcomer to the practice, Margo needed plenty of time for each step.

The more concrete and measurable the objectives, the more learners can visualize change or growth that comes with time. Within each objective, there will be a number of specific tasks. Sticking with the example of Margo's preaching goal, tasks would include spiritual or prayerful preparation for each sermon, study and exegesis of the Scripture text, writing drafts of the sermon, practicing the delivery, and/or going through the sermon with a trusted mentor or more experienced preacher. These tasks simply help break down the objective into manageable steps!

Margo also needed to identify resources to help her accomplish her tasks and objectives. Resources include people, such as professors, fellow seminarians, and ministry peers. In the case of preaching, resources also include study materials, spiritual and meditative practices, and perhaps other books about preaching as well as the community where she delivered her sermons. Having a list of resources and a sense of accountability will be essential for helping you actually engage the goals that you set.

Margo found the preaching experience exhilarating. However, when things did not go as expected with learning pastoral care, she needed to pause and revisit her learning goals. This is where accountability really came into play.

Seminary courses by design build in accountability. Field education in particular focuses on helping students integrate learning from many aspects of their seminary curriculum through setting goals and being accountable to peers, professors, supervisors, and ministry partners. After seminary, finding accountability takes more effort. New ministers can find themselves isolated and in need of both support and accountability. Taking time to recruit mentors and peers to back you up is worth the effort!

Margo set her goals, and then part of the way through the term, she needed to pivot. It was accountability to her class, her peers and professor, and the congregation she served that helped her make the most of a situation that did not go just as she was expecting.

Early in the internship, Margo made a few home and hospital visits. The pastoral care learning was slower than she wanted it to be, and she found herself discouraged and ready to throw in the towel. She asked for more guidance from her supervisor, but the response was minimal.

When I learned what was happening in the situation, I encouraged Margo to revisit her learning goals. This became a turning point in her internship. She decided it was time "to readjust my mindset . . . and to take ownership of my learning." She chose to invest herself more fully by interviewing congregation members about their experiences and expectations of pastoral care.

The choice to interview church folks led to one of the "the most unexpected moments" of her internship. Margo reached outside her comfort zone and interviewed people in all areas of the church.

What she found was this: "Many of my interviewees said that they believe both the pastor and congregation are equally responsible for caring for the world. However, they believed the kinds of pastoral care provided are different for each role."

This finding brought Margo up short because she went into the exercise believing "my interviewees would think pastoral care is solely the pastor's responsibility." She plans to take her new learning about shared ministry into her future ministry settings: "I hope I can bridge the gap of understanding about pastoral care between pastor and congregants."

Through the arts of preaching and pastoral care, Margo experienced profound moments of growth. Her big, squishy ministry goal has now expanded. Margo wants "to become a pastoral presence in the lives of others." She concluded her internship paper with this prayer:

> Creator God,
> For the preservation of sanity after these fourteen weeks,
> For the immense growing pains,
> I give thanks.
> For the word *woman*,
> And the word *pastor*,
> And the ability to use them together.
> I give thanks.
> Amen.

☙✠❧

Without some accountability, learning goals can certainly fall flat. Learning practices as complex and subtle as ministry do not work well in isolation or without good partners, mentors, and friends. Being accountable to them becomes especially important when things do not go as planned.

As Sarah Drummond says, learning goals and accountability can become part of "a lifelong pattern for learning."[5] When I work with new pastors, I encourage them to set learning goals for themselves. In the first few years, the immersion in practice is very likely to be overwhelming. The learning goal that many newer ministers need is related to how to care for their well-being amid all the demands on their time and energies. Every step considered here for ministry learning goals can also be useful for setting goals to nourish one's soul.

⤳ QUESTIONS FOR REFLECTION AND CONVERSATION

Consider the following to guide your journaling or spark conversation with mentors and friends:

+ Who can I draw into a conversation for feedback and accountability as I consider learning goals for ministry?
+ What objectives, tasks, resources, and accountability will I embrace to help me grow in my practice of ministry?
+ Where will I turn when I am discouraged or ready to throw in the towel on my plans for learning or self-care?

⤳ THREE MINUTE MINISTRY MENTOR

Watch episode 32, "Learning Goals: Seeking Accountability," https://3mmm.us/Episode32

33

Cultivating Questions

The important thing is not to stop questioning. Curiosity has its own reason for existing. One cannot help but be in awe when one contemplates the mysteries of eternity.... Never lose a holy curiosity.

—Albert Einstein

Pastor Greg is a white Lutheran man in his early thirties. When we interviewed him as part of the LPI Project, he was reflecting with us about his first full-time call to ministry. At that time, Greg was in his fourth month of serving a large, multistaff, suburban congregation.

We asked the new ministers gathered for the LPI Project interview that day to think with us about what had been important preparation for ministry. *What really matters for you now? What are you using and finding helpful?*

Pastor Greg told us about interviewing one of his seminary professors. The professor taught Scripture interpretation and said something that really stood out to Greg. The professor said he believed what students need to know is that they should become "cultivators of ministry questions."

A significant part of ministry, said the professor, is "being able to engage in thoughtful and meaningful ways the questions that people are having in their lives right now and being able to speak to them in a variety of creative and insightful ways."

Pastor Greg said that he did think his seminary education taught him to do just that: cultivate important questions. He said, "Something that I lean on quite regularly is listening for what questions people are asking and entering into those, *not* with the expectation that I'm going to provide answers but to validate the [questions] as good and holy work."

We asked him to "take us to a moment when that was what was happening recently."

Pastor Greg said, "Last night, when I was doing a study of Isaiah ... [people] were beginning to ask questions of the Bible and of God and what this means for me and being okay with the questioning."

Pastor Greg says he is excited to "see these lifelong believers begin to open up" to asking such important questions.

He prompts parishioners by seeding questions of his own in the Bible study. When he was leading them in the study of Isaiah 11, the peaceful kingdom vision, he raised these questions: "What does it mean that we don't see [the actual vision] yet? It is something we hope for, but yet people have been hoping for it forever. So how do we deal with that? How do we make sense of that and how is it not just a 'pie-in-the-sky' vision for us? How does it continue to be a word of hope for us?"

Not only does Pastor Greg seek to validate the questions of his parishioners; he also "takes advantage of being a newcomer," and he says, "I push back and I challenge. I wear the outsider hat because I'm still new and feel like I can ask questions and say, 'Well, why? What's the point?' or 'Why are we doing this?' and 'Have we thought of this?'"

Four months into his ministry, that approach was still working. A decade later, we interviewed Pastor Greg for a fourth time. It turns out that he is still asking new questions, pushing back, and challenging ideas in the same congregation.

A resource to help you deepen this aspect of your practice of ministry is your own personal journal. I hope you might pick up a blank journal and begin to make space in your ministry practice for writing down and cultivating your own questions.

⌒⥰⌒

When I took a public speaking course a couple of years ago, the instructor taught us to end our speeches by asking "Questions?" and holding out our hands or gesturing with a receptive posture. Then we were to wait for the audience to start asking.

In ministry, teaching, and lots of other professions, if we want our presentations to be more than one-sided monologues, both *asking* questions and *inviting* questions is important.

There are many ways I've learned that asking questions will get you further. Join me in thinking for a bit about *getting further with questions*. This approach is not just a matter of making progress but a matter of getting to the "more" of the situation.

When I speak of the "more" in a situation, I am not simply referring to something hidden, secretive, or what a critical theorist might call "deep structure." Instead, I am simply signaling that in speaking or acting, we often use shorthand. When we take time to pay attention patiently and deeply, we can discover that there is much more going on, much more to discover about the person or situation, much more to notice about the presence of the holy. Philosopher of religion William James makes an exploration of "the more," and he observes, "Apart from all religious considerations, there is actually and literally more life in our total soul than we are at any time aware of."[1]

Let's consider how cultivating good questions can get us further in noticing "more" about three crucial components of the practice of ministry: understanding, empathy, and discernment.

+ **Further in understanding:** When phrased right, thoughtful questions lead to more understanding in complex or escalating situations. Recently while my husband and I were navigating an unexpected situation with our daughter who was at sleepaway camp, we needed better understanding in order to make the best decisions. We needed to talk to more people and ask more questions. We asked clarifying questions, information-gathering questions, and direct yes or no questions. My husband and I asked each other questions about possible scenarios, and we wondered who could give us the help we needed. Fortunately, asking more questions led us to better information and more clarity.

+ **Further in empathy:** The situation like the one we faced with my daughter was complex and required greater understanding. Many ministry situations are multifaceted, and they call for skill in listening in order to understand people. Empathy takes patience and a willingness to "not know" until someone tells us or shows us what they are thinking, feeling, and experiencing. During the complicated situation with our daughter, I needed to ask many honest, open-ended questions to reach real empathy with my husband. He was having a very different emotional experience than I was having, and it took listening to grasp the "more" of what he was thinking and feeling. The more empathy I cultivated with him through the questions I asked, the more ready I was to support the direction that his intuition said we should go.

+ **Further in discernment:** In the end, we needed both greater understanding of the situation and greater empathy with each other in order to reach a decision about how best to care for our daughter. We asked a lot of versions of *What is the best/right/ most helpful thing to do?* We weighed out all the options, and in the end, it was abundantly clear what we needed to do. And we did it. Getting further with empathy for each other and grasping the complexity of the situation really helped us discern the right choice.

Whether you are an activist, chaplain, congregational minister, or nonprofit ministry leader, the practice of ministry nearly always requires discernment about how to lead a community; how to understand the "more" of the situation; how to hear the experiences, feelings, and ideas of the people involved;

and finally, how to decide what to do and how to take action. Thoughtful, intentional questions can lead the way in every case.

⟨ QUESTIONS FOR REFLECTION AND CONVERSATION

Consider the following to guide your journaling or spark conversation with mentors and friends:

- What kind of questions am I cultivating in my ministry?
- How can I affirm the questions of those I am leading? And how can I seed my leadership with questions that cultivate our shared ministry?
- What questions do I need to ask in order to see the "more" of the situation?

⟨ THREE MINUTE MINISTRY MENTOR

Watch episode 33, "Cultivating Questions," https://3mmm.us/Episode33

34

Action-Reflection for Beginnings

We only increase our self-knowledge in the process of making changes. We try something new and then observe the results—how it feels to us, how others around us react—and only later reflect on and perhaps internalize what our experience taught us. In other words, we act like a leader and then think like a leader.

—Herminia Ibarra, *Act like a Leader, Think like a Leader*

Action. Reflection. Action.

In any calling, from nonprofit leadership to chaplaincy to campus ministry to congregational pastoring, the model of action-reflection is a gift for learning the practice of ministry. Here are three stories of beginnings in ministry. Each brings the action-reflection model to life.

Pastor Debbie is a white-identified Lutheran pastor in her late twenties. When we interviewed her for the LPI Project, Debbie was only a few months into her new congregational role as an associate pastor, having recently completed her yearlong internship (see chapter 19, "Brick Walls").

Like many of the seminarians transitioning into ministry that we interviewed in our study, the experience of CPE came up often in our conversations as a site of major learning. Pastor Debbie told us, "Clinical pastoral education was the first place I encountered the action-reflection model. And I realized while in CPE that is how I best learn, but I always thought I was going about it wrong, so CPE was really helpful for me." CPE training gave Debbie a formal way to understand her learning preference: by trying something first and then reflecting on what happened.

Pastor Debbie says the action-reflection model was also "really helpful in finding my place in new communities, assessing myself, and working in the community." That's three important kinds of help!

"I've often heard people say that when you're new, you're just supposed to listen for the first year, but I don't really believe that," Debbie said, chuckling.

"And I think maybe part of it is being a woman in a place where there hasn't been a female pastor before, but I have always taken it upon myself—since CPE—when I'm in any new place to ask a lot of questions from the very beginning and to try out new things. My CPE supervisor gave me this wonderful phrase to use when you're in a new place. You have this wonderful advantage of being able to be 'dumb as sh**' for a given period of time and to really take advantage of that for as long as you can."

Debbie says she found it affirming to her learning style to "act and then reflect on it rather than spending a lot of time thinking about what ought to be done" or sorting out options. She believes the approach has worked well in new situations. She has been able to "step out of my own comfort zone or [the] comfort zone of the congregation and to just see what happens."

❧❧❧

When Esther interviewed for the campus pastor job at University Church, they asked if she played the guitar. Esther said, "You know, I can play like the eight chords that every youth director knows, but that's it."

That was all the hiring committee needed to hear. They thought it should be no problem for Esther to do the music, the preaching, and everything else in the "church within a church" campus ministry program. They hired her on a one-year contract. It turned out to be quite a year!

Esther was in her late twenties at the time and had just graduated from seminary. She recalls, "The first month or two was just the biggest disaster! We were worshipping in a fellowship hall: white walls, big metal chairs, fluorescent lights, preaching from a music stand." Students ate dinner before worship "around a big square table where you could only talk to the person on your right or to your left."

Esther says she felt like a "one-person show up there, with awkward transitions, and me banging my guitar as I'm taking it off and moving to the music stand." The students wanted traditional Presbyterian worship. Yet the traditional liturgy felt out of place in the very sterile room. "It just didn't feel like a worshipful space."

It was also a big year of personal transitions for Esther. In her final year of seminary, Esther met and began dating her first girlfriend, who was also in seminary. The summer after graduation, she came out to her parents around the time she took the new campus pastor position. And she sat for her first ordination exams, which she found "demoralizing and discouraging" when she did not pass.

Esther was the first *new* church staff minister in many years. Her senior colleagues seemed to have forgotten what it was like for someone to be new. Like Debbie, she found herself constantly needing to ask questions. Action was required to revitalize the campus ministry program. Yet Esther had few partners with whom she could process or reflect on the many changes. She also had to work to build trust with students and ministry colleagues. Her campus ministry team consisted of one ninety-year-old man who remembered campus ministry sixty years ago and one college student. Esther made it a priority to expand the leadership team in that year.

In her reflections toward the end of that year, Esther told us she experienced for herself just how much about ministry cannot be assumed. Seminary taught her that worship space should be worshipful. On the ground, she figured out it was up to her to take action. She needed to bring the creativity she learned in seminary to life in the new ministry setting.

By the time we interviewed Esther, she was nearing the end of that beginning year in campus ministry. Esther made many changes that fostered both community and communion. She drew in new people to support the work, including a new intern. With more people to share the work, Esther now had a sounding board to help her process and reflect on all the change and growth in that year.

She replaced the large square table for dinner with multiple round tables. Students could have more eye contact and more shared conversation. She fashioned both a pulpit and a font for the worship space, and she added banners, candles, and "fabric in different liturgical colors" to signal each season.

Esther was not only making significant changes to the physical space and the leadership structure of her ministry in that beginning year; she also came out to the church staff and the congregation, and she found lots of support.

⚜

It was winter. I took the pager home, laid it on my nightstand, and prayed it would not go off during the night. Of course, it did. I was not really prepared for what to say or do.

I fumbled in the dark and managed to dress in what seemed like appropriate clothes for the middle of the night: jeans and a nice sweatshirt. (It was the nineties. Fancy, decorative sweatshirts were so in.)

I do not remember the six-mile drive or which door I used to get into the hospital. Most likely it was the emergency entrance. But I remember the Reeboks I wore, the pager in my hand, and the knot in my stomach.

There was no time for reflection. It was an emergency. Someone was dying or in crisis. There was only time for action. Reflection would come later.

When I took my first unit of CPE, I was not the biggest fan of diving into the work of ministry with so little guidance on what to do. I had some experience with navigating crisis, but on the whole, I was young and very inexperienced.

How about some instructions? How about some ideas for what to say? How about someone to point us in the right direction? Spell out some expectations. Instead, we received only the barest bones of direction and were turned loose to bring pastoral care to patients and their families in the hospital.

I survived that first night on call. And I don't recall doing any harm. But intent and impact are different things, and I will never know for sure the impact I had. All these years later, I have long since let *that concern* drift away.

What I remember most about that first night of on-call duty as a hospital chaplain is that my lack of planning what to wear brought the most unsettling feedback. When morning came and my day shift was starting, I still had on the clothes I managed to put on in the middle of the night.

The program director pulled me aside to say that what I was wearing was not appropriate for a chaplain on call. I felt the sting of criticism.

What I wanted and needed was some feedback or affirmation for *getting up* in the middle of the night, *driving* to the hospital, *meeting* a family in crisis, *praying* with them, and *staying* with them. But instead I felt reprimanded and ashamed. It did not feel like a learning moment at all.

A big part of CPE is learning through messing up and recovering, taking action, reflecting, then taking action again. However, in earlier versions of CPE, setting expectations was often purposely left vague. That meant on that night long ago, my "messing up" was not in the way I cared for people but in the way I did or did not meet program expectations.

The idea of CPE was (and is) to help students discover rather than be spoon-fed the important directions and expectations for a ministry of chaplaincy. However, this model of learning could be harsh at times when the learning moments were filled with criticism that followed on the heels of systemic withholding of information.

I certainly learned my lesson about *what to wear*—even in the middle of the night—as a hospital chaplain. And the real downside was that it felt like unnecessary punishment when it would have been so easy to share the information about what to wear even when on call in the middle of the night. Although I never missed the cues for a daytime shift, the experience did help me learn to seek out expectations for myself.

In retrospect, the injunctions I received also felt sexist. Policing what women wear is a long-standing strategy for maintaining the gender status quo. While the sexism was real, I also feel relatively certain that the problem was the jeans, sweatshirt (no matter how dressy), and tennis shoes. These likely would have been called out if worn by any CPE student of any gender.

But I could have skipped all of that drama and shame, and I could have focused on the human crisis and my presence with a family, if someone had set that expectation clearly and explicitly. It took some reflection after the fact to sort out what was important and what needed letting go. Now, many years later, I can see how these nights of being on call and CPE were my plunge into the open-ended and underdefined quality of ministry.

In Montessori education, setting expectations and providing needed materials is called a *prepared environment*. In a prepared environment, students can learn through discovery rather than shame. However, there is so much we cannot control or prepare in ministry. We simply must act and later learn from what happened and how we engaged the situation. The moments that stick with us and give us pause for reflection are the ones that help us grow in wisdom and grace.

Debbie, Esther, and I each learned some important things in our beginnings of ministry. Like so much of life, ministry is open-ended and underdefined. Not all environments are prepared. Not all expectations will be set. So much must be learned through missteps and course corrections. Action now, reflection later. Good questions are important, as is reflection on what happens.

The *Journal of Pastoral Care and Counseling* makes space in its pages to foster the action-reflection model of learning.[1] The journal supports pastoral and spiritual caregivers in many ministry settings. This journal can be of use to you as you reflect on your practice of ministry.

QUESTIONS FOR REFLECTION AND CONVERSATION

Consider the following to guide your journaling or spark conversation with mentors and friends:

- What questions can I ask in my situation to uncover more of what is happening?
- How do I currently turn to action-reflection to learn and grow my pastoral imagination?
- Where in my ministry might I take action first and then reflect on the results?
- What in my past experiences or learning will help me deepen my reflection?

THREE MINUTE MINISTRY MENTOR

Watch episode 34, "Action-Reflection for Beginnings," https://3mmm.us/Episode34

35

Overcoming Isolation

If we don't know God, we don't know ourselves, because we are
made in God's image and likeness. That's who we are. Hence,
today many people are looking for their identity, for their place
in the world, for who they are. The only place we can find who
we are is in God.

—Albert Rossi, *Becoming a Healing Presence*

"Being in New England, one is very isolated from brother clergy." Not only was
Fr. Lucas feeling isolated from his fellow Orthodox priests; he was also feeling
worn down by his work in the parish.

Fr. Lucas, a white man in his midforties, serves as an Orthodox priest in
a church that is more than a century old. Raised a Southern Baptist, Fr. Lucas
converted to the Orthodox faith as a young adult. His current church is financially sound, yet the leadership patterns are challenging, and some very unfor-
tunate pastoral situations preceded Fr. Lucas's arrival. It seemed uncertain
to Fr. Lucas if the church could continue to function.

When we interviewed him five years out of seminary for the LPI Project,
Fr. Lucas told us about how he would occasionally lament to his wife, "What
am I doing wrong that people aren't getting it?" Serving the church was not
what he was expecting.

After years of teaching in boarding schools, Fr. Lucas says going to seminary was an exploration and confirmation of what was at the "center of my
identity and . . . related to my faith." That journey to seminary then flowed into
a pathway to ordination. But, he says, what he didn't expect after graduation
was to be entrusted as a minister of the gospel and to say to himself, "'This is
who I am. Let's go!' And then to have that slowly eroded over time."

Fr. Lucas told us what that erosion looked like daily. He said, "I get up,
I get my girls ready for school, I start working on whatever the task is for the
day, the three or four phone calls come in, emails. I go shopping, do a service,
depending on the day, make some visits, write a report, don't work on the

sermon, you know, don't do all the important things for the weekend, and then I pick up my daughters from school. I make dinner, spend time with the family, go to bed, and I've done that now twelve hundred or thirteen hundred times since we last met."

"And for me," says Fr. Lucas, "I guess the negative part of all of that is that . . . the erosion just slowly wears you down." He says the erosion "occurred at the heart of what ministry is all about, and that's proclaiming and preaching the gospel . . . and then to have every day, every other voice . . . saying, 'We don't really care, please do what we asked you to do, check off the boxes, get the stuff done, get the reports out, . . . send out these letters.'"

He coached new members into the congregation and brought them into leadership. Yet they, too, would be worn down by forces of congregational erosion and the difficulty of working with the old guard. Together these things took the "wind out of the sails," and says Fr. Lucas, it "carved away at the stone of my identity. My prayer life was a wreck."

❧

The sense of isolation in ministry struck a chord with other priests in the Orthodox cohort after Fr. Lucas shared his story during the daylong interview. At the end of the interview, we talked about themes from the day. Fr. Mark, also in his early forties and serving dual appointments of teaching and helping plant a small parish, chimed in about isolation. He says, "I've actually had good support from my dean and bishop and fellow clergy, so I do feel like I . . . have ports of call and somewhere to turn with difficult pastoral issues. It's been great. Yet like Fr. Lucas, in terms of isolation, big time! I do not feel like I've got close clergy peer friends in the area and, in fact, I would . . . almost say I don't even think I have friends in the area. And my wife is experiencing much the same."

Fr. Matthew also agreed. In his midsixties and single, Fr. Matthew is serving a small parish in the rural South. He says, "The closest Orthodox parish to me is sixty miles away. Takes an hour and a half to get there, so isolation, yes! You know, as each of you spoke about that, yes, I kind of know what that is. But it is . . . an issue for all of us."

Beyond the cohort of Orthodox priests, other clergy in the LPI Project tell us about the isolation they feel in their separation from family, particularly when their ministry call or graduate school moves them many states or an ocean away from their families. They tell us about the isolation of living in small towns where social interaction, or dating, or just finding friends outside their congregations is challenging. They tell us about the isolation of not having a call and trying to figure out their place and how to invest themselves. They told us about the isolation created by the 2020 pandemic.

❧

As we listened to Fr. Lucas, we learned how isolation became less of a concern for him. First, he said, "It was important for me to come to the realization about a year ago that it's okay if I'm the priest that closes this church. I have to be okay with that." He also had to be okay with his people, no matter what happened with them, even if they never understood him, even if they would not let him lead them. Fr. Lucas had to, as he said, "be okay, even if I'm the guy whose backside gets hit by the door when it closes."

How did he make the shift? Several things helped. Fr. Lucas says he stopped the erosion by making connections with someone he talks to weekly. In the Orthodox tradition, this is his "confessor." And this connection helped him renew his daily prayer life. The other thing that helped with change was that "God [kept] sending us new people." These new connections began to help renew the life of the congregation, even if they did not stay long. Finally, Fr. Lucas decided to go back to school and work on his doctor of ministry degree.

More intentional connection, more prayer, and more education—these were the healing balms for erosion in Fr. Lucas's practice of ministry.

Erosion. Entropy. Isolation.

Not pretty words to think about when it comes to chaplaincy, activism, congregational pastoring, or nonprofit leadership. And yet, they are real. The routines and daily rigors of the work can surely wear you down emotionally, relationally, and spiritually.

The resource to help you with isolation is not likely to be another book. The best resources to help you with overcoming isolation are the same ones that helped Fr. Lucas: locating someone to connect with consistently and speak the truth of your experience, finding a practice of prayer that will resonate for you, and reaching out to people and groups who are already available to you.

Professor of pastoral theology Dr. Albert Rossi says, "Our task in prayer is to unite the intellect and the heart, to find the place of the heart and draw the intellect down into it. There, when the heart has been found and the intellect is devoted to guarding it, true prayer, the prayer of the heart, becomes possible."[1] This is the kind of prayer Fr. Lucas found, the kind of prayer that became a central point for his self-acceptance and the end of his sense of isolation. If you are feeling isolated, perhaps you, too, will look inward to the work of prayer and look around and see where you can reach out to stop the erosion.

QUESTIONS FOR REFLECTION AND CONVERSATION

Consider the following to guide your journaling or spark conversation with mentors and friends:

- What am I doing each day to make life-giving connections in my ministry?
- Where am I finding the relationships and practices of prayer that help me guard against becoming isolated in ministry?
- Who are the go-to people who buoy me when I am feeling isolated?

THREE MINUTE MINISTRY MENTOR

Watch episode 35, "Overcoming Isolation," https://3mmm.us/Episode35

36

Improvisation

> Improvise.
> Rearrange and fit to size.
> Change. Adapt. And revise.
> Move it around as time flies.
> Pivot. Shift. Sidestep. Riff.
> Play it like jazz.
> Do you get my drift?
>
> —Eileen Campbell-Reed

A finely honed practice of professional tennis, vegan cooking, or performing upright bass can be beautiful to watch. Not simply for their perfections or even their mastery—these are essential. But the deeper and more profound beauty is to see them in action, changing, flowing, and improvising.

Such profound and fluid practice is something akin to wisdom, or kinesthesia or *phronesis*.[1] And practice at the level of unself-conscious improvisation across multiple domains as wide and far-ranging as writing, singing, driving, acting, and arts and sports of all kinds gives us a vision for how to practice ministry with improvisation.

Certain arts of ministry like preaching, teaching, leading worship, administering daily work, and leading people through change have a consistency and a definable arc of planning, creating, doing, and then reflecting to see if there are ways to improve later. Nevertheless, these routines of congregational ministry can become deadening and may erode one's sense of call and well-being (see chapter 35, "Overcoming Isolation").

Yet most of ministry, including these daily and weekly rounds of practice, is inflected with a character that is best understood as open-ended and underdefined. We don't really know what is coming or where it will lead. If we are attuned to see the holy depths of the situation, we will experience the demand for improvisation in our practice every day.

In truth, you never know when a dog will show up in the choir loft, your robe will nearly catch on fire from the altar candles, the offering plates will go missing, someone will confess they have been in a relationship marked by violence for two years, or the call will come that a young father in the congregation has died suddenly. Each of these are real moments I've experienced in the practice of ministry. Some of the lighter moments call for laughter. Others deliver an emotional punch in the gut. All require improvisation.

Early in the beginnings of a practice of ministry, the demand for improvisation becomes a necessity when one's planning, leading, skill, or experience falls short. Fluid and elegant forms of improvisation can render invisible the conditions that make improvising possible. To see this more clearly, I will lay out two stories that offer marked contrasts. Side by side, they will raise our consciousness about the background, the support systems, the assumptions, and the social and relational conditions that make flourishing and improvisation possible.

What follows is a tale of two beginnings in ministry. In the first, Pastor Greg must change his plans on the fly while teaching a Bible study. In the second, Roberto shifts and turns continuously, only to be reprimanded over and over. The two young men have similar educational backgrounds, years of experience, and seminary training, and yet the conditions into which they enter are vastly different.

❧❦❧

Pastor Greg is a white Lutheran man in his early thirties. He is married to Kim, a business executive in product development. When we interviewed Greg as part of the LPI Project, he described his work with a large, multistaff, suburban congregation. This was his first full-time call to ministry, and it was also the congregation he had served during his internship year. Greg was in his fourth month of ministry when we interviewed him.

He told us about a night when he was leading Bible study. He said with a laugh, "I was expecting eight people to show up and forty came. I think that's one of the benefits of being the new guy. People still want to come to check you out."

Greg began his presentation for the seventy-five-minute session, and when he had covered his material, he said it had only taken a half hour. He thought to himself, *Oh no!* We asked if anyone knew he had an "Oh no!" moment.

He said, "I don't think so, because I didn't hit 'Next' on my slideshow where it said 'end of slide show.'" What did Greg do instead? He improvised on the spot.

He told us, "So I got them into small groups and asked them to process and talk through some of the stuff in the text and asked some application questions. As they were doing that, I'm writing and figuring out, all right, so how am I going to fill up the rest of the time?"

He did figure out how to use the time, and significantly, it was a night when the engagement in small groups led to people asking good questions about the biblical text. In that moment, Pastor Greg improvised and went from "Oh no!" to "Oh wow!" when he handed over some of the leadership to the small groups attending the Bible study.

Greg learned some things about improvising on the spot. And he says he would be better prepared next time. He was learning "what worked and what didn't." It was another moment of learning through acting and then reflecting on the outcomes.

When beginning a complex practice like ministry, it's totally normal for a new minister to plan and work hard to meet expectations. But often moments happen, and we say, "Oh no!" Things we did not plan for transpire. Moments that *cannot* be expected rise up.

In those moments, we must improvise what we are doing if we are to continue leading. Eventually, as the practice of ministry grows, we may also grow in our ease and flexibility so that improvisation becomes an intuitive way of leading.

A resource that helps new ministers explore improvisation through play and imagination is the revised edition of *Becoming a Pastor: Forming Self and Soul for Ministry* by pastoral theologian Jaco J. Hamman. He says, "To become a pastor and leader means for you to playfully engage life and ministry, when alone or in the presence of others, and thereby to mature into a person who can create space where you and others can be transformed."[2] Being able to play freely and creatively is a significant ingredient of improvisation. It can only happen in a particular kind of "space" described carefully and thoughtfully by Hamman, a space that is "welcoming, forgiving, and nurturing," a space where "souls are affirmed, restored, and enlivened."[3]

While Greg experienced each of these space-making conditions, not every new minister does. There are many conditions that made the story told to us by Pastor Greg possible. Those conditions remain largely invisible until we have a contrasting story.

Roberto is in his early thirties, a Mexican American with family on both sides of the US-Mexico border, and third-generation Presbyterian. He is married to Miranda, who is a Euro-American, and they are a Presbyterian clergy couple. When we interviewed Roberto two years after his seminary graduation, he was just coming off a very difficult assignment that lasted several months. Miranda was in a two-year pastoral residency, so Roberto had been working part-time in short-term ministry positions until they both could look for more permanent calls.

No matter what Roberto tried to do in the small-town Texas church where he was sent to work on outreach to the Mexican community, it seemed his white female pastoral supervisor could find little to be happy with. He was trying out work he had never tried before, and everything had a steep learning curve. The pastor told Roberto to get out into the community and meet more people, work harder, and make things happen for the ministry. However, when he spent time in the trailer parks, restaurants, and meat markets where most of the Mexican Americans lived and worked, he was reprimanded for not keeping up with time schedules and being in the wrong places.

Instead of offering support, the pastor called him into her office over and over to ask him "What is wrong?" and "Why aren't you doing the things I instructed you to do?" Once, when there was a miscommunication about a meeting time, the pastor told Roberto, "You ruined ministry for me today." Roberto worked to make the criticisms constructive, and he constantly readjusted his work patterns and style. He improvised his work daily. Some friends and family advised him to "keep his head down, keep working, and get through this."

After weeks of walking on eggshells, trying to be responsive to each new set of directions, and never seeming to live up to his supervisor's expectations, Roberto received a five-page ultimatum. The pastor also asked him to make an immediate decision. He could agree to her demands or he could go.

Feeling like he was at a major crossroads, Roberto looked over the demands, and he felt like God was telling him, "You can't move forward. This is unhealthy." The next day, he returned to the pastor's office and said, "Well, I don't think we can move forward. I think this is unhealthy, and I don't think I can do this." He gave thirty days' notice, but the pastor made sure he was gone by the next Saturday.

Additionally, there were complicated presbytery politics. Roberto was left feeling isolated, unsupported, and disenchanted with the church. As he reflected on the events with us in an LPI interview day, he still focused on the ways that he had fallen short, but he also could see how the system was failing him. What he heard from the pastor and other leaders was *not* "Well, Roberto, we see you have these strengths. Here are some areas that you might be able to work on. Here's how I would go about doing that." Instead, the pastor and the presbytery staff repeatedly said, "You need to figure out what's wrong with you and you need to figure out how to go about fixing it."

To us, Roberto sounded like a young minister working hard within a difficult system to improvise and learn from minor mistakes (see chapter 10, "Failing Creatively"). The thinly veiled hostility and racism of the system only made him feel worse about himself and second-guess his gifts and skills (see chapter 19, "Brick Walls"). He was not part of a system that expected him to succeed. None of the space-making qualities that Hamman identifies as necessary for playful, imaginative ministry were available to Roberto.

Despite the terrible conditions, unfair disadvantages, ultimatums, and implicit biases of his faith community, Roberto demonstrated tremendous resilience. When he and Miranda left the state, they were both able to find pastoral calls, and Roberto found conditions, although not perfect, that gave him more space to flourish in ministry.

〰✕〰

Hearing the stories of Roberto and Greg side by side helps us name the conditions that were in place and easily assumed, or typically "invisible," for Pastor Greg. He is a white man entering into service in a predominantly white church. He was already known to the community, having completed an internship in the same church. Any missteps he made were hardly noticed in a system where everyone expected him to succeed. Additionally, learning from failure and improvisation were part of the culture at the particular church where he served. He had the full support of his coworkers and lay leaders in the church. He was paid adequately and received benefits for a full-time ministry position. His spouse had a relatively secure nonministry job.

The contrasting conditions and mostly invisible biases have a powerful effect on how these two young men got started in ministry after seminary. Our tendency is to credit individuals with their success and their ability to adjust and improvise in their situations. Placing these two stories side by side (there are more details than can be included here) highlights how conditions themselves are essential for making improvisation possible.

Improvisation is not simply what we do when we fail to plan (although that makes improvising essential); it is also planning fully and then making a change in response to the situation. This more seasoned kind of improvisation is the art and skill that makes any mature practice a delight to witness. It is wisdom in action. Yet all the beautiful improvising in the world may not be enough when a situation does not have the necessary conditions in place for a new minister to thrive.

In his book *Nobody Cries When We Die: God, Community, and Surviving to Adulthood*, Latinx professor, author, and activist Patrick Reyes recounts his story of growing up, answering a call to ministry, and becoming a theological educator against all odds.[4] He recalls, "I wanted to fit in. I wanted to serve in ministry. But the game is rigged. It is rigged to exclude those who navigate multiple worlds. It is rigged to keep out of the scholarly world the person who can identify with the biblical narrative on an embodied level. It actively seeks to re-create what it already is, and, in my case, that apparently meant being white, privileged, educated, and dressed appropriately."[5]

The space Reyes needed to thrive was crowded with stereotypes, biases, unjust practices, violence, and economic disparity. When he got to seminary, he was surrounded by progressive white Christians who saw him as a narrative, a story, and a stereotype rather than as a person. Nevertheless, he persisted. And Reyes's life has in fact been animated by an ability to improvise, survive, sometimes start over, and draw on the rich resources of family, imagination, and spiritual groundedness. Yet through the violence and struggles, Reyes leaned into working together with God's Spirit and his Latinx community to help him find his way and help him stay alive. And "living," he says, "is our primary vocation."[6]

"Only when I was finally given the freedom and space to discern what living into full human flourishing looks like," says Reyes, "was I able to discern a call to do or be anything other than just alive. When I had that freedom, I heard God call me to bring life to the marginalized, subjugated, and violated community from which I come."[7]

Like Patrick Reyes, Roberto needed to assess what was healthy, and when he came to a crossroads, he determined that to thrive, he needed to leave an untenable situation. Improvising for Roberto meant starting over and then finding space to thrive more fully.

QUESTIONS FOR REFLECTION AND CONVERSATION

Consider the following to guide your journaling or spark conversation with mentors and friends:

- What conditions support me as I learn the practice of ministry? And what conditions are a challenge to my learning and growth? Has there been a season in my life when improvising was required simply to stay alive or to start anew?
- How can I grow into trusting myself to improvise as I lead in ministry?
- Life in ministry will keep coming at me in the open-ended and underdefined ways it is prone to do. How will I keep leaning into those moments and learning to improvise my practice?

THREE MINUTE MINISTRY MENTOR

Watch episode 36, "Improvisation," https://3mmm.us/Episode36

Salience

> Distinctive to clergy education—in comparison with other
> forms of professional education—is the necessity of learning
> to make judgments in reference to some understanding of the
> presence or leading of God or the dynamics at work in the mys-
> tery of human experience in a given situation.
>
> —Charles R. Foster et al., *Educating Clergy:*
> *Teaching Practices and Pastoral Imagination*

Salience is a key aspect of the birth and growth of pastoral imagination. *Salience* means seeing what is important in a field of things or a situation. It means sorting through possible meanings to find the one that is pertinent, urgent, or more immediate in character.

If pastoral imagination is thinking in action—an embodied and relational capacity—and if it allows one to see the complexity of a situation in the pastoral life and know how to respond in a fitting way, then how does one know what to pay attention to? What is important in the situation? What can be ignored, and what details are crucial for responding in the best way?

What goes in the foreground and what goes in the background?

As you immerse yourself in the practice of ministry over time, you will potentially develop a greater sense of salience—that is, you will begin to see exactly what in a situation is most important and what to pay attention to. However, ministry does not start out that way.

As a new minister, you may find yourself feeling overwhelmed. It is challenging to decipher where to put your attention. Sometimes you pay attention to the wrong things, and sometimes you miss something big or important in the moment. Even when you are a seasoned minister, entering into a new or complex ministry situation can make salience quite hard.

Two ministers in very different contexts give us insight into how salience can begin to take shape. Malinda, in her late twenties, is a white Protestant pastor on the East Coast of the United States. Tim, in his early thirties, is a white Catholic lay minister on the West Coast of the United States. We met Malinda and Tim in separate LPI interviews. Each seminary graduate shared stories that highlight how one learns what exactly to pay attention to in ministry.

⊷⊱⊰⊷

When Malinda started out her first solo pastorate (see chapter 7, "Ministry as Embodied"), she told us that it took time to "discern what is important and unimportant." She was serving a small congregation in the Carolinas when we talked with her during a second round of interviews in the study. Her small rural congregation had around one hundred members.

In her first year, Pastor Malinda took on what she called a "steep learning curve" in the congregation. There was so much to figure out. She says she loved the preaching, the pastoral care, and "being a solo pastor." Yet the first year was also "a roller coaster."[1]

The lessons about salience started on her first day of work. Malinda says that when she arrived at the church office, she was not sure what to do. But she called friends from seminary, and they listened. They continued listening and talking with her throughout her first year as a pastor. They listened through the mundane decisions and moments and also the more critical situations of those early months.

Malinda shared with us many vivid examples of how salience emerged for her. For example, Malinda says she learned through trial and error how to set her weekly schedule and how to "develop some good boundaries" with her congregation in the midst of ever-present demands of email and phone calls, visitors, and meetings.

Setting a schedule was like walking a fine line, she said, "because if I'm too lax, then I end up writing sermons on my day off." If she was too rigid, she might miss important opportunities to be with people during the week. As her sense of salience grew, Malinda told us how she began to see that brief conversations over shaking hands on Sunday mornings at the back door of the church helped set her schedule for the week. She knew who needed a visit, what concerns were coming up in the community, and where she needed to invest herself with the congregation. As Malinda gained a greater sense of salience, she could see what was important and where to pay attention. Eventually, she was able to formulate a schedule with "flexible room" in it each week.

⊷⊱⊰⊷

Tim is a lay Catholic minister living and working in the northwestern United States. When we met him as part of the LPI Project, Tim told us about considering life in a religious order but discerning that his call was to serve the church through lay ministry. He especially enjoyed working with youth and eventually became a youth minister at a large urban Catholic parish.

Tim told us the story about how he came to see and understand the importance of a "ministry of presence." He began by sharing an image of how he had been thinking of his relationship with and dependence on God.

Tim says, "I'm definitely in the car with God. God's definitely in the driver's seat, but my experience of myself has been that I'm frequently saying, 'Move over, God.' And I'm trying to grab the steering wheel and saying, 'Ooh, let's go over here! And ooh, let's go over there!' It's a struggle for me to let go and let God drive the car!"

As a part of his discernment about joining a lay society of the Roman Catholic Church, Tim traveled to Nicaragua in his late twenties. He felt like it was a kind of road trip with God to a place where he could "barely speak the language and didn't fully understand the cultures."

When he arrived in Nicaragua, says Tim, "all of my notion of being in control or being at the wheel was completely gone!" He says that is when his "aha moment" happened (see chapter 17, "Aha Moments").

His work in Nicaragua was to spend time with young people who were in a state of crisis for many different reasons. "We're talking about kids who were orphans from war," said Tim. "Others had been abandoned, and these children had major spiritual and emotional and psychological issues." There was nothing he could do about their situations other than sit with them and listen.

In this experience of listening to children and young people in crisis, barely understanding or speaking their language, Tim says he felt grace filling in the gaps of understanding. And most significantly, he says, in those moments, "I stumbled into what the *ministry of presence* is all about . . . *being with* and *not needing to do or say or lead*, but being with people."

"And I think what caused me to stop talking and pay attention," says Tim, "wasn't so much the wisdom that's required, but it was my inability to speak." He says when he can "truly 'let go and let God,' that's when some really amazing things happen."

⁂

To dive deeper into the ideas of pastoral imagination and the importance of salience, consider the 2006 book *Educating Clergy: Teaching Practices and Pastoral Imagination* by Charles R. Foster, Lisa Dahill, Lawrence A. Goleman, and Barbara Wang Tolentino.[2] In this landmark study of theological education, you can see how seminary professors aim to instill capacities for salience in their students.

The authors of *Educating Clergy* studied the pedagogy of numerous professors from eighteen Christian and Jewish seminaries.[3] In the book, they introduce various approaches of seminary professors who set out to teach a process of discernment. Whether the discernment is for interpreting Scripture, designing Christian education in a congregation, or preaching preparation, each teacher offers a pathway to salience and specific instances of how to make judgments with criteria from a specific tradition.

For example, one exemplary professor, Mary Hughes of Trinity Lutheran Seminary, leads her students through a process that introduces them first into a community of learning in her classroom. Once they are clearly part of that community, she teaches her students how to cultivate a vision or working theory of Christian education. Then she helps them engage their pastoral imagination to evaluate curricula from various publishers to discern how their educational vision is present or absent in the materials. Beyond just curricular review, she is teaching students to "practice exercising judgments" about the educational work of their churches.[4]

These examples of salience in action demonstrate its key components: learning to pay attention, adopting and utilizing meaningful criteria, and making wise judgments. These particular kinds of skills of discernment help students and new ministers move toward a more flexible salience in their complex situations of ministry.

QUESTIONS FOR REFLECTION AND CONVERSATION

Consider the following to guide your journaling or spark conversation with mentors and friends:

◆ When I step into a new ministry situation, how do I discern what goes in the foreground and what goes in the background?

◆ How do I know what to pay attention to in my complex situation of ministry? What visions and criteria shape my judgment about what deserves attention?

◆ Recalling a moment when something of significance became newly clear to me, how did that moment unfold?

THREE MINUTE MINISTRY MENTOR

Watch episode 37, "Salience," https://3mmm.us/Episode37

38

Action–Reflection for Preaching

> Taking some hours of prime preparation time for reflection on a personal interest or concern has almost always born fruit in the final outcome of the sermon. Engaging one's own curiosity and desire as preacher leads to an intimate involvement with the sermon seldom lost on the listening congregation.
>
> —Robert Dykstra, *Discovering a Sermon*

The real learning for Derrick started when he hit a dry patch. Derrick is a young white minister in his early thirties. When we interviewed Derrick for the LPI Project, he was just finishing his yearlong internship in campus ministry at a Lutheran college. He was awaiting his first call as a full-time ordained pastor.

Prior to his campus ministry internship, Derrick said he had been through the same CPE program with the same supervisor that some of his classmates had experienced. He recalled that this supervisor emphasized the "action-reflection" learning model quite a bit. Derrick also realized that taking action and then taking time for reflection was an important part of the way he learns.

Derrick says that while he could journal, it was clear to him that his "reflecting and thinking critically about ministry" were better when he was "interacting with other people." He needed the reflection piece of the learning for preaching to truly be a "connective vital thing" for him. He said, "I want so much to learn from the mistakes I've made in preaching *and* the successes I've made in preaching." Fortunately, he worked with two colleagues in his internship who gave him different models for what ministry could look like and served as reflection partners for his learning.

From the year of working with Rev. Sue and Rev. Jan, Derrick learned something about how "the character of the individual pastor is pretty important to ministry." He could see beyond the idea that ministry is sharing some "ready-prepared thing . . . learned in seminary." In his supervisors, he witnessed how aspects of ministry like preaching are "embodied in your unique experience and personality." He said Rev. Sue and Rev. Jan are "very different people, and their personalities come through so well in their ministry. And it's not because they always tell stories about themselves." Rather, "it's that they, as individuals, are so embodied in their sermons and in how they lead." As a result of seeing this reality come to life, Derrick also felt like pieces of his own pastoral self-understanding began to fall into place.

He told us about a dry patch of sermons he preached the previous year. Derrick recalls, "It was in January, which is kind of a dry time on campus. It was low energy. A lot of people were gone for J-term. It's cold as sin. It's a rough time around campus, and my sermons in whatever way reflected that, and they just were ones that I think exhibited this quality of me being kind of bored." Derrick had a point of reference for understanding his boredom and also the dry quality of his sermons. In seminary, he had read *Discovering a Sermon: Personal Pastoral Preaching* by Robert Dykstra.[1]

In the book, Dykstra argues for engaging deeply and personally with a text before one ever preaches. Derrick says he learned from Dykstra "an intentional way that you personally engage in your experience, in your background, your insights, intuitions—all the stuff that isn't in commentaries." He also learned from Dykstra and his own experience that when one skips that intentional process, preachers can be "bored and boring in their sermons."

Later in the interview day, we asked Derrick if his need for shared reflection was somehow also related to his series of dry midwinter sermons. "Yes," Derrick told us. That dry patch also coincided with a time when Rev. Sue was busy and unavailable, and Derrick believes that not having adequate time with a reflection partner did play a role in "that particular season of the internship."

Eventually, Derrick was able to reflect with Rev. Sue about his dry patch of preaching. Rev. Sue conveyed to him "that she can look back on her sermons and kind of tell what was going on in her personal life—not from stories she told in sermons but from the *tone* of the sermons." She explained that "she can tell where she was emotionally and generally in life by the depth, richness, and concreteness or lack thereof in her sermons." This helped Derrick understand that when he was acting like a bit of a lone ranger that January, it showed up in the *tone* of his sermons.

During his internship year, Derrick also extended this learning about the need for good reflection partners into other areas of his ministry. He began going to spiritual direction in the second half of the year. The relationship with his spiritual director turned out to be "a really good thing." He knew that in his first call he would be seeking out further spiritual direction and conversation partners for reflection.

⟨∾⟩

"Ministry was never really on my radar," recalls Georgine. She grew up in Kentucky attending a Church of God (Anderson, Indiana) congregation. And although the Pentecostal denomination has a fair number of women preachers and pastors, Georgine did not feel drawn to it.

At several pivotal points in her life, she heard the quiet question "Have you considered seminary?" But Georgine wanted to be an attorney or a doctor. She doesn't "do blood," so law school it would be.

Georgine was in her early forties when we met her on an LPI interview day in the northwestern United States. She had reached her goal, graduating from Howard University undergrad *and* law school. "When I stand on Howard's campus," she recalls, "what I know is that as an African American, I stand on the shoulders of those who have gone before me and that many of those people died for me to sit there. This gives me chills."

She was an attorney with a small private practice. But Georgine was also about to graduate from seminary. Wait, what?

After law school, Georgine moved to the West Coast to begin her career in law and in the process found a new sense of self and belonging. One year turned into eighteen. She found work and a new life partner. When she went through the process of coming out as lesbian, she also found herself feeling further alienated from the church of her childhood.

Georgine recalls, "I still knew many ministers who felt as though homosexuality was a sin and an abomination." Their message to her? "You're on the express train to hell. Don't pass go, do not collect $200, go directly." Undoing this thinking became part of a long process of returning to church and seminary.

Along the way, Georgine spent years exploring her spirituality without the church. She had grown tired of feeling "pelted from the pulpit." So for thirteen years, she found spiritual nurture in places as divergent as Buddhism and the Nation of Islam. She found the most spiritual support in AA when she decided to choose sobriety. Her relationship with God never faltered through this journey—it only deepened.

When she felt an urge to return to church, Georgine began setting criteria and making a list of churches to try. "Nobody wants to go to church on Sunday and be preached at, preached under, or demeaned. I thought, you know, that's going to be a tricky thing because coming out of an African American tradition, many of our churches are fundamentalist. And I can count the number of times on one hand where I've been in an African American church and not felt as though there was *us* and *them*. There had to be somebody under *us* in order to be above somebody else. And in that community, homosexuals are the *them*."

Yet she still craved "community, connection, and fellowship of people," so she started visiting the congregations on her list, slipping in through the back and ready to bolt if she didn't like what she heard. Eventually, she found a Disciples congregation with a female pastor, and she stopped working through her list. She found her home and community of faith.

In this congregation, she discovered "a tremendous number of individuals who had been injured and harmed in other faith traditions, and it was a place that has a tremendous amount of healing power and healing energy." It was just what she needed.

Then the church started asking her when she was going to preach, despite her protests that she was an attorney and not a preacher. Inside her own heart and mind, the Spirit was back with the question about seminary. The church also asked Georgine to be an elder. She said yes.

Then one week before the pastor was going to be away, she asked Georgine to fill in at the pulpit while she was gone: "Just preach because you are an elder, okay?" Georgine said yes again.

She thought to herself, *Okay, I guess so. Why not? What the heck? What have I got to lose? They're a loving group of people. They'll forgive me for botching it.*

And so Georgine "prepared a little sermon and got up there and preached." And something very surprising happened. In her words, "It was like being raptured to preach, and it's such a holy dance of being lifted and dancing with the Spirit. It was an experience that was so affirming that I really have been called, that I can't deny it anymore. I really need to stand in the yes-ness of all of that."

Georgine was clear that the dance was between herself and the Spirit as she preached about Elisha and Elijah and being commissioned into service. She also knew that her first preaching moment was a dance with the people in front of her. They had been "delivering God's part of that conversation . . . in this long dialogue with the divine about me standing in that very spot." The congregation was with her, and they continued with her even as she answered the call to seminary.

Like Derrick and Debbie and Esther (see chapter 34, "Action-Reflection for Beginnings"), Georgine was taking action, stepping out and taking a risk, and becoming part of a moment that would leave an indelible mark on her. Her reflection on her first moment of preaching and the ensuing clarity of call to seminary continued on for years. She still feels a sense of dancing with the Spirit, an embodied kind of rapture whenever she steps into the pulpit to preach.

⟨≈⟩

A resource that may help you with your action and reflection for preaching is the one that Derrick found helpful for learning the practice of preaching. *Discovering a Sermon* by Dykstra is also one of my favorites. Dykstra raises important questions, and he offers concrete strategies for how our lives and interests intersect with the texts of Scripture in playful and thoughtful ways that help us discover the sermons we need to preach.[2]

Dykstra, who teaches pastoral theology at Princeton Seminary, draws on the work of psychologist D. W. Winnicott, and he points out the ways that traditions and their representatives (ministers) can bring forth new sermonic meaning by playing creatively with the text(s) and with their own life stories and experience. Meaning comes from action and reflection, being with others, and being alone. And meaning in a sermon, as well as in life, is both discovered and created.[3]

Recently I joined a few other preachers to talk about the craft of sermon writing. We held our conversation as a panel discussion in a Sunday morning worship service. Six women talked together about how they might plan for preaching about Mary and Martha (Luke 10:38–42). We discussed where we struggled, how we prepared, and what irritated and inspired us about the text. It was so much fun!

Preaching is not, however, always fun. Sometimes it is hard, as Derrick's story highlights. Sometimes it is a long resistance, as Georgine's story shows us. Occasionally it feels like no word from God is ever going to arrive. Sometimes it is anguishing to wrestle with the text and the context of our lives and wring a blessing from the experience. Sometimes preachers can find themselves feeling bored or in a dry patch.

Speaking is a major part of leading in the practice of ministry. It might take the form of delivering sermons, or working to inspire volunteers and employees, or telling the story of your organization and its purpose in the world, or leading a protest or rally, or simply chairing a committee meeting.

Like other aspects of the practice of ministry, it takes time and experience to learn the ins and outs of doing the work well. Honing the practice of speaking effectively and moving people to action takes attention, action, and reflection. It takes doing it over and over until you have a greater sense of timing, delivery, and connection. Having partners and supporters who will reflect with you before and after your preaching can really help you complete the loop of action-reflection-action.

QUESTIONS FOR REFLECTION AND CONVERSATION

Consider the following to guide your journaling or spark conversation with mentors and friends:

- What has my experience in preaching been like lately—more like rapturous dance or more like a dry patch? Why?
- How might I take a risk and try something new in my preaching?
- Who will I seek out as reflection partners who can help me think about my preaching, my preparation, and/or my practice of ministry?

THREE MINUTE MINISTRY MENTOR

Watch episode 38, "Action-Reflection in Preaching," https://3mmm.us/Episode38

39

Pulled Up Short

Our life of faith consists in moving with God in terms of:
(a) being securely oriented; (b) being painfully disoriented; and
(c) being surprisingly reoriented.

—Walter Brueggemann, *Praying the Psalms*

Keith is a participant in the LPI Project. He identifies as white, and he was in his midthirties when he began serving a United Methodist congregation as associate pastor. He preached on a regular basis but not every Sunday.

Keith had planned a four-week sermon series called "Recovering Our Economy" in a year when things had been tough financially in the community. With only about a dozen sermons under his belt, Keith prepared carefully for the first sermon of the series, preaching it in the early morning service.

Linda, a visitor new to the area, came to worship. Following the service, Linda lingered during the fellowship time until nearly everyone was gone. Then she approached Keith in tears. Inside, Keith was thinking, *Wow, the message must have been awesome. It must have really hit home. Yes!*

Then Linda said, "I just want you to know that was the most hurtful thing I've ever heard anyone say. I've never heard anyone sound so judgmental. I can't help it that I don't have a job."

Keith was pulled up short. He says, "I was flabbergasted because I had no idea where she got those things." He stood there, not knowing what to say.

Keith just experienced one of the most common yet essential moments in learning the practice of ministry. Being "pulled up short" is that moment when you are going along with your work and suddenly something happens that surprises you, throws you off balance, or confronts you with the limits of what you know. These moments have the potential to teach important aspects of ministry, and they can also be very unsettling.

Finally, Keith managed to say, "I am so sorry that you heard anything that was judgmental come from me. That would be the last thing in the world that I would hope that you would have gotten from that message."

After the apology, he continued to talk with her for another fifteen minutes, explaining his creative process in sermon writing. He worried, "If she's feeling that way, more than likely there are other people that would feel that way too." He said that after the conversation with Linda, he was a "wreck."

Keith made a beeline to find his mentor—the church's lead pastor, Larry—and told him he didn't think he could preach in the eleven o'clock service. Rev. Larry said, "What are you talking about?" Keith recounted his conversation with Linda.

Then Larry patiently helped Keith think about how people can receive the messages of sermons from where they are at the moment. Larry told Keith, "Sometimes people *hear* things that you would never say. Sometimes that will be great! And sometimes it won't."

Keith gathered up his courage and did the "most difficult thing." Following the admonition of John Wesley to "do no harm," he made a few small clarifications to the sermon. Then he climbed back into the pulpit and preached again.

It turned out that Linda had lost her job and her home and moved from another state to get a fresh start. She was in a lot of grief and pain. Over the next few weeks, the church received her, and she found a place of belonging. Through this experience, Keith made new connections about the impact of preaching.

⊰✦⊱

Orientation. Disorientation. Reorientation.

This pattern has been noted by many educators, and I use it in my classes regularly. I first learned the elegant yet powerful structure for imagining our learning from Hebrew Bible scholar Walter Brueggemann. He says, "Each of God's children is in transit along the flow of orientation, disorientation, and reorientation."[1]

For many people, the idea of orientation brings up thoughts of a new job or going back to school. Last autumn, when I started a new teaching appointment as a visiting associate professor of pastoral theology and care at Union Theological Seminary, I was plunged into several days of orientation right along with my students. I remember that before the week had hardly begun, I was pulled up short several times.

I arrived in New York City on a Sunday evening in late August, just in time for the last half hour of a picnic especially for new students and their partners and families. I literally parked my suitcase on the sidewalk and walked across the deep green grass to the food table, saying hello to a few people along the way. Most everyone was already eating or having postmeal conversations.

When I sat down with a table full of strangers, I said hello all around, and gradually I began learning who they were and sharing who I was. The weather was perfect, and the food was quite delicious. (I would definitely call it *advanced picnic*.)

Because I arrived late into the dinner hour, the picnic was all too soon over. But I had no idea how to reach the place where I would be staying. The buildings were something of a maze. I asked for some guidance from the students. They were also new, but soon they connected me with someone who could help.

We walked through a tunnel under the city streets of Morningside Heights. As we walked, I heard stories about Dr. Martin Luther King Jr. walking here to go from the school to the famed Riverside Church. Wow.

Then we arrived at a small lobby in the residence area, and a group of students was also arriving in the same place. We introduced ourselves, and they asked what I would be teaching. I told them I was teaching pastoral theology.

A third-year student asked, "*What* is pastoral theology?"

I was momentarily pulled up short. There was nothing like starting a new endeavor and hearing first thing a question about *what it even is!*

With every *orientation* to something new in our lives and in our practices of teaching and ministry comes what Brueggemann calls *disorientation*. That is, we find ourselves thrown off balance, confused or unsure of what to do, even stopped in our tracks. Rather than going along with life, we are suddenly *pulled up short*.

Philosopher of education Deborah Kerdeman, in her book chapter "Pulled Up Short: Challenging Self-Understanding as a Focus of Teaching and Learning," observes that being "pulled up short" entails a "deep recognition [that] confronts the fundamental limits of what human beings know and can do."[2] Kerdeman says these limits bring about pain that we must learn to live through, and we must orient ourselves to being pulled up short often if we are to learn from the moment and truly change our knowledge and self-understanding.

I've lived through quite a few such moments in my work. Being asked to explain who I am and what I do comes with the territory of being a woman called to ministry, a professor of practical and pastoral theology, and an academic entrepreneur.

After a split second of disorientation, I shared with the students how pastoral theology starts with where people live and the suffering and joy of their lives and considers how we care for one another. This is an important step on the pathway of understanding and constructing theology.

Systematic and doctrinal theology may prefer to foreground or begin with doctrine, Scripture, and/or history and proceed with how to understand the sacred and how to live. Pastoral theology prefers to begin with lived experience, including pain and suffering, and proceeds from there to theological reflections and constructive meanings. Theologies of many kinds engage both lived experience and texts as well as material culture and human psychology, yet the starting points are often unique, making the outcomes also particular. What most pulled me up short was being called on my first hour on campus, suitcase still in hand, to explain myself and my professional stance to students who seemed to have little apparent knowledge of these distinctions.

Kerdeman elaborates on the problems and discomfort of being pulled up short, a phrase she borrows and elaborates from philosopher Hans-Georg Gadamer. She says, "We do not choose the events that pull us up short. Neither do we choose whether this experience will expose self-distortions. Like it or not, being pulled up short shatters self-deceptions we would not perceive outside or in advance of this experience."[3]

Keith was unaware of how a sermon could impact listeners. I was pulled up short when I felt put on the spot to justify and explain my work as a pastoral theologian, causing me to momentarily question my choice. In both cases, we were misunderstood in ways that challenged our self-understandings, feeling thrown off balance and disoriented.

Such disorientations can come in surprising forms, sometimes causing great pain. Kerdeman says about this feeling, "Pain is not exclusively an injustice to uproot, a disorder to cure, or a wrong to set right. Pain is also an inevitable part of being alive. I call this kind of pain 'being pulled up short.' When we are pulled up short, events we neither want nor foresee and to which we may believe we are immune, interrupt our lives and challenge our self-understanding in ways we cannot imagine in advance of living through them."[4]

These kinds of unexpected and sometimes painful events of life are the starting place and fodder for much of practical and pastoral theology. In the practice of ministry, when our recovery goes well enough, we learn to practice ministry with improvisation (see chapter 36, "Improvisation"). Even when it does not go immediately well, we can learn from our missteps such that we grow in practice and expand our repertoire of possible responses, try new modes of recovery, and learn how not to lose our balance entirely (see chapter 10, "Failing Creatively").

What of the recovery from disorientation? Keith learned that the impact of his sermons is not always about him, and it can be an opportunity to learn with and from his listeners. I learned that students at Union ask questions when they want to know more rather than pretending to understand. How refreshing! Brueggemann says, "The other movement of human life is the surprising move from disorientation to a new orientation that is quite unlike the old status quo. This is not an automatic movement that can be presumed upon or predicted. Nor is it a return to the old form, a return to normalcy as though nothing had happened. It is rather 'all things new.' And when it happens, it is always a surprise, always a gift of graciousness, and always an experience that evokes gratitude."[5]

✎ QUESTIONS FOR REFLECTION AND CONVERSATION

Consider the following to guide your journaling or spark conversation with mentors and friends:

- When was the last time I was pulled up short? What did I learn from it?
- How have I experienced pain when discovering my limits?
- How can I hope and trust in the possibility of reorientation to life on the other side of the experience of being *pulled up short*?
- How am I recovering and learning from the experiences that disorient me?

✎ THREE MINUTE MINISTRY MENTOR

Watch episode 39, "Pulled Up Short," https://3mmm.us/Episode39

40

Change over Time

No instruction or program can simply transmit the wisdom and imagination that good pastors seem to have. Rather, these emerge over time in ministers who entrust themselves reflectively and well to participation in the life of faith and to the everyday work of ministry.

—Christian Scharen, "Learning Ministry over Time"

"I think the biggest thing, honestly, is just practice."

David is a white-identified leader in a nondenominational church. In his early thirties, David worked in youth ministry, and he also volunteered for various roles in more than one church. We met David in the LPI study when he was about to graduate from seminary.

When participants reached the five-years-out-of-seminary mark, we asked them to choose a particular aspect of ministry and talk us through how it has changed since graduating. They offered us lots of examples, from changes to their preaching style and giving pastoral care to their shifting prayer lives and preparation for teaching. David talked to us about how his "ability to teach has grown over time."

When he was "fresh out of seminary," David says his thought process went like this: "Oh, I've never done this before, so I'll get up and be really nervous, and I'll spit a bunch of stuff out that might or might not be helpful." Others in the interview chuckled in recognition.

David told us more about his early days of teaching Bible studies. He said, "I wanted to show how much I had learned, [how] I did all this study, and I wanted to make sure I get it all out there and that you were impressed by how much I learned about this Scripture or topic."

David says getting a few early teaching opportunities "under his belt" helped him become more comfortable and more confident. Then David experienced another transition. He began to focus less on himself and his own ego and more on what might be "important for actually helping the people."

David began thinking about how to tailor his lessons "more for the audience, whether it's ninth graders or retirees or people in a membership class at church." He took time to ask himself, "What do they need to learn from this material?"

A second thing changed about David's teaching preparation. He says, "For a long time, I was never consistently good at scheduling." After all, he *could* "write a sermon or make teaching plans *any time*." Because it didn't have to happen *right now*, emails, phone calls, and personal visits would divert David's attention at any given moment.

The result, said David, was that his preparation "would be disjointed . . . and all over the place." This was not all that satisfying. Eventually, he began "to schedule time during the week for each sermon prep or to work on his teaching lessons."

David said, "I would block the time off for teaching preparation in my calendar. And I would not check my email. I would close the door and focus in on the planning and protect that time, and that really helped me."

⚜

Whether it is a new call to ministry, a new semester in Seminary, or just the start of a new church year, beginning something new has a lot of emotion and expectation. Sometimes it carries a lot of freight.

Last fall, when I greeted students at Union Seminary's orientation, I told them, "I am just as new as you are! We will be learning together." And I could feel it. There was so much to learn on the steep, uphill curve of a new place, new people, and new systems. So much newness. So many firsts.

And hey, by the first day of orientation, I had already managed to lock myself out of my email account, lose my phone, break a key chain, and unintentionally donate $1.35 to the soda machine. These sound like everyday indignities. First World problems. White-privilege concerns. Yet when small trip-ups happen in a new situation, they feel bigger, more complicated, and more ominous than they really are.

My statement to the students was also not quite accurate. Sure, I was new to that institution, but I had been teaching at seminaries for more than a decade. I had been living into my call and purpose as a minister for longer than that. I was both new and also significantly more experienced all at once.

When we start something new, we cannot see where it is leading or predict the outcomes of our learning. Neither do we know how small choices made in the here and now may shape our future(s).

Each autumn, I feel a great resonance with new students. Going back to school means asking which books to buy, borrow, or rent. (Renting books, seriously? Wow.) Which books to read—paper, digital, audio? Going back to school means *all* the new technology to learn, *all* the new people to meet, and *all* the new systems and local cultures to grasp.

As I complete this book, going back to school in the fall means a whole new world for many institutions of higher education. The COVID-19 pandemic means many students and professors will be working together remotely. Not just through the crisis in the spring but for the entire fall term, we will be working together in new ways and learning new skills and new ways of relating over digital platforms.

Going back to school also means asking, How will I keep track of my own aims and goals? How will I keep up with exercise, eat right, and deal with other important aspects of basic self-care—like sleep? I also think about students from kindergarten through college who don't have the luxury of asking simple questions or the big life questions because they have to be concerned about what to eat, how to balance work and study, where they will sleep, and whether the teachers will take them seriously.

❧

Starting a new job in ministry can bring the same sense of being overwhelmed. In his article "Learning Ministry Overtime: Embodying Practical Wisdom," my research partner in the LPI Project, Christian Scharen, describes his own beginnings in ministry.[1] He traces the steps of the Dreyfus-Benner model for developing expertise. Scharen draws on moments of his own learning, starting with his time as a "beginner" working for a year in the Lutheran Volunteer Corps, serving with homeless people.[2]

Scharen describes his seminary education as a time of novice learning, understanding the "rules of the game," and having first experiences of preaching, leading worship, and giving pastoral care. He equates the stage of being an advanced beginner with his yearlong internship in an urban Black Lutheran congregation.[3]

In his first full-time pastoral call, Scharen plunged into the work of an urban New England congregation, presiding over twenty-two funerals, seven weddings, and thirteen baptisms in the first year. That year in the transitional neighborhood was like catapulting from the competence of knowing the rules into a kind of proficiency born of facing overwhelming leadership demands. Over and over, Pastor Scharen had to meet each new circumstance with both risk and responsibility.[4]

Scharen recounts the challenges he faced in the urban congregation and the way embodied learning became sedimented into his knowing. He was increasingly able to do his work by focusing less on the mechanics of any given task and more on seeing the immediate situation at hand. This shift also allowed him to see the bigger picture of the church and community as well. This kind of change and learning over time is the heart of cultivating a pastoral imagination.[5]

❧

Whether we are in college, doing an internship, working our way through seminary, or starting a new ministry call, we somehow know these endeavors will change us with all the classes and ideas, new people, ancient wisdom, broken traditions, injustices, and good and evil shaken, mixed, and stirred into our lives.

And yet change over time, growth, learning, and wisdom are not easy to see in the moment, much less predict or fully anticipate. We enter new worlds, and they are open-ended and underdefined. We find ourselves overwhelmed, struggling with our missteps, and pulled up short. Even when we courageously take risks and responsibility for our choices in these moments, the outcomes are not guaranteed.

We can only truly see how we change over time by looking back. Nevertheless (and this is a big one), by looking at the change over time that happens for others who are learning the same practices we are learning, there might be a way of making out at least a framework for change that is on our horizon. And not insignificantly, our own past experiences may also give us hints and clues about what is coming next or what may shift for us over time.

The only way practices such as learning, teaching, and ministry can lodge their best lessons in us is for us to persist over time, to reflect with our mentors and friends, to pay attention to the holy in the situation, and to take time for these things apart from the relentless demands of the work itself. So we move forward in trust, even if we cannot (and should not) leave our questions and doubts aside.

QUESTIONS FOR REFLECTION AND CONVERSATION

Consider the following to guide your journaling or spark conversation with mentors and friends:

- How is my practice of ministry changing and growing over time?
- If I look back, what course corrections do I see that I've made toward becoming more competent?
- Where were there any missteps in my early days of teaching, leading, preaching, or organizing? How did I recover?

THREE MINUTE MINISTRY MENTOR

Watch episode 40, "Change over Time," https://3mmm.us/Episode40

41

Two Vocations

> She thought of how precious it was to be able to know another
> person over many years. There was incomparable richness in it.
>
> —Alice Walker, *The Way Forward Is with a Broken Heart*

Vocation is a word that often evokes the idea of work. Yet vocation is not just work. Vocation may bring to the top of your mind the idea of calling. Yet vocation is more than calling. Vocation is often synonymous with ministry or religious service to the church. And yet vocation is not limited to working in or for the church.

The vocation of ministry is not simply a job. It is so much more than only a calling. And it works itself out in ways that are embedded and interwoven with other callings, or vocations, in your life.

Ministry is not a professional or spiritual practice that can or should be undertaken alone or in isolation. Remember, ministry as a practice is relational, embodied, emotional, and learned over time and with experience. It is best learned in an environment of support and love.

One of the realities about a call to ministry is that it always is accompanied by another call, one that will intertwine with it from start to finish. That other calling is the one related to how to live with others in family and/ or community.

Every time we sit down to interview the seminary graduates, pastors, and ministers in the LPI Project, they talk with us about a wide variety of ways that family and community are intertwined with the vocation and practice of ministry.

They tell us about taking care of special-needs children in their family or navigating a marriage with two pastors in partnership. They tell us about the demands of parenting, about the challenges of living in a parsonage in need of repairs, or about how to see young adult children through crises. And they talk about how they care for their elderly parents. Some of those parents were themselves in ministry. Some in our study are part of a multigenerational ministry family. One young Black pastor told us about his own struggle to understand

and accept that his wife is also experiencing a call to ministry. He was not sure how to cope with her vocation alongside his own. Some gay and lesbian ministers in the study have told us the challenges of coming out to their families and also how they have navigated that milestone through both generous support and painful rejections.

Some ministers and pastors in the LPI cohort have survived domestic violence and sexual trauma in their families. Others have lived through messy divorces, the loss of beloved family members, and the challenges of major mental and physical health crises. Ministers in the study are also impacted by joyful moments of family life with new babies, new partners and spouses, milestones for children, recoveries from illnesses, epic journeys to move to new places, renewed vocations, and the accomplishments of school and graduations.

In other words, ministers are like everyone else. They have lives and loves, struggles and celebrations, intimate partners, and real crises. They have relationships that are at once enthralling and maddening, life giving and sometimes draining.

And what about the priests and religious sisters and brothers or protestant pastors who choose a life of singleness? Well, those who choose a religious community or who set aside pursuits of marriage and children are also navigating a vocation and calling for how to live in a community of choice. Their relationships are still complex, challenging, sometimes supportive, and other times frustrating. Even the hermits of the fourth century who prayed in the desert and anchoresses who lived in tiny cells in the middle ages still needed the presence and care of a community to feed, clothe, and guard their sacred spaces. Thus the practice of ministry can only be learned and lived while also attending to the families and communities that support and uphold us daily.

Often the intertwining of two vocations can become knotted.

One minister in the LPI study offered an important insight. Pastor James, with many years of experience leading AME churches, said, "Ministry *will* put more on you than you can handle. You have to set boundaries. If you do not set boundaries, take it from me: We will put everything and everybody else first in the name of ministry. Ministry will put more on you than you can bear." Through a pastoral excellence program, James learned to pay attention to balance, to sabbaticals, and to giving more intentional thought to where family fits in. He says the program taught him "God first, family second, then church. If you're not careful, people will [believe] you say God first, church, then family."

Some traditions and theologies try to make the case that the only appropriate vocation for women is their work inside their homes or with their families. Many of the women in our study encounter people who still want to insist that women should only fulfill or prioritize a vocation that revolves around family concerns.

We need to reject the simplistic division of labor between women who work in home and family for no pay and men who work for wages outside the home. Even when this harmful and impractical ideal has been rejected and deconstructed, the Victorian division of labor, amplified by various forms of Christian complementarianism, still shapes expectations and sometimes invokes guilt in women.[1]

A much healthier and spiritually sound way to approach the questions about the two vocations of ministry and family is to examine them like overlays in an anatomy book: these two systems are unique and contained yet dependent and interconnected with one another in ways that are part of a larger whole we call *life*.

cᴙꙮɢ

New social configurations of family and work are emerging everywhere around us. Two resources that can help us go deeper into these questions around the two vocations are worth noting. First is the important people in your life. These may include your family by birth, adoption, marriage, or choice as well as your friends who are like family—sustaining you, laughing with you, having your back. These people in your life are a precious resource.

No matter how messy, shifting, or entangled these two callings are in our lives, we need both to sustain, uphold, and nourish us. When it comes to learning and embodying the practice of ministry and cultivating a flexible pastoral imagination, we need to know who our people are. We need people in our lives who have our backs and support our learning and with whom we share compassionate, mutual obligations.

The second resource to take us deeper into understanding the complexity of our own vocations and the vocations of people we serve is the Marilynne Robinson trilogy of books: *Gilead*, *Lila*, and *Home*.[2] In this series—and we could say the same about many other fine novels—we glimpse the depths of human relationship. The fascinating aspect of Robinson's intertwined families is that two of the main characters are pastors who are flawed and complicated at best. Her sagas, which take place over decades, capture the interconnected layers of love, loss, enmity, forgiveness, guilt, betrayal, and the enduring tragic and graceful character of life.

QUESTIONS FOR REFLECTION AND CONVERSATION

Consider the following to guide your journaling or spark conversation with mentors and friends:

+ How am I navigating these two vocations of family/community and ministry in my life?

- How am I setting appropriate priorities and boundaries with my community, friends, and family in relation to my practice of ministry?
- What novels, movies, or poems capture the complexity of these two vocations for me?

🪶 THREE MINUTE MINISTRY MENTOR

Watch episode 41, "Two Vocations," https://3mmm.us/Episode41

42

Blueprint Stories

By blindly following the script, we forfeit the power to shape
our own lives and identities.

—Sue Monk Kidd, *The Dance of the Dissident Daughter*

"I will not get the help I need." Despite evidence to the contrary and years of
work to change it, that story lingers in my life like a blueprint that resists change.

Sometimes when you engage in the practice of ministry, you may notice
that certain kinds of stories keep repeating themselves in your life. Stories
about the ways people have let you down, certain patterns of community conflict, or the ways you have been embraced or rejected in your ministry context.
Unattended, these "blueprint stories" can cause havoc and pain.

Although I learned eventually to ask for help from people in my work as
a professional minister and teacher by recruiting volunteers, organizing events,
and raising money, I also continued to find myself struggling to ask for the help
I needed in more personal ways.

A few years ago, early on a Saturday morning, I took off to go on a run. I
only made it as far as the end of my driveway. I was trying to secure my phone in
my running belt when I looked up to see a medium-sized brown dog growling
at me. Startled and slightly panicked, I began backing away. When the dog
barked and snapped in my direction, I stepped backward, falling into the ditch
that runs through my front yard, twisting my ankle badly.

I heard a voice behind me asking, "Are you okay?"

"No. I really don't think I am," I said, feeling relief that another human
was there. "I'm not sure if I can stand up."

I looked over my shoulder to see the elderly woman from across the street.
We had lived in our house less than a month. I did not know her name. She
had her white dog on a leash. I asked about the brown dog. She said it lived two
doors down. I thought she was coming to help me.

I could not have been further from the truth. When I looked around
again, she was walking up the street with her dog.

That is my blueprint story in a nutshell. Asking for help gets me nowhere except sitting in a ditch by myself in pain and crying.

So I did what I usually do. I got up and tried to "walk it off." I even ran a little because I assumed my injury would be less problematic if I just kept moving.

I was wrong. The ankle swelled. So did my grudge against my neighbor. Ice and ibuprofen did not help much. The next day's eight-hour plane ride to a professional conference did not help at all. I spent a week hobbling around Great Britain, searching daily for elusive ice.

I'm not usually a grudge-holding person. But I was very slow to let this one go, and I think it's because the story had something to teach me. A few therapeutic conversations helped me unpack it.

You see, help was actually everywhere. My husband and daughter were home. They were sleeping, yes, but help was only 150 feet away. My phone was in my hand. I could have called for help. Old strategies to "walk it off" didn't work physically or emotionally. Attaching my frustration to a stranger did not work either.

My failure to see what was available to me was the work of my unconscious to keep the story I inherited alive and kicking. This is the power of blueprint stories. The roots of harm were not in my neighbor, not in the growling dog, and not in my sleeping family but in my own deep-seated belief that I would not get the help I needed.

❧

Sometimes help is literally in the palm of our hands, and we cannot see it. Sometimes our ability to see or imagine or welcome the things we need in life is blocked by the kind of deeply seated beliefs and narratives that I am calling *blueprint stories.*

I could not connect my need for help with the phone that was in my running belt. I let the experience of my neighbor walking away drown out the possibilities for help plainly at my fingertips.

When interviewing ministers over the last decade, I sometimes hear stories from them that sound remarkably similar from situation to situation across the arc of their lives. When I worked with women in addiction recovery living in a residential treatment center, I heard beliefs they carried with them that were not adaptive. These beliefs came out in words like "I have a character flaw" or "I deserved punishment from my parents" or "Things just don't ever go my way."

I heard stories that seemed to repeat themselves in each new relationship—stories that blocked each woman's recovery from her addictions. And when they got clean, the volume on these stories would often crank up louder and louder.

The drug or alcohol use started as a coping strategy to help the women ignore and avoid the painful blueprint stories. The stories were often grounded in survival strategies from very early in their lives. But the childhood strategies became maladaptive coping mechanisms in adulthood. Together, the blueprint stories and coping strategies caused the women to be more invested in avoiding trauma and pain. Eventually, the blueprint stories, coping mechanisms, and use of substances to avoid pain and trauma became a toxic mix that helped fuel and maintain the addictions.

Addiction is not the only way people deal with blueprint stories. These stories show up and do their work in all kinds of sneaky ways. These stories have a way of infiltrating every area of our lives, including, for ministers, their very work in ministry.

Earlier in my life and ministry, my blueprint story—about not getting the help I needed—showed up when I tried to do everything by myself. In those beginning days in ministry, I often failed to ask for the help I needed from volunteers or colleagues because I did not fully believe that help would come. Quite the opposite was actually true—many people were ready to help, but I was not ready to believe in them.

Sometimes people in ministry—and other professions, of course—find explicit ways to overcome the harms of negative blueprint stories in their work. I did this by putting effort into finding and nurturing professional relationships that reversed my belief that I would not get the help I needed. I cultivated my tolerance for asking for money, volunteers, and other resources and getting the occasional "no." The more I asked, and the more I heard "yes," the more the power of my blueprint story released its grip on my work.

Yet for those of us in helping professions—and this is important—our work is so deeply entangled with our relationships and our emotional and spiritual well-being that the blueprint stories may do their most harm around our abilities to give compassionate care to ourselves.

The day I fell in the ditch, something was shifting in me, and my blueprint story asserted itself in a powerful and painful way. I was working intentionally to change my beliefs, but they are hard to change.

The grudge against my neighbor seemed to hang on, and when I would see her walking her dog, I would relive the moment. Yet attaching my frustration to a stranger did not work to move me toward healing. A few therapeutic conversations helped me unpeel the layers and bring me down to that cellar of my soul where the blueprint was most clear. While my ankle healed in the weeks after my fall into the ditch, I also worked to let go of a story that no longer served me.

I came to recognize the blueprint story clearly so when it shows up in my life—and it will again and again—I can recognize it for what it is. And I can also thank that blueprint story for the ways it served me and saved me at some point earlier in my life. In my case, it helped me become competent at many things early in life. I can also let the story be without letting it control me. I can make a different choice about what to believe and how to interpret my situation. And I *can* receive the help I need.

A resource that may help you explore the blueprint stories of your life or in the lives of people you care about is the book *The Body Keeps the Score* by Bessel van der Kolk.[1] If you are struggling with stories that keep repeating ancient harms, even the kind of harms that are passed down for generations, this book may offer insight for recognizing and eventually healing from those stories that no longer serve your well-being. Van der Kolk says, "Trauma is much more than a story about something that happened long ago. The emotions and physical sensations that were imprinted during the trauma are experienced not as memories but as disruptive physical reactions in the present."[2] After prioritizing a sense of safety and trust with a professional therapist, revisiting the events and harms that shaped one's narrative can lead to profound healing.

Those blueprint stories and the deeply held beliefs most likely protected you at some point earlier in your life, perhaps when you were very young or very vulnerable. And perhaps the stories are no longer adaptive in everyday, grown-up life. So be kind to yourself as you unpack those stories that you live by, and also access compassion for the ways blueprint stories function in the lives of others you love and serve. May you find peace and power to make the liberating changes you need for your well-being and your work in the practice of ministry.

✎ QUESTIONS FOR REFLECTION AND CONVERSATION

Consider the following to guide your journaling or spark conversation with mentors and friends:

+ How can I notice possible blueprint stories in my life? What responses do I have to difficult circumstances that seem automatic or like unquestioned rules that seem to guide my life?
+ When I know one of my blueprint stories, where does it seem to show up most often?
+ In what ways are these patterned stories impacting my practice of ministry?
+ Who is a trusted person with whom I can talk about the ways these stories are shaping me?

✎ THREE MINUTE MINISTRY MENTOR

Watch episode 42, "Blueprint Stories," https://3mmm.us/Episode42

43

Facing Fears

Our bodies have a form of knowledge that is different from our cognitive brains. This knowledge is typically experienced as a felt sense of constriction or expansion, pain or ease, energy or numbness. Often this knowledge is stored in our bodies as wordless stories about what is safe and what is dangerous. The body is where we fear, hope, and react; where we constrict and release; and where we reflexively fight, flee, or freeze.

—Resmaa Menakem, *My Grandmother's Hands*

Cathy is a participant in the LPI Project. She is a white woman in her thirties, and she grew up in a Roman Catholic family in the southwestern United States. We met her just near the time of her graduation from seminary.[1]

During college and graduate school and several ministry-related jobs, Cathy engaged with vulnerable groups of people in homeless shelters and on the streets. During a summer of CPE, Cathy worked with poor and formerly homeless people living in transitional housing and in a group home for children and adolescents.

Her peers in CPE were all Protestants and on various ordination tracks in their denominations. Women's ordination was a regular topic of conversation that summer, and Cathy faced her calling in a new way. Family and friends urged her to consider joining a religious order, and she supported women's ordination in the abstract.

Up to that point, Cathy's ministry felt like something she offered "through the back door." But one day, all the pieces of the puzzle came together. Previously, her own feelings were somewhat flat and unemotional when she considered the question of ordination for herself, but sitting alone in her office that day at the group home, she saw for the first time that she felt afraid.

She worried that "God was going to tell me no, that I couldn't have it." Once the realization of fear dawned, then she felt like God spoke to her, saying, "You can have it if you want it, if this is where your love and your life are."

Cathy recalls, "For me, becoming a *sister* was the sacrifice I was *supposed* to make, but it was like letting go of everything that I wanted, and it was not a good feeling." However, that day in her office, Cathy's understanding of sacrifice changed substantially.

Now she could see it as "giving to God everything you love and your whole life and living that, and *that's* what sacrifice is." She says, "In that moment, it felt like *I want to be ordained and that's where I want to go.*"

The same evening on the phone, her dad offered an unsolicited affirmation: "Cathy, you know, I was at mass and I was watching Fr. Tom . . . and if that's what you want, if you want to be a priest, then you should have it."

That autumn, Cathy found her way to a newly formed community of the Old Catholic Church, a group that broke away from the Roman church in 1870 in protest over doctrinal differences. After joining the congregation, she had her first opportunity to read the Gospel lesson and preach a sermon. She says she was feeling overly conspicuous wearing a white alb (liturgical robe). However, a friend said to her, "That's your baptismal identity. Wear it!"

She felt the profound blessing of that gift from her friend. A year after her first sermon, the church ordained Cathy as a deacon. Three years ago, Cathy was ordained as a priest in the Old Catholic Church, where she regularly exercises her gifts of leadership, preaching, and pastoral care in the congregation.

❧❦❧

Kaleb, in his early forties, was by any standard a highly successful minister at High Plains Community Church, a large megachurch in the southwestern United States. He was involved with the church many years before we met and interviewed him in the LPI Project. The Black congregation supported and cheered him on to seminary and to complete his MDiv. When he graduated, the church hired him to come work with young adults, from college age to age thirty-five.

The young adult ministry grew from just two dozen people to well over six hundred. The staff increased from Kaleb alone to more than twenty full-time, part-time, and volunteer leaders. Kaleb was also in charge of training one summer for the large extended staff of the High Plains Community Church. The training included designing, developing, and implementing the program. This event led to the senior pastor promoting Kaleb to be the executive pastor and director of ministries. In the new role, his duties expanded to serve all the ministries and ministerial staff, including the oversight of worship. His role was to make sure that worship ran smoothly each week at four separate campuses.

He often led worship and preached as well. On Mother's Day, Kaleb preached a sermon, and by the end of two full services, his voice had given out. He didn't know it at the time, but this would be the beginning of an eighteen-month medical leave.

"God has taken me on a journey," says Kaleb about those months away from work.

He spent a year in bed or in the side chair in his bedroom, losing weight, growing weak, and unable to eat or sleep with little explanation. He was wasting away, and he didn't know why. He felt like he was in a mighty struggle, a spiritual warfare in his mind, body, and spirit. Somehow God provided for him and his immediate family in this time with a patchwork of support from extended family, friends, and his wife taking a part-time job.

Finally, Kaleb reached a low point and asked his wife to call on the faith community to pray for him. They did. And then things turned . . .

Kaleb recalls, "One day I was listening [to music] in my chair, and a song came on: 'Let Go' by Dewayne Wood. And I remember getting up out of the chair, raising my hands to God, and telling God, 'I trust You. I trust You.'" The Scripture, Romans 8:26, came to him: "In the same way, the Spirit helps us in our weakness. We don't know what to pray for, but the Spirit intercedes for us with groans and words we cannot express." Kaleb says, "A groan came out of me that I have no idea how to explain, and I fell prostrate to the floor, and I said, 'God, I trust You.'"

Kaleb felt himself surrender utterly and completely to God.

When we interviewed Kaleb about six months after this day, he told us about that turning point and complete moment of surrender and deliverance. He says from that time on, he began to heal and recover his strength. He changed his diet, began to work with new health care providers, and made new habits of caring for his body.

Kaleb said the year of suffering and illness helped him "understand how much my physical health plays in ministry. During the time, I learned you can have as much theological training as you want. You can be as spiritual as you want. But how useful are you if you can't even do anything because your health is so out of line?"

I asked Kaleb if there was any connection between the internal spiritual war he felt and the day the song "Let Go" came on, and what brought him to the point of surrender and the new path of healing?

Fear.

There were multiple layers of fear that were holding Kaleb captive. He had "a vision—or a *dream*—that my soul was not only being bound but also tortured and terminated. And it scared me." He felt a long-standing fear of death and eternity (any time without an ending). He felt fear not only for his spiritual well-being but also for his physical well-being.

During the months of suffering, Kaleb says his theological education helped him recall what is "theologically sound" and stop his mind to see what did and did not "line up with the word of God." When everything came together and he heard the song "Let Go," Kaleb says, "That moment freed me from that fear, and I came to discover that fear is what I had been dealing with."

On that day, a new prayer was born in Kaleb's heart and mind: "I trust You, Lord. I trust You to deliver me, to make sure that nothing harms me." Although he says he will likely never be completely "over it," Kaleb now walks in freedom and trust and knows the presence of Christ on his path.

⳩

It can be hard even to admit our fears, much less face them.

Fear of loss. Fear of disappointment. Fear of not getting what you want and fear of getting it. Fear of walking down the street. Fear of making the wrong decision. Fear of staying in a relationship. Fear of leaving it.

Fear is a powerful motivator for action *and* inaction.

Fear can play a role in every aspect of the practice of ministry, in congregational life, in the work of chaplaincy, activism, college ministry, preaching, leading change, and so on. Why? Because fear is human, and humans are the heart of every ministry (see chapter 31, "Learning Goals: Redirecting Fear").

Unfortunately, many people around the globe and in the United States live in a constant state of fear, including your neighbors and closest friends. This is a painful and debilitating way to live. During 2020, in the time of the pandemic, the uprising of protests, and tremendous economic upheaval, we witnessed the effects of both personal and collective fear.

Like anger, fear is a part of our emotional and psychological warning systems for good reasons. It should not be ignored or avoided. Fear helps keep us alive every day (by keeping us on the sidewalk and not stepping in front of that truck). But if someone lives in a constant state of threats, trauma, or abuse, then their system of fear may be functioning much less effectively. It can be debilitating.

We are also impacted by social and psychological systems of fear and anxiety in which we live. For example, the systems of white supremacy and heteropatriarchy are systems that depend on fear to keep the status quo. In other words, fear of change, fear of losing power, and fear of anyone or anything different are powerful motivators to keep harmful beliefs in place. Those of us with adequate amounts of food, shelter, social capital, relationships, and privileges can and often do still get stuck in systems of fear that are paralyzing.

A resource for taking this theme deeper is *My Grandmother's Hands* by Resmaa Menakem.[2] In this book, Menakem describes the transmission of trauma over generations, and he considers the significance of dealing openly and forthrightly with our fears and traumas so that they do not control us overtly or covertly. He gives attention to the different ways fear and trauma manifest themselves in Black and Brown bodies and the ways they show up in white bodies. These differences are socially prescribed by a long history of "white body supremacy."[3]

Cathy's fear related to sacrifice and Kaleb's dream of being bound give us hints about how the feeling of fear is often about more than just the feeling itself. Both Cathy and Kaleb experienced social marginalization, which set the stage for their experiences of navigating fear. Many people carry generations of harm and profound needs for healing. In particular, people who have been marginalized carry in their bodies legacies of trauma that can go beyond words. These legacies of fear and trauma can manifest themselves in multiple ways physically, mentally, and emotionally.[4]

Menakem, who works with many groups, including police officers and first responders, offers practical ways to get in touch with our need for healing, to care for our bodies, and to release inherited fears. Menakem recommends many practices with breath and movement for becoming attuned to our bodies, feelings, and traumas and then intentionally addressing and releasing the pain we carry in our bodies and our collective social fabric.

The practice of ministry often entails accompanying people who are suffering and in need of healing. Many of them live with debilitating fear. Becoming aware of our own experiences of fear and anxiety and of our need for healing as human beings is important, as it was for Cathy and Kaleb, if we are to bring life and love to the people with whom we serve.

QUESTIONS FOR REFLECTION AND CONVERSATION

Consider the following to guide your journaling or spark conversation with mentors and friends:

+ When I am afraid, what is my gut reaction most of the time: fight, flight, freeze, or faint?
+ How am I facing my fears in ministry or in life?
+ What fears do I need to face in order to take my next steps in cultivating the practice of ministry?
+ What deeper fears are built into the systems around me and stand in need of healing?

THREE MINUTE MINISTRY MENTOR

Watch episode 43, "Facing Fears," https://3mmm.us/Episode43

Defining Moments

Many moments of insight are serendipitous. Lightning strikes, and there's no explaining why. You can't schedule epiphanies.

—Chip Heath and Dan Heath, *The Power of Moments*

Defining moments are the ones that cause us to change, turn, go in a new direction. In Greek, the word *metanoia* can be translated as "repentance" or "conversion." When something dramatic happens, we pivot, turn, and set off on a dramatically new path. Such pivotal points of our lives and ministries can also become touchstones to which we return over and over.

The power of such moments can come from a "peak" or a "pit" experience, according to Chip and Dan Heath in their book *The Power of Moments*.[1] Let's consider two defining moments for two women engaged in the practice of ministry: one peak and one pit.

Martha is one of five clergywomen featured in my book *Anatomy of a Schism*.[2] Martha came to seminary in the late 1990s as a second-career student with a résumé full of part-time church staff experience. She did not feel the need to meet the field education requirement. However, the professors insisted and encouraged her. She took a job at First Baptist Church (FBC) Benson, where she also planned to do her field education.

What began as a way to earn income and fulfill a seminary requirement soon became a pivotal experience in Martha's self-understanding and identity as a pastor. Martha felt happy and enjoyed her work at FBC.

Although the church ordained women as deacons and ministers already, electing Linda, who grew up at FBC Benson, as deacon chair was a first. This surprised Martha, who thought of the church as "way beyond women deacons."[3]

One evening, Linda invited Martha to dinner to discuss changing the structure of FBC's deacon ministry. Linda believed Martha could help create "stability and warmth in the congregation." As the evening continued, however, the conversation with Linda shifted, and she began sharing about growing up at FBC, her teenage rebellion, and her eventual marriage and divorce. Linda was "pouring out this beautiful story of . . . how God has worked in her life."

Martha says she felt "equipped" to hear the story, yet inside, she was saying to herself, "This is a moment that cries out for benediction!"

As the conversation continued, Martha realized, "Linda was identifying with me as a woman in ministry. And in her ministry as the chair of deacons, she wanted to share that with me. That's the whole purpose of calling the meeting. I thought it was to lead off at the deacon's forum and set the tone. But really what she wanted to do was receive my blessing."

Martha recalls thinking, "You need to talk to your minister about this because this is that kind of moment." Then it hit her, "Oh man, she thinks I'm a minister!'" Martha says that evening was her "moment of call." It was a peak moment that gave definition to her pastoral identity for years to come.

When she began seminary, Martha considered college chaplaincy but never pastoral ministry. Four years at FBC Benson gave Martha "opportunities to preach" and to try on being a minister.

Martha became part of the "heart and history" of the church. That evening of conversation with Linda clarified Martha's sense of calling. And it felt like a "miracle" for the way everything came together to prepare Martha for full-time pastoring. She said about her connection to FBC Benson, "It's really difficult to predict . . . but those really mystical moments do occur, and they don't occur all the time. I guess that's what makes them so special."

❧❦❧

Mariana was in her late twenties when we met her as a study participant in the LPI Project. She was born and grew up in Brazil and decided with her husband, Alex, a US citizen and also a seminary student, to return to South America and do an internship. First, they tried going to a fishing village, but they ran into problems, including the lack of ministry-related work for Mariana to do. So they took a new direction and traveled to the city where Mariana went to college. She tells the story here:

We decided to work with a very poor church in a very urban setting. They did a lot of work with homeless people, and prostitutes, and drug addicts, so we thought that was going to be interesting. We got there and the pastor was completely against me, and Alex didn't know how to speak Portuguese, so I had to be involved in everything and translate, and the pastor wouldn't talk to me.

He would talk to Alex, and I had to translate, and that was hard because when I left Brazil to come here (to the United States) to go to seminary, it was because in Brazil I couldn't go to seminary. So I went to seminary in a dilemma because I felt the call, but I didn't understand how I could be called if I was a woman. It didn't make sense.

Then I went to seminary and realized I can do this! You know, women are called too. But then whenever I went into the field, I wasn't accepted in the church where we were working. The pastor would invite Alex to come preach and go visit people in the hospital and go to the prison with him, and I couldn't do anything, not even go with him. They wouldn't let me.

The only thing they would let me do was . . . it's a very poor church and . . . so once a week I was allowed to go there and wash the church—like literally wash the walls, the floor, all the chairs, wash the bathrooms, which I actually enjoyed. [She chuckles.] I mean, you know, I wasn't able to do anything, so at least while I was there, it was like I might just be washing the bathroom, but at least it's still the house of the Lord.

Ada María Isasi-Díaz argues that a key challenge facing Latina women is "invisible invisibility."[4] The phrase refers to the experience of being ignored by those who do not even recognize the reality of the destructive contempt they inhabit. Mariana's powerful story of nonrecognition in her calling demonstrates what Isasi-Díaz means by the phrase "invisible invisibility."

This extended moment of invisibility in Mariana's life was clearly a "pit" moment. Yet it was also entwined with a peak moment of her epiphany in seminary when she saw for the first time, "I can do this!" Somehow the pit may have seemed deeper with the contrast of the recent seminary moment of affirmation.

What needs to happen in pit moments, according to the Heath brothers? Care and support to help someone come out of the pit. Heath and Heath know what religious communities have known for millennia. Pit moments happen—death, separations, losses, and pains—and communities of faith can come around the person, family, or group so they do not have to be in the pit alone.[5]

For Mariana and people who are rendered invisible like she was in this experience, the moment often remains hidden to the larger community. Mariana reframes her experience of being confined to "washing the bathroom" as a way to serve the Lord, yet her work was literally invisible to that church as well as to other communities. Thus care and support were limited. Fortunately, she willingly gave testimony to her experiences in Brazil as part of her conversation with us in the LPI study. This becomes part of her work of claiming her voice and calling. And retelling her story becomes part of the resistance to churches and religious leaders who keep trying to make certain people, especially women, invisible.

∙҉∙

To learn more about Martha's journey into the pastorate, you can read her story in *Anatomy of a Schism*. To learn more about the power of recognizing and fashioning moments that define people's lives, take a deeper dive into *The*

Power of Moments by the Heath brothers. The story of ministry for Mariana is still unfolding, and it seems fair to say that she has struggled to find a clear way to answer her calling. We look forward to learning more as we continue following her life and ministry in the LPI study.

 ## QUESTIONS FOR REFLECTION AND CONVERSATION

Consider the following to guide your journaling or spark conversation with mentors and friends:

- What are the defining moments that have brought me to this place in ministry?
- What, if any, pit and peak moments have turned my life in a new direction?
- What are the defining moments and epic experiences, small or large, that have changed the way I practice, define, or articulate ministry?

THREE MINUTE MINISTRY MENTOR

Watch episode 44, "Defining Moments," https://3mmm.us/Episode44

45

Navigating Conflict

> I pray to a God that calls people to life.
> I pray that you are called to life.
> I give you my breath—because, at times, that is all I
>   have to give.
> I give you my listening heart—because, sometimes,
>   that is all we need.
> I give you my hands, because showing you my
>   wounded hands is an act you first afforded me.
> Continue to show me your wounds in your hands and
>   I will believe.
> This is a call to life.
> Don't let it be choked out by the suffering of the world.
>
> —Patrick B. Reyes, *Nobody Cares When We Die*

Every ministry setting has its share of conflict. So how do we navigate it?

Bishop Carlos is in his early fifties and a participant in the LPI Project. He likes to say he is "Bronx born and bred." His parents came to New York from Puerto Rico. Carlos is now a multivocational pastor and bishop in his Pentecostal denomination.

Carlos used to say he was "bivocational," then he went to "trivocational," and now he says "multivocational." He holds down multiple jobs in higher education administration, and he is also pastor of a church that is growing with a lot of new people coming in.

In our second interview, he called himself "a bishop with training wheels." And when we interviewed him five years out of seminary, he says he still likes the "training wheels on." Mostly, he says, his role as a bishop is more of a healer.

When we asked Carlos to tell us about how his practice of ministry had changed over time, he said, "I'll lead off by saying when meeting with folks before, I was very quick to give an answer. Sometimes I would not listen enough to know exactly what they were going through."

"Now," he says, "I've learned just to let them talk . . . and share everything that's in their heart. Then at the end is when I intervene." He asks clarifying questions, but he has learned to "throw his assumptions out the window and listen with a blank page." This allows him to really hear "what someone is trying to say."

Bishop Carlos takes this approach with congregants and also with other ministers. "Because," he says, "I've found that pastoring a church is easy compared to leading a bunch of ministers."

As a result of this shift to more *listening*, Carlos says his "relationships are better." He is able to "build bridges" and "work together for common goals" with people formerly opposed to him.

On the flip side, *speaking* more directly has also transformed his leadership. He says more of what he needs to share. He holds back less and doesn't get overly worried about feelings or saying the "politically safe thing." This approach helps him with many difficult situations.

"Direct conversations are better than acting like the five-hundred-pound gorilla does not exist. Let's talk about the gorilla," says Bishop Carlos, "and let's see what we can do with it."

He told us about a particular moment of navigating a difficult situation.

There was a father and mother who were the pastors of a church in his jurisdiction. They wanted Bishop Carlos to ordain their son so they could retire and the son could take over leadership of the congregation.

There were two problems. Usually ordination is reserved for someone already pastoring a church. The son was not the pastor. To get around this, the bishop needed two letters—one from the current pastors and one from the congregation. Problem number two: they refused to write the letters. But Bishop Carlos kept listening. And he heard problem number three: the son said he did not want to be ordained or even be in ministry.

Then came problems four, five, and six. The church chose to go through the proceedings on their own, asking another minister to ordain the son independently and install him as the pastor. On "ordination day," they hired a police presence to keep Bishop Carlos out of the church.

Carlos had no interest in going to prison. Neither did he want a fight. He did not go anywhere near the church. Now legal issues and property rights are coming to light in the same congregation. The denominational body owns the church property, so all the issues will eventually come back to the bishop's desk.

How has he handled this? Bishop Carlos says, "I'm just staying quiet, waiting for everything to happen, but I did have the right conversation with them. And I didn't lose my composure." He says he did not accept the role of "angry administrator" or go in "to take over and fix everything."

Instead, Carlos listened. He has learned "to be silent, and to speak up [at the right time], and also to play the waiting game."

❧

Conflict in ministry is hard.

It is hard because it often feels personal. It is also hard because it can evoke feelings like anger, self-doubt, fear, or shame—feelings that are unpleasant to digest. And it is hard because change of any kind is often accompanied by some conflict. When marginalized groups face conflict, they can be saddled with additional burdens of systemic racism and strained resources. Most of the churches under Bishop Carlos's care are made up of first-, second-, and third-generation immigrants (see chapter 31, "Learning Goals: Redirecting Fear").

Yet change is also essential for flourishing in ministry. And it follows that healthy conflict cannot be avoided, as it is often a key aspect of health and growth. So how do we navigate conflict well and with pastoral imagination?

I know only a small handful of ministry leaders who go looking for conflict in ministry. A minister who seeks out conflict or likes to stir up discord may not last long in their calling. I know more ministers who would prefer to avoid conflict whenever possible.

Even activist ministers who are called to lead protests and agitate for social change do not necessarily want to be constantly dealing with conflict among or between those they are leading in movements for change.

Given these observations, perhaps we can reframe the normalcy of conflict. Rather than being something we seek out, or try to avoid at all costs, conflict is better understood as a regular and unavoidable by-product of everyday change, renewal, and growth.

Learning to navigate conflict and give leadership through conflict is a persistent and challenging aspect of the practice of ministry. Some of the most interesting stories we hear in the LPI Project are the ones where someone talks about a conflict they faced.

Listening is a key to navigating conflict, as explained in the powerful resource, *Leading a Life with God.*[1] In this book, pastor and teacher Daniel Wolpert invites readers to think about how to lead in multiple kinds of ministry situations by starting in contemplative silence and deep listening. Rather than following business principles designed to make better consumers, why not follow the lead of the Spirit to make better disciples?

The art and practice of leading people of faith is one that starts with listening to God in silence. While leadership based on business models or social change may commend skills of motivating people, casting vision, or organizing resources, there could be another starting point for leading disciples. What might happen if you entered each meeting, ritual service, or task of your organization's life with patient attention to silence and holy presence?[2] What if, following Bishop Carlos, you tried "listening with a blank page"?

Wolpert's book grounds pastoral leadership in the practices of prayer, contemplation, and deep listening. He is offering yet another way to see and respond to the holy depths of a situation (see chapter 2, "Seeing Holy Depths"). In this approach, the kind of complex conflicts that Bishop Carlos describes become opportunities for listening rather than rushing to fix or flee the situation.

QUESTIONS FOR REFLECTION AND CONVERSATION

Consider the following to guide your journaling or spark conversation with mentors and friends:

- In what ways will I listen and speak when I must navigate conflict in ministry?
- What might happen if I entered each meeting, ritual service, or task of my organization's life with patient attention to silence and holy presence?
- How might I become a bridge to people who position themselves in opposition to my leadership?

THREE MINUTE MINISTRY MENTOR

Watch episode 45, "Navigating Conflict," https://3mmm.us/Episode45

46

Knowledge Use

The kind of knowing at the core of the Christian life is closer to practical than to theoretical reason—closer, that is, to embodied, situated knowing-in-action than to disembodied, universal knowledge.

—Christian Scharen, *Christian Practical Wisdom*

Seminary education is a time when students acquire a great deal of knowledge. Having knowledge without a good idea about how to make use of it makes it less valuable. In my research about the practice of ministry, it is clear that the use of knowledge is just as important as acquiring knowledge.

When we interviewed Pastor Sondra for the LPI Project, she had been senior pastor of a small AME church in Texas for ten years. She led the congregation to engage in many firsts, including the fact that she was their first female pastor.

Pastor Sondra told us she thought one of the "greatest resources" she received in her seminary education "was how to use information, how to find it, and how to discern the information," especially when she was preparing a sermon.

She said a member of her congregation commented to her, "Pastor, I know you study!" He said, "You always have a good story to tell us [in your] sermon and how it just ties in. How do you do that?"

Pastor Sondra said her first thought was "Oh, it's nothing but the Lord." Yet, she says, she also appreciated deeply "learning how to . . . relate the daily things that are happening around us and find those things that fit with the sermon so that people have a practical connection [with Scripture]."

Learning about how to use resources went beyond preaching and teaching. She says her "personal study" and "personal devotion time" became essential to nourishing her well-being as a minister. Referring to her spiritual nourishment, she says, "You know, I can go eat, too, and I can eat well."

Pastor Sondra read devotionally before seminary. Yet, she says, "I didn't know *what* to read." She got ideas about what to read devotionally while in seminary, but her diet of reading "evolved" over time. Pastor Sondra said to herself, "You know, I share a lot; how am I going to maintain my own spiritual health?"

She was busy "feeding the hungry" as a pastor and began to see that she also "needed to eat." She says she often asks people, "How many times a week do you eat?" They say, "I eat every day!" Unsurprising.

Pastor Sondra says she began to pay attention to her own needs, and she says, "I need to eat every day, not just physically, but spiritually . . . That helped me come to a conclusion that I need to find devotional material for myself. And if I'm healthy, then I can help others be spiritually healthy."

Pastor Sondra reads some form of daily devotional *each day*. And the last time we spoke, she was leading her "whole church to read together." She wants to "get people used to eating spiritually every day."

Pastor Sondra took away from seminary a deep well of knowledge about biblical study, theological reflection, and practical ministry. She also took with her buckets to help her draw up that knowledge in ways that are life giving to her parishioners and to her own soul.

⸎

When I was in college and seminary, I took a lot of tests. I earned good grades on most of them. I memorized dates, names, cities, battles, theorems, species, formulas, genealogies, periodic tables, chemical compounds, and rules of grammar in multiple languages.

Much of this wealth of knowledge is now forgotten—long forgotten. I am not suggesting that these things are unimportant. They are quite important to many particular domains of knowledge. They make human life more practical or more livable.

What was missing from most of the specific realms of knowledge that I learned in college or seminary? I learned the *what*, but I did not learn *how* to make use of that knowledge at the same time. Knowledge acquisition without knowledge use can be, well, useless.

My daughter and her friends are at a stage where they have to memorize their math facts: add, subtract, multiply, and divide small whole numbers. Memorization is essential to be able to make quick use of math facts for more complex math like algebra and geometry and also for science as well as everyday tasks like shopping or cooking.

For my daughter, knowing math facts at this stage of learning is essential, but it is not enough. She also needs to make use of them by solving problems. The same can be said of knowledge about the Bible, theology, history, pastoral care, spiritual formation, preaching, and all the other subjects of a seminary education. Just learning the *what* may be interesting, but it is insufficient. It is not the same as learning *how* this knowledge is useful at the same time.

To be sure, I am not recommending that seminary training be solely "technical" or "how-to" education. What I am commending is that deep wells of knowledge, the *what* of theological education, deserves to be paired with the *so what?* of everyday ministry and living lives of faith in the world. Theological education should be a deeply integrative enterprise.

The use of knowledge, or the *So what?*, is helping students experience the practical, embodied, relational, and emotional aspects of what they are learning. Contrary to the popular idea that rational thinking is the highest form of knowing, in fact it is a rather low level of knowing. Knowing ideas and facts and arguments is the beginning of wisdom, not the end.

If such knowledge is needed to live in the world, we need also to know—and even experience—how human beings live in, make use of, and expand what they know in their lives and in service to their neighbors.

⟋⟍⟋⟍

The following resources can support you by feeding your soul on a regular basis. *The Upper Room Disciplines: A Book of Daily Devotions* features weekly themed reflections on Scripture from the Revised Common Lectionary and is written by ministers, spiritual directors, and theologians.[1] An online resource, www.d365.org (which also has an app), features music and prayers every day online or on your device.[2] The third resource I recommend is *The Words of Her Mouth: Psalms for the Struggle*, edited by Martha Spong and featuring ten women who "call out, talk back to, and come alongside the biblical psalms" as a "roadmap through the psalms or a field guide for the life of faith."[3]

When searching for a devotional guide, look for one that includes a depth of knowledge from the Bible, history, theology, spirituality, and life in ways that will nourish and support you as a faith leader. Search for resources written to provide fresh insight into the *What?*, the *How?*, and the *So what?* for ministry and life.

✒ QUESTIONS FOR REFLECTION AND CONVERSATION

Consider the following to guide your journaling or spark conversation with mentors and friends:

- How am I making practical use of knowledge to serve others and nourish myself?
- What buckets do I depend on to help me draw from the well of resources I need in my practice of ministry?
- How am I feeding myself spiritually each day? And how am I pointing others to the spiritual nourishment they need in their lives?

✒ THREE MINUTE MINISTRY MENTOR

Watch episode 46, "Knowledge Use," https://3mmm.us/Episode46

47

Congruence

For me, social justice work is integral to who we are called to be, as people of faith.

—Asha

I think it's sustaining to me to have some basic congruence between what I'm doing and what I think is important.

—Rebecca

Congruence is that notion of consistency, integrity, and alignment between what one thinks and what one does. Many of the participants in the various studies of ministry that I have conducted have a concern for integrity. This concern goes by many names, yet it consistently shows up in the way people discern their vocations and reflect on the ways they do their work.

Two stories demonstrate congruence, integrity, and alignment, showing how these values are important in two very different kinds of ministry practice. Rebecca has spent more than fifteen years in congregational leadership. The last time we interviewed Asha, she was working at a community nonprofit leading women's programming. Both women put a high priority on practicing ministry that aligns with their values.

Rebecca was in her early forties when I interviewed her for the Baptist clergywomen study. She is one of five white women whose stories about calling and ministry are told in depth in my book *Anatomy of a Schism*, showing what was at stake in the split of the Southern Baptist Convention.[1]

Rebecca was baptized in a predominantly white Southern Baptist church at the age of six. In those early years, Rebecca says, "I got a really good grounding in Scripture and the stories in the Bible and that God loves me. And I got a really good grounding in women being inferior." She says, "The messages about women were never spoken . . . you saw what women did and didn't do in the church: osmosis."[2]

Osmosis is a chemical process in which molecules pass through semipermeable membranes, such as animal cells. It can also mean cognitive absorption or slow and unconscious adoption of knowledge, social norms, or values.

Looking back over fifteen years of congregational ministry, Rebecca says one of her most sustaining experiences has been "the knowledge that wherever I am, I'm being the role model that [my] generation didn't have." Rebecca says one of her "very favorite possessions in the world" is a church bulletin from a Sunday when she preached.

A church member "noticed two young girls sitting behind her in church passing notes back and forth." After the service, the church member scooped up the note, which said, "What I love about this church is that a girl preached today. Girl power!" Reading it reminded Rebecca, "No girls will grow up in this church believing women can't preach because they have seen it."

"I hope that I'm good at what I do," says Rebecca, "and that there's some sense in which the fact that I do it is almost more important: just to embody that feminine role."

On another Sunday at the same church, Rebecca found herself presiding at communion. She says, "It didn't seem like any big deal to me, and yet elderly women came up to me in tears saying that they had never known how powerful it would be to sit there and watch a woman play that role. I really am sustained with the thought that I represent something that's beyond me." She said, "It's like this message of *you're okay* because somebody like you is standing in the pulpit."

Rebecca says, "One of the privileges we have as ministers is to represent things, and no one of us can represent all that needs to be represented, but it's a very powerful thing for me when I'm able to do that. I think it's sustaining to me to have some basic congruence between what I'm doing and what I think is important."

❧

When she graduated from divinity school with somewhat uncertain plans about how she would share all she had learned (see chapter 24, "Vocational Discernment"), Asha moved into a year of hospital residency in a CPE program. In the ten years since she graduated, she has also worked as a church staff minister and expanded her family. The last time we interviewed her, and five years post-seminary, Asha was directing the education office at a community nonprofit and leading women's programming.

Toward the end of the interview, while following up on themes, I asked Asha if parenthood had changed her understanding of ministry or vocation. She focused first on vocation: "I think what fuels me to do this work, what makes me so passionate about it, is my own perspectives on faith and my faith foundation."

She says that faith is "not as explicit in the work that I'm doing because very little of what I do focuses on faith or ministry directly," except when she is involved in the retreat center's chapel programming. What she understands her work to be, however, is a "ministry of raising the questions about issues and creating spaces where women can be empowered to find their voices. And *that*," she says, "definitely feels like ministry to me."

Asha imagines that other people might not consider the work she does to be ministry. Yet, she says, "personally, I see it as ministry." We asked Asha to tell us, in a nutshell, what theological understanding motivated her commitment to the kind of work she's doing.

Asha did not hesitate: "I think it goes back to how my faith intersects with social justice. It was one of the things that drew me to divinity school, knowing that I could pursue work outside the church, but it could still be ministry. And so I think raising and shining a light on some of these issues of human trafficking and reproductive justice and reproductive rights feels like the necessary work that we're not talking enough about in our church communities *or* larger communities."

She also believes that the community center's stakeholders see the work she leads as "an outpouring of their faith." For Asha, it comes down to this: "Social justice work is integral to who we are called to be, as people of faith. And so that's why faith is integral to the work that I'm doing."

As for the impact of her work on parenting and vice versa? Asha says, "I want to be the best person that I can be, because I think when I feel that way, I'm able to give the most to my kids. But I think it's more about thinking vocationally and trying to find the best opportunity to do the most life-giving work so that I can be . . . my best self in all aspects of my life."

☙✠❧

Both Rebecca and Asha aspire to embody congruence and integrity in their practices of ministry. Questions about vocation and integrity lead both women to talk about the people to whom they minister and the children they are raising and nurturing in faith. Spiritual nurture is built into the practice of ministry. Faith formation and spiritual legacy are significant aspects of what we leave to the generations that come after us.

With that in mind, I'll share a bit of my own spiritual formation from my teenage years. I was very devoted to my church youth group. And I definitely felt my first sense of pastoral calling while I was on a summer-long series of youth ministry trips. That is how I spent every summer from seventh grade through high school.

Part of my material faith was that I liked taking what I learned and making it into posters or signs. I liked putting them up in my room. And I would hang them where I could see them upon waking each morning and before sleeping at night. It seems a little hokey looking back, but I suppose they were the memes of the 1980s and '90s. The messages I created captured ideas that I was learning *from* and *for* my spiritual journey as a teenager.

The one I recall most vividly is one with just two words: *Be Consistent.* I used big block letters and hung the eight-and-a-half-inch-by-eleven-inch sign from the canopy over my twin bed. I saw it every morning and night. The message to *Be Consistent* was a reminder to let what I said and did, what I thought and how I acted, who I was every day, and who I aspired to be, all to come into alignment and into congruence in my life.

The phrase became a mantra for me in my last couple years of high school. It also lasted beyond that time. *Be Consistent* is an idea rooted in the saying of Jesus to "let your yes be yes and your no be no" (Matt 5:37, Sermon on the Mount).

Be Consistent helped me cultivate integrity in my life. It helped me avoid quick answers and commitments that I might not really intend to complete. Saying yes and no to life's questions pushed me to own more responsibility for my choices.

As an enthusiastic young person, this message also slowed me down and kept me (occasionally) from taking on things that would have been too much. (*Slow Down* was another sign that hung in my room.) Of course, I do not always live up to these aspirations. But learning to try again after failing was part of being consistent. Not perfect, but present. Not right, but responsible.

QUESTIONS FOR REFLECTION AND CONVERSATION

Consider the following to guide your journaling or spark conversation with mentors and friends:

+ Where is the congruence in my practice of ministry between what I am doing and what I think is important?
+ Where do I need more consistency or better alignment?
+ How am I cultivating congruence for my own spiritual journey?
+ How am I teaching it to the young people in my life and ministry?

THREE MINUTE MINISTRY MENTOR

Watch episode 47, "Congruence," https://3mmm.us/Episode47

Holy Fierceness

For we are attempting to say something fully life sustaining in a world that often affirms death over life. Before we can ever take such a risk, we ourselves have to believe that something more is possible and that it is a holy possibility demanding a holy risk.

—Lisa Thompson, *Ingenuity*

"If I trust that I can't kill the church, and if I trust that it is not in my power to suffocate the Holy Spirit, then church just may look really different! I have benefited from the church, and I want to name that privilege, but it's never really served me well. So I have a lot of excitement about how we may move next and where the church may be going."

Theresa was responding to her mentor, Rev. Loretta, near the outset of her two-year residency program following divinity school. Her mentor had observed, "You're at the stage of your career when you should be so excited about serving the church! So how did you get to be you?"

Theresa said, "I am excited to serve!"

"But how did you start asking these questions?" wondered Rev. Loretta.

"I've been forced to ask the questions," replied Theresa, who understands that she has both benefited from her privilege as a white woman and also been marginalized as a woman and a queer person. She says about the church, "I think, from the margins, decline is actually really exciting, because it means that something new is being born."

Theresa shared this conversation with her cohort of divinity school alums on an interview day when they were five years past graduation. The group was responding to a question about what they are drawing on and what has prepared them for their current practice of ministry.

Cassandra, an African American woman in her early thirties, is back in graduate school. She has also continued in an associate minister role in each city where she has lived since graduation. She says she learned in divinity school to identify discriminations early. But she wishes someone would have prepared her for what to do when the discrimination was turned against her on the job market. She wishes someone would have warned her and other women that they might not be able to find sustainable work in ministry after graduation. Because, as she puts it, "church is the one place where you are totally allowed to discriminate, based on whatever you like."

All the women around the room agreed that more mentoring about this reality would have been a gift. As Theresa says, "It didn't matter that I got an A on my New Testament paper. [Churches] didn't care!" It was hard to know who of their successful professors might have been able to engage them in conversations about the difficulty of finding and keeping a sustainable place of ministry—"I wish I had known who to call when it was just so utterly painful and difficult."

The preparation they received was powerful, yet each graduate also shared with us ways that sustaining the level of intensity was not easy. Mary, who is in her midthirties, is experienced in global and multicultural ministries. She identifies as white, and she has been an associate pastor in the same multiethnic congregation since graduation. She told us about learning to be wiser when confronting injustice. She said that "learning how to ask good questions is sometimes more powerful than sitting on a committee and saying, 'Let me call you out on your racism.'" She's learned instead "to discern what question to ask to get a group thinking and questioning things for themselves."

Reflecting back to divinity school and its social justice ethos, Mary says, "I think my education prepared me for when I need to challenge something, take a risk, or question authority. I feel prepared to do that. I know how to [take a] risk and challenge the system when I need to."

Theresa really resonated with Mary's experience of feeling intense righteousness during divinity school but then experiencing uncertainty about how and whether to sustain this elevated mode of engagement. She said she couldn't maintain that level of "righteous indignation because no one likes you and you are just tired." Immediately, knowing laughter broke out in the circle.

Asha, in her thirties, identifies as African American, and she works in a community nonprofit (see chapter 24, "Vocational Discernment," and chapter 47, "Congruence"). She believes that divinity school and CPE made her "more astute in terms of interpersonal skills." She also believes that her education helped her develop "a rapport with folks." She uses her perspective on intersectionality for evaluating difficult issues. Many womanist scholars offer analyses of intersectionality, or the ways that gender identity, race, sexual orientation, class, ability, and other identity markers do not exist in isolation or with discrete definitions. These identities are entangled and operate to maintain white privilege and power, and open the gap on healthcare and economic disparities.[1]

For example, Asha says, "you can't talk about reproductive rights without thinking about class and culture and gender." Asha takes into consideration all the critical tools from her training as well as skills of discernment while she is planning community programming. It helps her get a wider diversity of voices into the conversations. Asha says, "I'm being really intentional about who's at the table and whose voices might not traditionally be heard, and that we might give a space for those voices to be heard."

Naomi says she is working on discernment, too, regarding her own voice. She does not feel empowered to change her entire city council with its racist policies and low wages, yet she interacts with these systems daily. To do her work of advocacy, she is finding that she uses the voice she found in conversations at divinity school even though she is sitting around new tables with new people. That voice for her comes out through careful listening and occasional insights and questions that steer the conversation.

Theresa expressed gratitude for models witnessed in divinity school of what she calls "holy fierceness," yet she knows she can't live there continuously and also sustain relationships with everyday communities of faith. To her, holy fierceness is "what it is to be prophetic and to be holy and sacred in your fierceness." She admits to some feelings of guilt about the limits, yet she knows she "can't operate that way all the time."

Each woman in the group was identifying the complexity of sustaining holy fierceness. It cannot be sustained simply by naming or calling out injustice. It also needs to include a fierceness of care for one's self and one's well-being. To tend to the well-being of others, one needs a holy fierceness that encompasses compassion for one's own soul.

Near the end of the rich conversation, Theresa said, "I think I was educated to serve a church that doesn't exist anymore." Being in the northwestern United States for her two-year residency felt to Theresa as if she had "been to the future!" The group chuckled with her. "Ten years, twenty years into the future, and it's fine! It's different, and you probably won't be able to do it as your full-time job, but you'll be great, and Jesus is still there!"

◈

What does *holy fierceness* look like? Based on the experiences of the women and their conversation, I would say holy fierceness has these characteristics:

+ crafting a way of seeing the world that accounts for its power structures, social locations, and lenses through which people see that world, and not forgetting that "we have power over the narratives that shape our lives" (Theresa)
+ speaking prophetically and also knowing how to ask the fitting questions at fitting moments (Mary)

- seeking justice yet knowing how to build trust with people who might not share your exact view of the world (Cassandra)
- seeing how one has been both privileged and marginalized and speaking honestly from that space (Theresa)
- helping communities see and own their complicity in racist and sexist and heterosexist ideologies and being bold, taking risks, and speaking truth to power (Mary)
- "naming *wrongs*" and also remembering that "we still have to live among these wrongs" (Cassandra)
- knowing how to live faithfully in a particular place with a particular people, without insisting that they be "totally right" by our standards (Cassandra)
- cultivating interpersonal skills for building rapport with people and also the capacity to look at the intersectionality of a system where you are working for change and using power to get a wider diversity of people to the table (Asha)
- knowing when to insist on changing language for inclusivity and when to "mix up the metaphors" in other ways (Naomi)
- giving thoughtful and intentional compassion to one's own well-being in order to sustain holy fierceness

❧

Preacher, professor, and practical theologian Lisa Thompson in her 2018 book *Ingenuity: Preaching as an Outsider* calls on people of faith to move the preaching voices and experiences of women from the margins to the center.[2] In particular, she is advocating for the preaching voices of Black women. We have so much to learn from the wisdom, ministry, insights, and compassion of women of color and women who identify as lesbian, bisexual, and trans—women who are routinely excluded from pulpits and positions of leadership in the church. Thompson's argument is especially concerned with hearing the preaching voices of Black women descended from generations of slavery and trauma that is yet to fully end.

Thompson says, "Attending to the lives of black women calls us to reshape both our view and practices of preaching. When we consider the thriving and well-being of black women as primary, it affords an opportunity to consider how a distinct group of people often denied full personhood helps us rethink our approach to biblical interpretation and the process of proclamation."[3] Recentering marginalized women's voices in both the pulpit and other places of leadership offers not only insight and courage but also hope, wisdom, and holy fierceness, as the excerpts of the previous conversation demonstrate.

"For we do not truly gain fresh air in our communities," says Thompson, "until we attend to the most vulnerable and they, too, can breathe untainted air, courtesy of speech that shapes our behavior and beliefs for the wellbeing of our body politic."[4]

🪶 QUESTIONS FOR REFLECTION AND CONVERSATION

Consider the following to guide your journaling or spark conversation with mentors and friends:

- ◆ What courage do I need and what risks must I take in order to lead with holy fierceness?
- ◆ What insights or critiques am I called to make with risk and responsibility in my current ministry situation?
- ◆ Where and how do I need to make space for the holy fierceness of voices that remain marginalized in my community?
- ◆ What are the tensions of holy fierceness that are most challenging for me?

🪶 THREE MINUTE MINISTRY MENTOR

Watch episode 48, "Holy Fierceness," https://3mmm.us/Episode48

49

Boundaries

> How might we create spaces in our homes, churches, and temples, to face life's hardest questions? How might our sense of identity, purpose, and legacy change if these seemingly insular communities asked: Who are we? What is our gift?
>
> —Gregory C. Ellison II, *Fearless Dialogues*

One of the first things Pastor Randall noticed when he came to the church is that it was completely surrounded by a large wrought-iron fence. He wondered about what it communicated to the community.

Pastor Randall is an elder in the CME Church. When we last talked to him, he was in his early forties and serving Riverside CME, an urban congregation with a long history and a new building. He had been appointed by the bishop to serve there just about a year before we met for the interview.

The neighborhood where the church is located lacks resources. It is home to many people who live in poverty, although some members of the congregation drive into the city for worship from middle-class suburbs. Because Pastor Randall had been around the block a few times, he had a better idea about how to approach boundaries than when he started out in ministry.

Riverside CME had a reputation for being aggressive. Its culture allowed business sessions to seem more like a union hall meeting than a church conference. Before moving to Riverside, Pastor Randall said he regularly "slipped into these little, nuanced tug-of-wars" when conflicts arose. But this time he had an opportunity to start fresh. He said to himself, *I don't want to get into that kind of exchange here, so I'll just ask questions.*

On his very first Sunday of preaching, Pastor Randall waited at the back near the office following the service. He saw the treasurer walking out of the finance room, and he said, "Hi. We had a great day today! Do you have a package for me?"

The treasurer said, "Oh no, we don't pay you. We hadn't voted to pay you."

Pastor Randall remembers what flashed through his mind in just a matter of seconds: *I just moved out of a parsonage. I just secured another place, and I spent any savings that I had because I wasn't anticipating this move . . . and this guy is telling me they hadn't voted to pay me. What?*

Then he came to himself and stepped a little closer to the treasurer and said, "You know, I don't understand."

The treasurer said, "I can go in here and write you a check."

In that moment, Pastor Randall remembered, *We have a church conference that happens every month, and it is actually going to happen tomorrow night.* He said, "No, don't write me a check. Don't worry about it."

The next night, Pastor Randall opened the meeting by asking those gathered to sing "Lord, I Want to Be a Christian in My Heart." He led them in prayer, and then he explained simply how disappointed he had been in how the pay was handled.

Of course, some members piped up with the seven last words of the church: "That is how we've always handled it." Pastor Randall took time to explain to them the process of budgeting. He used some questions to lead them into a better understanding: "Was a church budget approved for the previous conference year? What amount was allocated for the pastor? Does anyone want to object to the church continuing its operation with those guidelines until a new budget can be established for this conference year?" He patiently helped them see how approving a church budget is done to take care of the needs of the church, including the salary for the pastor—not a particular pastor, but whoever the current pastor is.

Looking back, he says, "That was a way to set the tone even when I didn't fully understand certain things about their culture." Pastor Randall used an approach of education and questions rather than a heavy-handed approach of insisting things be done a certain way. In the past, when people threw darts at him, he would not throw darts back, but this time he avoided the "tug-of-war." Rather than defending himself, Pastor Randall was committed to asking more questions as the way forward.

In the early months of his pastorate, he used lots of questions to learn his way around the culture of the congregation. In this congregation, one thing was clear: the power struggles would be real, and boundaries were going to be a challenge.

⚜

One day in Bible study, Pastor Randall decided to learn more about the wrought-iron fence. He asked those gathered, "What is the purpose of this fence?" And they simply looked at him.

Then he asked, "Is the purpose of the fence to keep us safe or to keep people out?"

They said, "Oh, well, it's meant to keep us safe."

Pastor Randall said, "Well, look—it communicates that people are not welcome."

226 ◆ Pastoral Imagination

"Well," they said, "that is why we left the gate open."

"Hm," Pastor Randall said. "Tell me how it's kept you safe."

They said, "Well, you know, when cars are left in the parking lot, we close the gate."

Then Pastor Randall asked, "So how has that been working?"

The people said, "Well, we had a church van."

Pastor Randall said, "You *had* a church van?"

"Yes," they said. "Somebody jumped over the fence and stole the van and drove it through the gate. That's why the first gate was always left open."

And Pastor Randall said, "So, really, the gate doesn't keep you that safe, does it?"

And that's when they finally embraced Pastor Randall's point that the fence was serving as a barrier with the community rather than security for the church. And it would be better for the gates "to be open to show people they can come in at all times."

Pastor Randall challenged his congregation to look at how they had done church. He challenged them to think about their boundaries with the community. His new relationship with Riverside also challenged him to think about his relational boundaries and his leadership style—as he put it, "To look at how I was pushing people." He decided that his new approach of leading with questions was working pretty well.

⚭⚭

Boundaries can serve us well in the practice of ministry. When boundaries give clarity to relationships and prevent the abuse of power, they are worth maintaining. Boundaries can also become barriers in the work of ministry. A boundary that Riverside CME intended to enhance the church's safety had turned into a barrier with the neighborhood that they wanted to serve. As with most boundaries, our purpose and motivation impact the usefulness or harmfulness of the boundaries we set.

Is the aim of a personal boundary to keep relationships clear and steer us away from the misuse or abuse of power between people? For example, clergy and the people they lead can be served well by maintaining healthy boundaries when it comes to the areas where human beings are exceedingly vulnerable. Money, sexuality, and power are areas that need clear and well-maintained boundaries to prevent harm and help people relate lovingly and safely together.

In her latest book, *The Big Deal of Taking Small Steps to Move Closer to God*, AME bishop Vashti Murphy McKenzie writes about the importance of connection.[1] She tells a story about women she met while traveling in the Middle East. The Israeli and Palestinian mothers transcended the boundaries of their religious traditions to become genuine neighbors and protectors of one another's safety.

The women in her story are geographical neighbors living across the road from one another, yet their connections are limited by the boundaries between their religious history and traditions. They transgressed the boundaries—which had become barriers—to make friendships. They created a shared enterprise, and they lived into the values of their connections with one another. McKenzie notes, "Connection provided an energy that repurposed their behavior and actions beyond cultural and religious restrictions. Each group was seen, heard, and valued, and as such the groups were strengthened and sustained by that association."[2]

Just as Pastor Randall asked small questions that led to important changes, Bishop McKenzie encourages small steps toward spiritual growth, intimacy with God, and service of family, church, and community. Noticing the boundaries, barriers, and potential connections in our lives and ministries is an important skill for bringing the practice of ministry to life.

🪶 QUESTIONS FOR REFLECTION AND CONVERSATION

Consider the following to guide your journaling or spark conversation with mentors and friends:

- How are the boundaries in my practice of ministry hindering or making space for growth?
- With Pastor Randall we can ask, Do these boundaries still serve us? Do they help us serve and love our neighbors? Or have they become barriers between us and the very people with whom we desire connection?
- What relational or leadership boundaries need to be shored up in my practice of ministry?
- What questions can I ask to bring clarity to the community where I serve?

🪶 THREE MINUTE MINISTRY MENTOR

Watch episode 49, "Boundaries," https://3mmm.us/Episode49

50

Embracing Joy

> Don't ask yourself what the world needs, ask yourself what makes you come alive. And then go and do that. Because what the world needs are people who are alive.
>
> —Howard Thurman

"Your call is what brings you energy and joy." This advice from her professor helped Chloe begin to embrace joy more fully in her vocation and practice of ministry.[1]

Chloe, who was twenty-nine and the pastor of a small Baptist congregation when I interviewed her for my book *Anatomy of a Schism*, identifies as white. She was born and grew up in the southern United States. Ministry was a second career after a brief time in television news and marketing. Chloe told me about her seminary internship. She arrived at seminary totally committed to the work of social justice. She wanted to work in the community. However, the school required her to do one field placement in a congregation. Fortunately, she found Milesdale Baptist Church, a congregation with many social justice programs serving its southern city.

Morgan, Chloe's mentor and Milesdale's pastor, said, "This is going to be a buffet of ministry experiences. And I want you to taste from preaching and teaching and pastoral care." This lined up with her field education requirements. Chloe would sample ministry in "all sections of the church." She was surprised by her love of worship, and she enjoyed using her creative energies to write sermons. She loved pastoral visits.

Chloe grappled throughout seminary to reconcile her clear call to social justice, on one hand, with the "joy and energy" she experienced in the local church, on the other. Chloe felt committed to embody Christ in the world by feeding people, helping them find homes, and making social change. She worried that if she spent her energy and time on preaching or pastoral care, the needs for justice would go unattended.

She wondered, "Is God calling me to one thing and what I want to do is another thing? Is God going to be disappointed or upset if I don't do this work that needs to be done?" Then one of her professors helped shift her thinking. He said, "Chloe, your gift is to empower and inspire and mobilize the church. You are one person. You can go out and work in those places if you want. Or you can choose to bring this work that needs to be done to the church and inspire and empower the church to do this work."

Her field education supervisor, an Episcopal priest, also helped. He said, "Your call is what brings you joy and energy. That's how you know what your call is."

A saying of Howard Thurman also helped her sort it all out. He said, "Don't ask yourself what the world needs, ask yourself what makes you come alive. And then go and do that. Because what the world needs are people who are alive." Chloe decided, "Maybe it wasn't heresy; maybe all these people were right." She embraced the "energy and joy" of serving the church. Chloe continues more than fifteen years after I interviewed her, still joyfully pastoring a congregation committed to justice and social change.

Pastoral theologian Mary Clark Moschella spent several years studying the significance of joy in coping with grief and in working for liberation. She spent years dreaming of a project about this topic, awakening to it early in her career. Although she delayed it for the sake of tenure, when she came around to the study of joy, Moschella brought to the study a deep wisdom from her own pastoring, studying congregations and ministers, and years of seminary teaching. In *Caring for Joy*, Moschella weaves together a sturdy theology in action out of her perceptions, reflections, and constructions with narrative strands from six lives, including her own.[2]

Moschella tells the stories of ministers who find joy in the work of church, justice, social transformation, and compassionate care for God's people and all of creation. Moschella traces the practice of ministry, unfolding in the lives of Henri Nouwen, Heidi Neumark, Gregory Boyle, Pauli Murray, and human rights activist Paul Farmer. Each person Moschella profiles was deeply influenced by faith, and they found ways to access joy in their work of justice, preaching, writing, organizing, and advocating.

Like Chloe, yet in a very different time and set of circumstances, Pauli Murray felt a deep concern for social justice. Born in Baltimore, Maryland, in 1910, Murray's grandmother Cornelia Smith Fitzgerald was a child of an enslaved mother and a slave-owning father. At three years old, Murray moved to North Carolina to be raised by aunts and cousins after her parents died.[3] Bright, curious, and an avid learner, Murray learned to read and write early on and used her powers of communication to advocate for justice and social change throughout her life.[4]

Murray grew up in the traumas and indignities of Jim Crow. She pressed hard to challenge injustices along a pathway that led her through writing and poetry, being among a small handful of Black women to graduate from the all-women's Hunter College and the first Black woman to graduate from Howard Law first in her class.[5] She was also the first Black person to graduate from Yale Law in 1965.[6] While in school at Howard, she coined the term *Jane Crow* as a counterpoint to Jim Crow, "the twin evil of discriminatory sex bias."[7] She was rejected by the graduate programs at University of North Carolina and Harvard University because of her gender and race.[8] She cofounded the National Organization for Women and later left it because it failed to take seriously the concerns of Black women and women of color.[9] In 1977, she became the first Black woman ordained as an Episcopal priest.[10]

Pauli Murray is so much more than a list of accomplishments. She was ahead of her time in an enormous number of ways. She also struggled throughout her life with poverty and its insecurities. She was on the receiving end of discrimination, arrests, and rejections not only "due to her sex" but also in relation to her struggle with her gender identity and sexual orientation.[11] Yet Murray pressed forward and continued to advocate, write, study, and lead. She led sit-ins twenty years before they became a mainstay of the 1960s civil rights movement in the South. She contributed legal opinions that helped change segregation laws.

A few weeks after her ordination, Murray was invited to preside at Holy Communion for the first time at Chapel of the Cross in Chapel Hill, North Carolina, founded in 1848.[12] She read from a Bible that belonged to her grandmother Cornelia Smith Fitzgerald, who was baptized in that very church at age ten in 1854.[13] The church was the home to both Murray's grandmother Cornelia and other enslaved family members who worshipped from the balcony. It was also the church home of the white family who enslaved Cornelia and her siblings and family members. In the service, Rev. Murray read from a lectern engraved with the names of her white ancestors, Ruffin and Smith.[14] It was a momentous occasion. She even called it a joyous occasion, hard-won and full of both grief and grace. As Moschella observes, "Murray proclaimed a lived theology of joy that emerged over time as she practiced resistance to injustice."[15]

In her own words, Murray said of that moment in her life, "All the strands of my life had come together. Descendant of slave and of slave owner, I had already been called poet, lawyer, teacher, and friend. Now I was empowered to minister the sacrament of One in whom there is no north or south, no black or white, no male or female—only the spirit of love and reconciliation drawing us all toward the goal of human wholeness."[16]

❧⁂❧

How do we embrace joy in a world full of so much overwhelming sorrow and pain? How do we practice ministry grounded in joy when so much of the ground we stand on shifts and quakes in fear and despair?

We have big work to do in the world. Pain, harm, social injustices, and brokenness are everywhere. How can we even think about joy when these challenges are at every turn in our lives? Embracing the joy of our callings as ministers, activists, pastors, chaplains, and religious leaders is no simple or frivolous task.

Pastor Chloe found guidance for these questions from mentors and supervisors while she was a seminary student. A minister, a professor, and a spiritual theologian helped guide her. Together they pointed her to the idea of leaning into the places that stirred up joy, helped her come alive, and gave her energy for her work. Rev. Pauli Murray drew on tenacity and determination to change the world. She also drew strength from a vast group of friends, colleagues, and supporters to help her face the challenges and history of her life and the systems of injustice that shaped it and to wrestle out a hard-won blessing.

In a world that is dying and death dealing, floundering in crisis and despair, we need people, as spiritual theologian Howard Thurman puts it, "who are alive!" And people who are alive find joy in what they are doing. Joyful *doing* and joyful *being* mean participating in change and justice making, hope and healing, bringing new and renewed life to the people and places we serve.

Without sinking a taproot into the joys of life and the deeper sources of joyful living, we will quickly grow weary of ministry and lose hope in life itself. Mary Moschella puts it this way: "As I understand it, joy comes down to this: to being awake and deeply alive, aware of the love and grace of God, and of the gift of life, both in and around us. Joy in pastoral ministry is the same thing, but magnified by the blessing of a high and holy calling that challenges one to step outside of one's self into relationships of care and communion. The themes and practices that I have found that characterize joy in the settings I have studied include presence, attentiveness, gratitude, release, hope, creativity, liberation, and love."[17]

Go out in hope, live in joy, and work with the Spirit to renew and revive the world using all of your best pastoral imagination to bring the practice of ministry to life.

QUESTIONS FOR REFLECTION AND CONVERSATION

Consider the following to guide your journaling or spark conversation with mentors and friends:

- What in my practice of ministry is bringing me life and joy?
- How am I embracing joy amid sorrow, tragedy, and injustice? Where am I sinking my taproot?
- What makes me come alive? What brings me joy in the doing?
- Where is the gladness in my deepest sense of being and belonging?

THREE MINUTE MINISTRY MENTOR

Watch episode 50, "Embracing Joy," https://3mmm.us/Episode50

Appendix

QUESTIONS FOR REDEMPTIVE CHANGE

The view and broad understanding of ministry in the United States, including the research of the Learning Pastoral Imagination Project, are beholden to a white, privileged, and westernized model of how to manage and organize the church as well as how to educate for ministry. Although pastoral imagination is cultivated as all adult human learning is and is thus universal, the particular context of learning ministry in the United States is shaped by a long and entrenched history that maintains and upholds privilege, money, and power as being primarily the domain of whiteness and maleness. This flaw in the way ministry is conceived and practiced in the US context is noted and explored throughout this book. Problematizing the ways that Christian ministry upholds dominant white culture is a start. Questioning how ministry in its current forms may not be purely biblical, spiritual, and wise is another step in the right direction. Stepping back to reimagine the kinds of change that are needed and to envision new possibilities is also necessary. Keeping in mind that new visions for a redemptive and inclusive church will not emerge all at once will help us see how old structures also remain operative and inflict harm even as change is underway. Perhaps among the greatest needs for pastoral imagination in our day is to take on a complete reconsideration of ministry itself.

This appendix offers a starter set of questions to help deconstruct personal habits and social structures that inhibit bringing ministry fully to life. The list is by no means exhaustive but rather serves as a beginning point for your own work of imagining how to deconstruct harmful structures that hinder practical wisdom for ministry. Each person who is learning the vocation and practice of ministry lives within the multiple structures of racism, sexism, homophobia, transphobia, classism, and ableism. From our particular social locations, we need to ask different questions to break loose of the structures. Every question has a starting point, and it may be considered respectfully and fruitfully by everyone. What will you add?

Especially for congregations and religious organizations:

+ How do the policies and practices of this organization and its leaders uphold and/or support structures of racism and maintain normative white values?

- In what ways does this organization work to be antiracist and aim for changing policies, practices, and ways of thinking and speaking about race and racism?
- In what ways will we commit to solidarity with Indigenous Peoples (i.e., making land acknowledgments, repudiating the doctrine of discovery, paying "real rent," offering free facility use, etc.)?[1]
- In what ways will our community seek to better integrate accessibility into our spaces (i.e., curb cuts, ramps, closed captions, transcriptions, etc.)?
- How do the structures of the organization maintain beliefs, practices, policies, and traditions that marginalize women and LGBTQIA folks?
- How is labor treated in this religious group? Is all labor compensated equitably? Who is asked to work for lower pay or only as volunteers? What is the hierarchy of compensation and benefits?
- How does the physical space and accessibility of our buildings, programs, and printed materials welcome or limit the participation of leaders and members of the organization?

Especially for ministers and religious leaders who identify as Black, and/or Brown, and/or as Indigenous Peoples, and/or as BIPOC:

- How will I safeguard my well-being, maintain my sanity, and reserve my energy for the work of ministry?
- How do I make a space for care and building up the people of my faith community so they can endure the onslaught of personal and systemic racism in many or most parts of our lives?
- How am I empowering younger generations to resist the structures and messages that try to define and confine them while also honoring the wisdom and legacies of elders in my community?[2]
- How do we organize to protect our children from mass incarceration, police brutality, and generational trauma?
- What structures of ministry are shaped by white supremacy and white privilege that need lamenting, releasing, and reimagining? How does my resistance to those structures help me reshape my vocation and purpose as well as the context of ministry itself?

Especially for ministers who are women-identified BIPOC:

- Where am I finding personal, spiritual, and pastoral support for working within and against systems that try to diminish or erase me?

- How am I setting boundaries and seeking support for the sake of my well-being and the well-being of my family and community?
- How am I refusing the expectations and demands others place on me that ignore my contributions and needs?
- How am I prioritizing my health and well-being—physically, mentally, and spiritually?

Especially for ministers living with disabilities:

- What conditions do I need to have in place so I am seen and heard and I can flourish in ministry?
- What specific kinds of support and/or accommodation do I need from partners in ministry as I bring my vocation to life?
- What particular gifts and insights do I bring to my organization and community?

For ministers who identify as LGBTQIA:

- How am I seeking spaces of support, welcome, and relative safety where I can show up fully as myself to renew and recharge my energy for the work of ministry?
- In what ways will I help my organization resist its language, practices, and traditions of theology, relationship, and family by modeling and embodying these important relationships in new ways?

For ministers who identify as white:

- What am I doing to deconstruct the white privileges and structures of white supremacy that shape the places I live and minister?
- How will I decolonize my own thinking, actions, and complicity in harming or erasing people?
- In what ways will I embrace being present, being a follower, decentering myself, and deferring with honor to BIPOC in ways that do not reinforce white privilege?
- How will I move beyond being "not racist" to becoming "antiracist" and work actively against my participation and my organization's complicity in trauma and harm?
- How am I making use of my privilege and position(s) of power to reduce harm, resist centering whiteness, initiate change in white spaces, and ask important questions?

For ministers who identify as women and white:

- In what ways will I prioritize my health and well-being—physically, mentally, and spiritually—while resisting expectations and demands that tell me I can do it all?
- How are my identity markers seen as normative in some ways and marginalized in other ways?
- How can I live creatively and compassionately in the tension of inhabiting both a place of social power and a place of exclusion and marginalization?
- How is this tension itself a theological and spiritual space where practice can be forged?

Gratitude

A single apple sits atop a stack of books. The books rest on a neatly organized desk. The desk stands in front of a clean chalkboard silently waiting for a lesson.

A teacher looks calmly at her learners with a glimmer in her eye. Is it curiosity? A secret only she knows? Perhaps a mystery she plans to unravel?

I look at the apple. It is perfectly ripe, elegantly shaped, and deliciously inviting. I want to run to the front of the room and sink my teeth into it. One juicy bite.

"Apples are a wonderful metaphor," the teacher says. My mind weighs each one: *an ideal fruit, contained and portable, not easily bruised, nutritious, full of recipe possibilities.*

"They symbolize good teaching," she says with a smile. "And happy learners."

"More importantly, this apple," she says, picking it up and examining it, "represents the single most important idea in any lesson, any assignment, any book." She tosses the apple into the air one time.

"The apple represents the core of the matter." She chuckles, catching it. "Pun intended." Then, more seriously, she continues: "Every time you plan a project, a new piece of writing, or a day of class, ask yourself, *What is the apple?*"

This story came to me when I worked as a master teaching fellow at Vanderbilt University. I no longer know its origin, yet the question continues to serve me well. When I begin writing projects, lesson plans, and weekly episodes of 3MMM, I often ask myself, *What is the apple?*

Here and now the apple is *gratitude.* A book never comes to life without the help of countless people. Being educated, disciplined, and hardworking helps an author. But writing is more than the sum of those parts. So when I feel bereft or let down, disappointed or frustrated, unable to see a way through the process, the thing that nearly always rescues me is *gratitude.*

For all that led to this book, my gratitude must begin with everyone who is part of the LPI Project. This book is dedicated to the study participants. For Chris Scharen, who invited my insights, ideas, and imagination into this project; who continues to offer generative and generous partnership; and who has asked countless times with me *What is the apple?* I remain profoundly grateful. For Catrina Ciccone, who is steadfastly game to think aloud, learn transparently, look after details, and meet me at the state fair, I am joyously thankful.

238 ◆ Gratitude

For our LPI advisors over the years, Patricia Benner, Chuck Foster, David Wood, Rick Foss, Kathleen Cahalan, and Terri Elton, thank you for pushing and inspiriting us to think more deeply and make important connections. Thanks to the Lilly Endowment for generously launching and supporting our research, and thanks to John Wimmer (1957–2020) and Chris Coble for oversight and engagement. Craig Dykstra's fountainhead of ideas, including the concept of *pastoral imagination*, and his plentiful support stand behind this entire project.

Numerous colleagues, theological educators, and denominational leaders have invited talks and presentations about the LPI Project over the last decade, giving me a chance to hone and sharpen my thinking about the research, writing, and implications for ministers and theological educators. Two groups in particular continue to invite me back. Thanks for your partnership in the support of new pastors, Landon Whitsitt and the Presbyterian Synod of Mid-America and Scott Hudgins and the Helping Pastors Thrive initiative through the Cooperative Baptist Fellowship of North Carolina.

For opportunities to present and take in feedback, I am deeply grateful to my colleagues and members of the Society for Pastoral Theology; the Psychology, Culture, and Religion Unit of the American Academy of Religion; the Association of Practical Theology; and the Association of Theological Field Education (ATFE). From ATFE I am especially thankful for encouragement from Matt Floding and Danielle Tumminio Hanson. For Pete Ward, Tim Snyder, and numerous colleagues in the Ecclesiology and Ethnography work group, I am enlivened by ongoing conversations and jam sessions.

For opportunities to work with students who are in the thick of learning ministry in practice, I am grateful to Molly T. Marshall, Sally Dean Holt, Pamela Durso, Angela Jackson, and colleagues at Central Seminary. For new opportunities to teach and learn, I am grateful to Pamela Cooper-White, Serene Jones, and colleagues at Union Theological Seminary in the City of New York. For every metaphorical apple shared with students, mentors, and field education supervisors, I am delighted by all that you teach me.

Over the last two years, both of my teaching institutions provided direct and indirect support to 3MMM, extending my classroom to a great many more ministers, activists, chaplains, and religious leaders. For beautiful film work and for pushing me to write scripts early in the process that became the core of this book, thank you Ben Saunders, Kyle Jonas, and Rachel Ford of Adelicia Company. For creating the technological and social media recipes for 3MMM and for delivering inspiration week in and week out, my deepest gratitude to Adam D. J. Brett and Erin Robinson Hall. For research, social media assistance, and long talks about vocation, I am grateful to Colleen Maki. For providing an audit of this book to disrupt the structures of racism, sexism, homophobia, and ableism that haunt it, I am grateful to Nick Donkoh. Any remaining oversights and gaps are mine.

When it comes to my growth as a writer, my orchard is sprawling. Coaching from Erin McCarthy, Kayla Rae Whitaker, and Michael McGregor made this book so much better. For more than a dozen years of accountability and community, I cannot say enough thanks to theological writing colleagues Duane Bidwell, Emily Askew, Janet Schaller, Mary Clark Moschella, Tim Robinson, and Frank Thomas. In the department of everyday encouragement, support, and accountability, I offer apples all around to the "advisory board" of my Academic Writing Club group, where I am a player-coach: BadWolf, Ben B, Brilly, Heyali, ion, LucindaM, marguerite, Sarah T, Stacey_T, and TinaC.

To Scott Tunseth at Fortress Press who believed in *Pastoral Imagination* from our first conversation in 2018, a bushel of thanks. And to book cover artist and former student Amber Simpson, I am grateful for our shared collaboration and inspiration. What gifts!

Finally, to my parents, Juanita and Ron Campbell; to my spouse, Lynn Reed; and to our daughter, Marissa, you make my life possible. And to all our extended family, friends, church community, and neighbors, you keep me going. Every day you hand me the most fantastic, life-giving fruit. Most days I have the good sense to enjoy it. Thank you one and all.

Notes

INTRODUCTION

1 Eileen R. Campbell-Reed, *Anatomy of a Schism: How Clergywomen's Narratives Reinterpret the Fracturing of the Southern Baptist Convention* (Knoxville: University of Tennessee Press, 2016).

2 David Voas and Mark Chaves, "Is the United States a Counterexample to the Secularization Thesis?," *American Journal of Sociology* 121, no. 5 (2016): 1517–56, https://doi.org/10.1086/684202.

3 Janelle Wong, *Immigrants, Evangelicals, and Politics in an Era of Demographic Change* (New York: Russell Sage Foundation, 2018), 5: "Evangelical churches are without a doubt the largest, fastest-growing Asian American and Latinx organizations in the United States, and they are fueling demographic change within the larger evangelical community."

4 Richard P. DeShon, *Clergy Effectiveness: National Survey Results* (Nashville: General Board of Higher Education and Ministry of the United Methodist Church, 2010).

5 Dykstra's most complete treatment of the topic can be found in Craig Dykstra, "Pastoral and Ecclesial Imagination," in *For Life Abundant: Practical Theology, Theological Education, and Christian Ministry*, ed. Dorothy C. Bass and Craig Dykstra (Grand Rapids, MI: William B. Eerdmans, 2008), 41–61.

6 Kathleen Cahalan, *Introducing the Practice of Ministry* (Collegeville, MN: Liturgical Press, 2010), 99–117; Christian Scharen and Eileen R. Campbell-Reed, "The Learning Pastoral Imagination Project: A Five-Year Report on How New Ministers Learn in Practice," *Auburn Studies*, no. 21 (Winter 2016): 6–8.

7 Eileen R. Campbell-Reed, *State of Clergywomen in the U.S.: A Statistical Update*, 2018, http://www.stateofclergywomen.org.

8 William A. Daniel, *The Education of Negro Ministers* (New York: Doran, 1925); William Adams Brown and Mark A. May, *The Education of American Ministers*, 4 vols. (New York: Institute of Social and Religious Research, 1934).

9 Examples of these studies include the following: Jackson W. Carroll et al., *Being There: Culture and Formation in Two Theological Schools* (New York: Oxford University Press, 1997); Kevin R. Armstrong and L. Gregory Jones, *Resurrecting Excellence: Shaping Faithful Christian Ministry* (Grand Rapids, MI: William B. Eerdmans, 2006); and Don S. Browning, *A Fundamental Practical Theology* (Minneapolis: Fortress, 1991).

10 DeShon gives a brief overview of the earlier studies in *Clergy Effectiveness*, 3–4.

11 DeShon, 9–12.

12 DeShon, 5–9, 17.

13 Matt Bloom, *Flourishing in Ministry: How to Cultivate Clergy Wellbeing* (Lanham, MD: Rowman & Littlefield, 2019).

14 Seward Hiltner, *Preface to Pastoral Theology: The Ministry and Theory of Shepherding* (Nashville: Abingdon, 1948); Edward Farley, *Practicing Gospel: Unconventional Thoughts on the Church's Ministry* (Louisville: Westminster John Knox, 2003); Christie Cozad Neuger, *The Arts of Ministry: Feminist and Womanist Approaches* (Louisville: Westminster John Knox, 1996); Mary Clark Moschella and Lee H. Butler Jr., eds., *The Edward Wimberly Reader: A Black Pastoral Theology* (Waco: Baylor University Press, 2020); Jaco Hamman, *Becoming a Pastor: Forming Self and Soul for Ministry* (Cleveland: Pilgrim Press, 2007).

15 For example, Marilynne Robinson's award-winning trilogy about the intertwining stories of two ministers and their families, *Gilead* (New York: Picador, 2004); *Home* (New York: Farrar, Straus & Giroux, 2008); and *Lila* (New York: Picador, 2014). Exemplary memoirs include Heidi Neumark, *Breathing Space: A Spiritual Journey in the South Bronx* (Boston: Beacon, 2003); Eugene H. Peterson, *The Pastor: A Memoir* (New York: Harper Collins, 2011); Samuel DeWitt Proctor, *The Substance of Things Hoped For* (New York: Putnam, 1996); and Renita Weems, *Listening for God: A Minister's Journey through Silence and Doubt* (New York: Simon & Schuster, 1999).

16 For more about "theological ethnography," see Christian Scharen and Aana Marie Vigen, *Ethnography as Christian Theology and Ethics* (London: Continuum, 2011).

17 Beyond the LPI Project, other material in this book comes with permission from students, mentors, and participants in several other studies with whom I have worked over the last fifteen years in various capacities.

18 Research with ministers included in this book was conducted following the protocols of Institutional Review Boards at Vanderbilt University (Nashville, TN) and Luther Seminary (St. Paul, MN).

19 Most longitudinal studies—clinical-medical, qualitative–social science, or otherwise—must be intentional about retaining participants over the years of a study, and many factors can interrupt the retention rate. One of the best-known longitudinal studies follows 268 male graduates from Harvard University, starting when they were sophomores in 1938. See George E. Vaillant, *Triumphs of Experience: The Men of the Harvard Grant Study* (Cambridge, MA: Belknap, 2015).

20 The LPI study employs regular contacts and requests for updates. We occasionally make site visits and conduct virtual and in-person interviews to maintain contact with study participants. In one meta-study, researchers identified the following effective retention strategies: "study reminders, study visit characteristics, emphasizing study benefits, and contact/scheduling strategies. The

research teams were well-functioning, organized, and persistent. Additionally, teams tailored their strategies to their participants, often adapting and innovating their approaches." See Martha Abshire et al., "Participant Retention Practices in Longitudinal Clinical Research Studies with High Retention Rates," *BMC Medical Research Methodology* 17, no. 30 (2017), https://doi.org/10.1186/s12874-017-0310-z.

21 When first and last names are given in this book, they represent the identity of a person by that name. By default, pseudonyms, often titles and first names like Pastor Debbie, are used for people and places to represent the LPI research participants and their stories. Permission was secured from each living and available minister featured in the book. All other students and ministers whose stories are included are shared with permission. In many cases, a note indicates details of individual identities.

22 To learn more about integration, see Kathleen A. Cahalan, Edward Foley, and Gordon S. Mikoski, *Integrating Work in Theological Education* (Eugene, OR: Wipf & Stock, 2017).

23 Scharen and Campbell-Reed, "Learning Pastoral Imagination Project," 5, 18–20.

24 Patricia E. Benner et al., *Educating Nurses: A Call for Radical Transformation* (San Francisco: Jossey-Bass, 2010), 42.

25 Eileen Campbell-Reed and Christian Scharen, "'Holy Cow! This Stuff Is Real!' From Imagining Ministry to Pastoral Imagination," *Teaching Theology and Religion* 14, no. 4 (2011): 323–42.

26 Seven of the LPI study participants who identify as men are Asian American, Black, or Latinx or emigrated from India. Compared with the Euro-American men in the study, these men of color tell us more stories of work- and health-related challenges, microaggressions, and financial sustainability struggles. This difference resonates with the overall experiences of racism in the United States. While they tell us more of these stories, their experiences are not homogenous, and the eighteen white-identified men also have some work, health, and financial struggles; however, they tell us significantly fewer stories of this type.

27 Monica A. Coleman, *Making a Way out of No Way: A Womanist Theology* (Minneapolis: Fortress, 2008).

28 See Ken Bain, *What the Best College Teachers Do* (Cambridge, MA: Harvard University Press, 2004), 46–47; Benner et al., *Educating Nurses*, 79–85; and Cahalan, Foley, and Mikoski, *Integrating Work*, 75–89.

29 Eileen Campbell-Reed and Christian Scharen, "Ministry as Spiritual Practice: How Pastors Learn to See and Respond to the 'More' of a Situation," *Journal of Religious Leadership* 12, no. 2 (Fall 2013): 125–44.

30 See Eileen Campbell-Reed and Christian Scharen, "Ethnography on Holy Ground: How Qualitative Interviewing Is Practical Theological Work," *International Journal of Practical Theology* 17, no. 2 (2013): 1–28.

31 Campbell-Reed, *Anatomy of a Schism*, 2–3.

32 Jean Lave and Etienne Wenger, *Situated Learning: Legitimate Peripheral Participation* (New York: Cambridge University Press, 1991), 35.
33 Campbell-Reed, *Anatomy of a Schism*, 4–7.
34 To learn more about Three Minute Ministry Mentor, visit https://3mmm.us/welcome

CHAPTER 1

1 Patricia Benner, *From Novice to Expert: Excellence and Power in Clinical Nursing Practice, Commemorative Edition.* (Upper Saddle River, NJ: Prentice-Hall, 2001), 13–38.
2 Cahalan, *Introducing the Practice of Ministry*, 1–2.
3 Cahalan, 130–41.
4 Cahalan, 99.

CHAPTER 2

1 Scharen and Campbell-Reed, "Learning Pastoral Imagination Project," 15.
2 Scharen and Campbell-Reed, 15–17.
3 Weems, *Listening for God.*
4 Weems, 17.
5 Weems, 15.
6 Weems, 42–49.
7 Weems, 44.
8 Weems, 44.
9 Weems, 45.
10 Weems, 45–46.
11 Weems, 46.

CHAPTER 3

1 "Jake" is a pseudonym. The story is told from my memory.
2 Darnell L. Moore, *No Ashes in the Fire: Coming of Age Black and Free in America* (New York: Bold Type, 2018), 7.
3 Moore, 227.
4 Moore, 157.
5 Moore, 170.
6 Moore, 191.
7 Carrie Doehring, *The Practice of Pastoral Care, Revised and Expanded Edition: A Postmodern Approach* (Louisville: Westminster John Knox, 2015).
8 Doehring, 52.
9 Doehring, 52.

CHAPTER 5

1 John O'Donohue, "For Presence," in *To Bless the Space between Us: A Book of Blessings* (New York: Doubleday, 2008), 42. Used by permission.

CHAPTER 6

1 See the wider story of the Southern Baptist schism between biblicist and autonomist parties between 1979 and 2000 in Campbell-Reed, *Anatomy of a Schism.*

2 I am grateful for many years of friendship with Amy Mears, currently pastor of Glendale Baptist Church, and Beth McConnell, currently pastor of Kathwood Baptist Church.

3 Penny Long Marler, ed., *So Much Better: How Thousands of Pastors Help Each Other Thrive* (Nashville: Chalice Press, 2013).

4 Marler, 5.

5 Marler, 5.

6 Marler, 5–6.

7 Marler, 63–71.

CHAPTER 7

1 Hubert L. Dreyfus, *On the Internet*, 2nd ed. (New York: Routledge, 2009), 20–21.

2 See Ric Burns and Gretchen Sullivan Sorin, dir., *Driving While Black: Race, Space and Mobility in America* (New York: Steeplechase Films, 2020).

3 Christian Davenport, Sarah A. Soule, and David A. Armstrong II, "Protesting While Black? The Differential Policing of American Activism, 1960 to 1990," *American Sociological Review* 76, no. 1 (2011): 152–78.

4 Lisa L. Thompson, *Ingenuity: Preaching as an Outsider* (Nashville: Abingdon, 2018), 19.

5 In *On the Internet*, Dreyfus says that practical wisdom is "the general ability to do the appropriate thing, at the appropriate time, in the appropriate way" (46). This definition comes from Aristotle's notion of *phronesis*. Pastoral imagination as we understand it in the LPI study is also *phronesis*, or practical wisdom.

6 Bonnie J. Miller-McLemore et al., *Christian Practical Wisdom: What It Is, Why It Matters* (Grand Rapids, MI: William B. Eerdmans, 2016).

CHAPTER 8

1 Delores Carpenter, *A Time for Honor: A Portrait of African American Clergy-women* (St. Louis: Chalice Press, 2001); Barbara Brown Zikmund, Adair T.

Lummis, and Patricia Mei Yin Chang, *Clergy Women: An Uphill Calling* (Louisville: Westminster John Knox, 1998).

2 See Campbell-Reed, *State of Clergywomen in the U.S.*

3 Carpenter, *Time for Honor*, 99–103, 131–37.

4 Campbell-Reed, *State of Clergywomen in the U.S.*, 4–5.

5 Debora Jackson, *Meant for Good: Fundamentals of Womanist Leadership* (Valley Forge, PA: Judson, 2019), 67.

CHAPTER 10

1 Sarah Lewis, *The Rise: Creativity, the Gift of Failure, and the Search for Mastery* (New York: Simon & Schuster, 2015), 12.

2 Kelly Moreland Jones is a graduate of the Women's Leadership Initiative MDiv program at Central Seminary. She also served as a ministry intern in the congregation where I am a member. This story is shared with permission.

3 Lewis, *Rise*, 7–8, 19–24.

4 Lewis, 10.

5 Lewis, 7–8.

6 Lewis, 8.

7 Lewis, 8.

8 Lewis, 20.

9 Lewis, 11–12.

10 Lewis, 12–13.

CHAPTER 11

1 Karynthia Glasper-Phillips is a graduate of the Women's Leadership Initiative MDiv program at Central Seminary. Rev. Patricia Brock, DMin, served as her mentor for three years. This story is shared with their permission.

2 Teresa Fry Brown, *Can a Sistah Get a Little Help? Encouragement for Black Women in Ministry* (Cleveland: Pilgrim Press, 2008), 103.

3 Nelle Morton, *The Journey Is Home* (Boston: Beacon, 1985), 128.

CHAPTER 12

1 Dorothy Leonard and Walter Swap, *Deep Smarts: How to Cultivate and Transfer Enduring Business Wisdom* (Boston: Harvard Business School, 2015).

2 Leonard and Swap, 2.

3 Leonard and Swap, 9.

4 Walter Swap et al., "Using Mentoring and Storytelling to Transfer Knowledge in the Workplace," *Journal of Management Information Systems* 18, no. 1 (Summer 2001): 95–114.

5 Swap et al., 96.

CHAPTER 13

1 The fuller story of Gary's death and my longer-term care for Julie can be found in Eileen R. Campbell-Reed, "Wisdom at the Crossroads (Text: Proverbs 8:1–11)," in *This Is What a Preacher Looks Like: Sermons by Baptist Women*, ed. Pamela R. Durso (Macon, GA: Smyth & Helwys, 2010), 99–106. Rev. Dr. Jim Strickland was the senior pastor of the church.

CHAPTER 14

1 Thomas Keating, *Open Mind, Open Heart: The Contemplative Dimension of the Gospel* (New York: Amity House, 1986). The Contemplative Outreach website (http://www.contemplativeoutreach.org) is also rich with support for learning the practice.

2 Poem © Eileen Campbell-Reed, July 2012.

CHAPTER 15

1 Pete Docter, dir., *Inside Out* (Burbank: Walt Disney Pictures, 2015).

2 Daniel Siegel, *Brainstorm: The Power and Purpose of the Teenage Brain* (New York: Penguin, 2013), 81–84.

3 Siegel, 10–11.

4 Siegel includes a discussion of getting agitated and losing control of the executive functions of one's brain, known in shorthand as "flipping your lid" or "flying off the handle" (101–5).

CHAPTER 16

1 Shane Claiborne and Michael Martin, *Beating Guns: Hope for People Who Are Weary of Violence* (Grand Rapids, MI: Brazos Press, 2019).

CHAPTER 17

1 More of Monica's story is available in Eileen R. Campbell-Reed, "Living Testaments: How Catholic and Baptist Women in Ministry Both Judge and Renew the Church." *Ecclesial Practices* 4, no. 2 (2017): 178–80.

2 Kate Bowler, *Everything Happens for a Reason: And Other Lies I've Loved* (New York: Random House, 2018).

3 Bowler, 115–19.

4 Bowler, 119–20.

🦢 CHAPTER 18

1 Jamie Arpin-Ricci, "Preach the Gospel at All Times?," *Huffington Post*, July 1, 2012, accessed August 20, 2020, https://tinyurl.com/y6eubhec.

2 Amy-Jill Levine, *The Misunderstood Jew: The Church and the Scandal of the Jewish Jesus* (New York: HarperOne, 2006).

3 Levine, 7.

4 Levine, 7.

🦢 CHAPTER 19

1 Cody Sanders and Angela Yarber, *Microaggressions in Ministry: Confronting the Hidden Violence of Everyday Church* (Louisville: Westminster John Knox, 2015).

2 Lillian Daniel and Martin B. Copenhaver, *This Odd and Wondrous Calling: The Public and Private Lives of Two Ministers* (Grand Rapids, MI: William B. Eerdmans, 2009), 19.

3 Sanders and Yarber, *Microaggressions in Ministry*, 2–6.

4 Sanders and Yarber, 18–20.

5 Sanders and Yarber, 95–97.

6 Sanders and Yarber, 75–77.

🦢 CHAPTER 20

1 Shaun Gallagher, *Action and Interaction* (New York: Oxford University Press, 2020), 4.

🦢 CHAPTER 22

1 Chanequa Walker-Barnes, *I Bring the Voices of My People: A Womanist Vision for Racial Reconciliation* (Grand Rapids, MI: William B. Eerdmans, 2019).

2 Walker-Barnes, 206.

3 Walker-Barnes, 206.

4 Walker-Barnes, 206–7.

5 Walker-Barnes, 207.

6 Walker-Barnes, 207–8.

🦢 CHAPTER 23

1 J. Dana Trent, *For Sabbath's Sake: Embracing Your Need for Rest, Worship, and Community* (Nashville: Upper Room, 2017), Kindle.

2 Trent, 126–31.

3 Chris Mooney, Brady Dennis, and John Muyskens, "Global Emissions Plunged an Unprecedented 17 Percent during the Coronavirus Pandemic," *Washington Post*, May 19, 2020, accessed August 27, 2020, https://tinyurl.com/y9cmloua.

CHAPTER 24

1 Parker Palmer, *Let Your Life Speak: Listening for the Voice of Vocation* (San Francisco: Jossey-Bass, 2000), 4.
2 Palmer, 14–15.
3 Palmer, 15.

CHAPTER 25

1 "Margaret" is a pseudonym, and this story is shared with her permission.
2 Daniel Wolpert, *Creating a Life with God: The Call of Ancient Prayer Practices* (Nashville: Upper Room, 2003).
3 Numerous translations and reprints of *The Spiritual Exercises* are available online and in print. These quotes come from an online version translated by Louis J. Puhl in 1951. Ignatius of Loyola, *The Spiritual Exercises*, trans. Louis J. Puhl, Loyola Press, accessed August 27, 2020, https://tinyurl.com/p455vay.
4 Ignatius, *Spiritual Exercises*, "First Week" III (316).
5 Ignatius, *Spiritual Exercises*, "First Week" IV (317).
6 Ignatius, *Spiritual Exercises*, "First Week" III (316).
7 Ignatius, *Spiritual Exercises*, "First Week" IV (317).

CHAPTER 26

1 Andrew Lester, *Hope in Pastoral Care and Counseling* (Louisville: Westminster John Knox, 1995).
2 Lester, 29.
3 Lester, 88–94.

CHAPTER 28

1 Anne E. Streaty Wimberly, *Soul Stories: African American Christian Education*, rev. ed. (Nashville: Abingdon, 2005).
2 Wimberly, preface, n.p.

CHAPTER 29

1 Neumark, *Breathing Space*.
2 Neumark, 233.

CHAPTER 30

1 Malcolm Gladwell, *Outliers: The Story of Success* (New York: Back Bay, 2011), 39–42.
2 Tony Schwartz and Catherine McCarthy, "Manage Your Energy, Not Your Time," *Harvard Business Review*, October 2007, accessed August 31, 2020, https://tinyurl.com/jpo2r8c.
3 Schwartz and McCarthy.

CHAPTER 31

1 Martin Laird, *Into the Silent Land: A Guide to the Christian Contemplation* (New York: Oxford University Press, 2006), 97–107.
2 Laird, 104.
3 Laird, 104.

CHAPTER 32

1 "Margo" is a pseudonym. This story is shared with her permission.
2 Sarah Drummond, "Assessment and Theological Field Education," in *Welcome to Theological Field Education!*, ed. Matthew Floding (Lanham, MD: Rowman & Littlefield, 2014), 169–89.
3 Drummond, 173.
4 Drummond, 174–76.
5 Drummond, 189.

CHAPTER 33

1 William James, *The Varieties of Religious Experience: A Study in Human Nature*, centenary ed. (New York: Routledge, 2002), 395.

CHAPTER 34

1 The *Journal of Pastoral Care and Counseling* is available at http://www.jpcp.org.

CHAPTER 35

1 Albert S. Rossi, *Becoming a Healing Presence* (Chesterton, IN: Ancient Faith, 2014), chapter 3, 542, Kindle.

CHAPTER 36

1 *Phronesis* is a word from Aristotle best translated as "practical wisdom." It is the same concept the LPI Project is exploring with pastoral imagination.

2 Hamman, *Becoming a Pastor*, 149.

3 Hamman, 149–50.

4 Patrick B. Reyes, *Nobody Cries When We Die: God, Community, and Surviving to Adulthood* (St. Louis: Chalice Press, 2018).

5 Reyes, 54.

6 Reyes, 12.

7 Reyes, 13.

CHAPTER 37

1 To learn more of Malinda's story, see Campbell-Reed and Scharen, "Ministry as Spiritual Practice."

2 Charles R. Foster et al., *Educating Clergy: Teaching Practices and Pastoral Imagination* (San Francisco: Jossey-Bass, 2006).

3 Foster et al., 384–87.

4 Foster et al., 116, 120–23.

CHAPTER 38

1 Robert Dykstra, *Discovering a Sermon: Personal Pastoral Preaching* (St. Louis: Chalice, 2002).

2 Dykstra, 6–9.

3 Dykstra, 12–16, 50.

CHAPTER 39

1 Walter Brueggemann, *Praying the Psalms: Engaging Scripture and the Life of the Spirit* (Eugene, OR: Cascade, 2007), 3.

2 Deborah Kerdeman, "Pulled Up Short: Challenging Self-Understanding as a Focus of Teaching and Learning," in *Education and Practice: Upholding the Integrity of Teaching and Learning*, ed. Joseph Dunne and Pádraig Hogan (Malden, MA: Blackwell, 2004), 154.

3 Kerdeman, 155.

4 Deborah Kerdeman, "Pulled Up Short: Challenges for Education," in *Philosophy of Education 2003*, ed. Kal Alston (Urbana, IL: Philosophy of Education Society, 2003), 208.

5 Brueggemann, *Praying the Psalms*, 11.

❧ CHAPTER 40

1 Christian Scharen, "Learning Ministry over Time: Embodying Practical Wisdom," in *For Life Abundant: Practical Theology, Theological Education, and Christian Ministry*, ed. Dorothy Bass and Craig Dykstra (Grand Rapids, MI: William B. Eerdmans, 2008), 266–67.

2 Scharen, 270–71.

3 Scharen, 271–75.

4 Scharen, 277–82.

5 Scharen, 283–84.

❧ CHAPTER 41

1 For a discussion about complementarity and ministry, see Campbell-Reed, *Anatomy of a Schism*, 57–60, 81–85.

2 Robinson, *Gilead; Home;* and *Lila.*

❧ CHAPTER 42

1 Bessel van der Kolk, *The Body Keeps the Score: Brain, Mind, and Body in the Healing of Trauma* (New York: Penguin, 2015).

2 van der Kolk, 204.

❧ CHAPTER 43

1 More of Cathy's story is available in Eileen R. Campbell-Reed, "Living Testaments: How Catholic and Baptist Women in Ministry Both Judge and Renew the Church." *Ecclesial Practices* 4, no. 2 (2017): 183–86.

2 Resmaa Menakem, *My Grandmother's Hands: Racialized Trauma and the Pathway to Mending Our Hearts and Bodies* (Las Vegas: Central Recovery Press, 2017).

3 Menakem, 4–6.

4 Menakem, 129–30.

❧ CHAPTER 44

1 Chip Heath and Dan Heath, *The Power of Moments: Why Certain Experiences Have Extraordinary Impact* (New York: Simon & Schuster, 2017), 96.

2 Campbell-Reed, *Anatomy of a Schism*, chapter 2.

3 The story of Martha and Linda appears in Campbell-Reed, 53–54.

4 Ada María Isasi-Díaz, *En la Lucha / In the Struggle: Elaborating a Mujerista Theology* (Minneapolis: Fortress, 1993), 188.

5 Heath and Heath, *Power of Moments*, 27–33.

CHAPTER 45

1 Daniel Wolpert, *Leading a Life with God: The Practice of Spiritual Leadership* (Nashville: Upper Room, 2006), 17–19.
2 Wolpert, 19–22.

CHAPTER 46

1 *The Upper Room Disciplines 2020: A Book of Daily Devotions* (Nashville: Upper Room, 2019).
2 "d365: Devotionals 365 Days a Year," Passport, accessed August 20, 2020, http://www.d365.org.
3 Martha Spong, ed., *The Words of Her Mouth: Psalms for the Struggle* (Cleveland: Pilgrim Press, 2020).

CHAPTER 47

1 Rebecca's story is told more fully in Campbell-Reed, *Anatomy of a Schism*, chapter 4. Quotes come from pages 94–95, 101. Asha's story is told in part in Campbell-Reed and Scharen, "Holy Cow," 323–42.
2 Quotes from the stories about Rebecca are from Campbell-Reed, *Anatomy of a Schism*, 94–95, 101.

CHAPTER 48

1 For example, homiletics professor and practical theologian Lisa L. Thompson, in her book *Ingenuity*, says, "One aspect of black women's history in North America is the experience of being a captured—or caged—group for the social and economic gain of other individuals. The most recognizable aspects of this captivity are in the transatlantic slave trade. The less visible, but no less stigmatizing, aspects of being caged are the domestic servitude that followed the era of slavery and its ongoing mutations; their offspring yield income gaps, healthcare disparities, and higher death rates for these women in the twenty-first century" (13).
2 Thompson, 2, 39.
3 Thompson, xiii.
4 Thompson, xiii.

CHAPTER 49

1 Vashti Murphy McKenzie, *The Big Deal of Taking Small Steps to Move Closer to God* (New York: FaithWords, 2017).
2 McKenzie, 29–30.

CHAPTER 50

1 Chloe's story appears in Campbell-Reed, *Anatomy of a Schism*, chapter 5.
2 Mary Clark Moschella, *Caring for Joy: Narrative, Theology, and Practice* (Boston: Brill, 2016), 16.
3 Moschella, 162.
4 Moschella, 162, 165–67.
5 Moschella, 162, 169.
6 Moschella, 182. "In 1965 [Murray] was, in her words, 'the first Negro—male or female—to be awarded the J.S.D. from Yale Law School.'"
7 Moschella, 170, 182.
8 Moschella, 163–65, 175–76.
9 Moschella, 183.
10 Moschella, 185.
11 Moschella, 186.
12 Moschella, 185.
13 Moschella, 185. Dates reported in Pauli Murray, interview by Charles Kuralt, *On the Road with Charles Kuralt*, 1985, accessed May 30, 2020, https://tinyurl.com/yytq87ej.
14 Murray, interview.
15 Moschella, *Caring for Joy*, 187.
16 Moschella, 185–86.
17 Ray Waddle, "Mary Clark Moschella: Surprised by Joy," Yale Divinity School, March 12, 2009, accessed June 10, 2020, https://tinyurl.com/yxvvz4tn.

APPENDIX

1 To learn more about land acknowledgment and the *doctrine of discovery*, visit the Doctrine of Discovery website: https://doctrineofdiscovery.org.
2 Thanks to Dr. Stephanie Crumpton for this insight. See more at episode 74, "Activism and Legacy," https://3mmm.us/Episode74

Bibliography

Abshire, Martha, Victor D. Dinglas, Maan Isabella A. Cajita, Michelle N. Eakin, Dale M. Needham, and Cheryl Dennison Himmelfarb. "Participant Retention Practices in Longitudinal Clinical Research Studies with High Retention Rates." *BMC Medical Research Methodology* 17, no. 30 (2017). https://doi.org/10.1186/s12874-017-0310-z.

Allman, Mark. "Eucharist, Ritual & Narrative: Formation of Individual and Communal Moral Character." *Journal of Ritual Studies* 14, no. 1 (2000): 60–68.

Armstrong, Kevin R., and L. Gregory Jones. *Resurrecting Excellence: Shaping Faithful Christian Ministry*. Grand Rapids, MI: William B. Eerdmans, 2006.

Arpin-Ricci, Jamie. "Preach the Gospel at All Times?" *Huffington Post*, July 1, 2012. https://tinyurl.com/y2zpmfhl.

Bain, Ken. *What the Best College Teachers Do*. Cambridge, MA: Harvard University Press, 2004.

Benner, Patricia. *From Novice to Expert: Excellence and Power in Clinical Nursing Practice, Commemorative Edition*. Upper Saddle River, NJ: Prentice-Hall, 2001.

Benner, Patricia E., Molly Sutphen, Victoria Leonard, Lisa Day, and Lee S. Shulman. *Educating Nurses: A Call for Radical Transformation*. San Francisco: Jossey-Bass, 2010.

Berry, Wendell. "Manifesto: Mad Farmer Liberation Front." In *The Selected Poems of Wendell Berry*. Berkeley: Counterpoint Press, 1999.

Bloom, Matt. *Flourishing in Ministry: How to Cultivate Clergy Wellbeing*. Lanham, MD: Rowman & Littlefield, 2019.

Bowler, Kate. *Everything Happens for a Reason: And Other Lies I've Loved*. New York: Random House, 2018.

Brown, William Adams, and Mark A. May. *The Education of American Ministers*. 4 vols. New York: Institute of Social and Religious Research, 1934.

Browning, Don S. *A Fundamental Practical Theology*. Minneapolis: Fortress, 1991.

Brueggemann, Walter. *Praying the Psalms: Engaging Scripture and the Life of the Spirit*. Eugene, OR: Cascade Books, 2007.

Burns, Ric, and Gretchen Sullivan Sorin, dir. *Driving While Black: Race, Space and Mobility in America*. New York: Steeplechase Films, 2020.

Cahalan, Kathleen. *Introducing the Practice of Ministry*. Collegeville, MN: Liturgical Press, 2010.

Cahalan, Kathleen A., Edward Foley, and Gordon S. Mikoski. *Integrating Work in Theological Education*. Eugene, OR: Wipf & Stock, 2018.

Campbell-Reed, Eileen. *Anatomy of a Schism: How Clergywomen's Narratives Reinterpret the Fracturing of the Southern Baptist Convention.* Knoxville: University of Tennessee Press, 2016.

———. "Living Testaments: How Catholic and Baptist Women in Ministry Both Judge and Renew the Church." *Ecclesial Practices* 4, no. 2 (2017): 167–198.

———. *State of Clergywomen in the U.S.: A Statistical Update.* 2018. http://www.stateofclergywomen.org.

———. "Wisdom at the Crossroads (Text: Proverbs 8:1–11)." In *This Is What a Preacher Looks Like: Sermons by Baptist Women,* edited by Pamela R. Durso. Macon, GA: Smyth & Helwys, 2010: 99–106.

Campbell-Reed, Eileen, and Christian Scharen. "Ethnography on Holy Ground: How Qualitative Interviewing Is Practical Theological Work." *International Journal of Practical Theology* 17, no. 2 (2013): 1–28.

———. "'Holy Cow! This Stuff Is Real!' From Imagining Ministry to Pastoral Imagination." *Teaching Theology and Religion* 14, no. 4 (2011): 323–342.

———. "The Learning Pastoral Imagination Project: A Five-Year Report on How New Ministers Learn in Practice." *Auburn Studies,* no. 21 (Winter 2016): 6–8.

———. "Ministry as Spiritual Practice: How Pastors Learn to See and Respond to the 'More' of a Situation." *Journal of Religious Leadership* 12, no. 2 (Fall 2013): 125–144.

———. "The Unfolding of Pastoral Imagination: Prudence as Key to Learning Ministry." *Reflective Practice: Formation and Supervision in Ministry* 32 (2012): 71–86.

Carpenter, Delores. *A Time for Honor: A Portrait of African American Clergywomen.* St. Louis: Chalice, 2001.

Carroll, Jackson W., Barbara G. Wheeler, Daniel O. Aleshire, and Penny Long Marler. *Being There: Culture and Formation in Two Theological Schools.* New York: Oxford University Press, 1997.

Claiborne, Shane, and Michael Martin. *Beating Guns: Hope for People Who Are Weary of Violence.* Grand Rapids, MI: Brazos Press, 2019.

Coleman, Monica A. *Making a Way out of No Way: A Womanist Theology.* Minneapolis: Fortress, 2008.

Daniel, Lillian, and Martin B. Copenhaver. *This Odd and Wondrous Calling: The Public and Private Lives of Two Ministers.* Grand Rapids, MI: William B. Eerdmans, 2009.

Daniel, William A. *The Education of Negro Ministers.* New York: Doran, 1925.

Davenport, Christian, Sarah A. Soule, and David A. Armstrong II. "Protesting While Black? The Differential Policing of American Activism, 1960 to 1990." *American Sociological Review* 76, no. 1 (2011): 152–178.

DeShon, Richard. *Clergy Effectiveness: National Survey Results.* Nashville: General Board of Higher Education and Ministry of the United Methodist Church, 2010.

Docter, Pete, dir. *Inside Out.* Burbank: Walt Disney Pictures, 2015.

Doehring, Carrie. *The Practice of Pastoral Care, Revised and Expanded Edition: A Postmodern Approach.* Louisville: Westminster John Knox, 2015.

Dreyfus, Hubert L. *On the Internet.* 2nd ed. New York: Routledge, 2009.

Drummond, Sarah. "Assessment and Theological Field Education." In *Welcome to Theological Field Education!*, edited by Matthew Floding, 169–189. Lanham, MD: Rowman & Littlefield, 2014.

Dykstra, Craig. "Pastoral and Ecclesial Imagination." In *For Life Abundant: Practical Theology, Theological Education, and Christian Ministry*, edited by Dorothy Bass and Craig Dykstra, 41–61. Grand Rapids, MI: William B. Eerdmans, 2008.

Dykstra, Robert. *Discovering a Sermon: Personal Pastoral Preaching.* Nashville: Chalice, 2002.

Ellison, Gregory C., II. *Fearless Dialogues: A New Movement for Justice.* Louisville: Westminster John Knox, 2017.

Farley, Edward. *Practicing Gospel: Unconventional Thoughts on the Church's Ministry.* Louisville: Westminster John Knox, 2003.

Foster, Charles R., Lisa Dahill, Lawrence A. Goleman, and Barbara Wang Tolentino. *Educating Clergy: Teaching Practices and Pastoral Imagination.* San Francisco: Jossey-Bass, 2006.

Fry Brown, Teresa. *Can a Sistah Get a Little Help? Encouragement for Black Women in Ministry.* Cleveland: Pilgrim Press, 2008. Kindle.

Gallagher, Shaun. *Action and Interaction.* New York: Oxford University Press, 2020.

Gladwell, Malcolm. *Blink: The Power of Thinking without Thinking.* New York: Little, Brown, 2005.

———. *Outliers: The Story of Success.* New York: Back Bay, 2011.

Hamman, Jaco. *Becoming a Pastor: Forming Self and Soul for Ministry.* Cleveland: Pilgrim Press, 2007.

Heath, Chip, and Dan Heath. *The Power of Moments: Why Certain Experiences Have Extraordinary Impact.* New York: Simon & Schuster, 2017.

Hiltner, Seward. *Preface to Pastoral Theology: The Ministry and Theory of Shepherding.* Nashville: Abingdon, 1948.

Ibarra, Herminia. *Act like a Leader, Think like a Leader.* Cambridge, MA: Harvard Business Review, 2015.

Ignatius of Loyola. *The Spiritual Exercises*, 1523. Translated by Louis J. Puhl, 1951. https://tinyurl.com/p455vay.

Isasi-Díaz, Ada María. *En la Lucha / In the Struggle: Elaborating a Mujerista Theology.* Minneapolis: Fortress, 1993.

Jackson, Debora. *Meant for Good: Fundamentals of Womanist Leadership.* Valley Forge, PA: Judson, 2019.

Jackson, Donald. *The Saint John's Bible.* Collegeville, MN: Hill Museum & Manuscript Library, St. John's Abbey, 2007.

James, William. *The Varieties of Religious Experience: A Study in Human Nature.* Centenary ed. New York: Routledge, 2002.

Keating, Thomas. *Open Mind, Open Heart: The Contemplative Dimension of the Gospel.* New York: Amity House, 1986.

Kerdeman, Deborah. "Pulled Up Short: Challenges for Education." In *Philosophy of Education 2003*, edited by Kal Alston, 208–216. Urbana, IL: Philosophy of Education Society, 2003.

———. "Pulled Up Short: Challenging Self-Understanding as a Focus of Teaching and Learning." In *Education and Practice: Upholding the Integrity of Teaching and Learning*, edited by Joseph Dunne and Pádraig Hogan, 144–158. Malden, MA: Blackwell, 2004.

Kidd, Sue Monk. *Dance of the Dissident Daughter: A Woman's Journey from Christian Tradition to the Sacred Feminine*. San Francisco: HarperOne, 1996.

Laird, Martin. *Into the Silent Land: A Guide to the Christian Contemplation*. New York: Oxford University Press, 2006.

Lave, Jean, and Etienne Wenger. *Situated Learning: Legitimate Peripheral Participation*. New York: Cambridge University Press, 1991.

Leonard, Dorothy, and Walter Swap. *Deep Smarts: How to Cultivate and Transfer Enduring Business Wisdom*. Boston: Harvard Business School, 2015.

Lester, Andrew. *Hope in Pastoral Care and Counseling*. Louisville: Westminster John Knox, 1995.

Levine, Amy-Jill. *The Misunderstood Jew: The Church and the Scandal of the Jewish Jesus*. New York: HarperOne, 2006.

Lewis, Sarah. *The Rise: Creativity, the Gift of Failure, and the Search for Mastery*. New York: Simon & Schuster, 2015.

Marler, Penny Long, ed. *So Much Better: How Thousands of Pastors Help Each Other Thrive*. St. Louis: Chalice, 2013.

McKenzie, Vashti Murphy. *The Big Deal of Taking Small Steps to Move Closer to God*. New York: FaithWords, 2017.

———. *Strength in the Struggle: Leadership Development for Women*. Cleveland: Pilgrim Press, 2001.

Menakem, Resmaa. *My Grandmother's Hands: Racialized Trauma and the Pathway to Mending Our Hearts and Bodies*. Las Vegas: Central Recovery Press, 2017.

Miller-McLemore, Bonnie, Dorothy Bass, Bonnie Cahalan, Christian Batalden Scharen, and James Nieman. *Christian Practical Wisdom: What It Is, Why It Matters*. Grand Rapids, MI: William B. Eerdmans, 2016.

Mooney, Chris, Brady Dennis, and John Muyskens. "Global Emissions Plunged an Unprecedented 17 Percent during the Coronavirus Pandemic." *Washington Post*, May 19, 2020. https://tinyurl.com/y9cmloua.

Moore, Darnell L. *No Ashes in the Fire: Coming of Age Black and Free in America*. New York: Bold Type, 2018.

Morton, Nelle. *The Journey Is Home*. Boston: Beacon, 1985.

Moschella, Mary Clark. *Caring for Joy: Narrative, Theology, and Practice*. Boston: Brill, 2016.

Moschella, Mary Clark, and Lee H. Butler Jr., eds. *The Edward Wimberly Reader: A Black Pastoral Theology*. Waco: Baylor University Press, 2020.

Murray, Pauli. Interview by Charles Kuralt. *On the Road with Charles Kuralt*. CBS News, 1985.

Neuger, Christie Cozad. *The Arts of Ministry: Feminist and Womanist Approaches.* Louisville: Westminster John Knox, 1996.

Neumark, Heidi. *Breathing Space: A Spiritual Journey in the South Bronx.* Boston: Beacon, 2004.

O'Donohue, John. *To Bless the Space between Us: A Book of Blessings.* New York: Doubleday, 2008.

Palmer, Parker. *Let Your Life Speak: Listening for the Voice of Vocation.* San Francisco: Jossey-Bass, 2000.

Passport. "d365: Devotionals 365 Days a Year." http://www.d365.org.

Peterson, Eugene H. *The Pastor: A Memoir.* New York: Harper Collins, 2011.

Proctor, Samuel DeWitt. *The Substance of Things Hoped For.* New York: Putnam, 1996.

Reyes, Patrick. *Nobody Cries When We Die: God, Community, and Surviving to Adulthood.* St. Louis: Chalice, 2018.

Robinson, Marilynne. *Gilead.* New York: Picador, 2004.

———. *Home.* New York: Farrar, Straus & Giroux, 2008.

———. *Lila.* New York: Picador, 2014.

Rossi, Albert. *Becoming a Healing Presence.* Chesterton, IN: Ancient Faith, 2014.

Sanders, Cody, and Angela Yarber. *Microaggressions in Ministry: Confronting the Hidden Violence of Everyday Church.* Louisville: Westminster John Knox, 2015.

Scharen, Christian. "Learning Ministry over Time: Embodying Practical Wisdom." In *For Life Abundant: Practical Theology, Theological Education, and Christian Ministry,* edited by Dorothy Bass and Craig Dykstra, 266–267. Grand Rapids, MI: William B. Eerdmans, 2008.

Scharen, Christian, and Eileen Campbell-Reed. "The Learning Pastoral Imagination Project: A Five-Year Report on How New Ministers Learn in Practice." *Auburn Studies,* no. 21 (Winter 2016): 6–8.

Scharen, Christian, and Aana Marie Vigen. *Ethnography as Christian Theology and Ethics.* London: Continuum, 2011.

Schwartz, Tony, and Catherine McCarthy. "Manage Your Energy, Not Your Time." *Harvard Business Review,* October 2007.

Siegel, Daniel J. *Brainstorm: The Power and Purpose of the Teenage Brain.* New York: Penguin, 2013.

———. *Mindsight: The New Science of Personal Transformation.* New York: Bantam Books, 2010.

Spong, Martha. *The Words of Her Mouth: Psalms for the Struggle.* Cleveland: Pilgrim Press, 2020.

Swap, Walter, Dorothy Leonard, Mimi Shields, and Lisa Abrams. "Using Mentoring and Storytelling to Transfer Knowledge in the Workplace." *Journal of Management Information Systems* 18, no. 1 (Summer 2001): 95–114.

Thompson, Lisa. *Ingenuity: Preaching as an Outsider.* Nashville: Abingdon, 2018.

Trent, J. Dana. *For Sabbath's Sake: Embracing Your Need for Rest, Worship, and Community*. Nashville: Upper Room, 2017.

The Upper Room Disciplines 2020: A Book of Daily Devotions. Nashville: Upper Room, 2019.

Vaillant, George E. *Triumphs of Experience: The Men of the Harvard Grant Study*. Cambridge, MA: Belknap, 2015.

van der Kolk, Bessel. *The Body Keeps the Score: Brain, Mind, and Body in the Healing of Trauma*. New York: Penguin, 2015.

Voas, David, and Mark Chaves. "Is the United States a Counterexample to the Secularization Thesis?" *American Journal of Sociology* 121, no. 5 (2016). https://doi.org/10.1086/684202.

Waddle, Ray. "Mary Clark Moschella: Surprised by Joy." Yale Divinity School (March 12, 2009). https://tinyurl.com/yxvvz4tn.

Walker, Alice. *The Way Forward Is with a Broken Heart: Stories*. New York: Ballantine, 2001.

Walker-Barnes, Chanequa. *I Bring the Voices of My People: A Womanist Vision for Racial Reconciliation*. Grand Rapids, MI: William B. Eerdmans, 2019.

Weems, Renita. *Listening for God: A Minister's Journey through Silence and Doubt*. New York: Simon & Schuster, 1999.

Wimberly, Anne Streaty. *The Courage to Hope: Empowering Adolescent Joy amidst the Challenges of Life*. Yale Youth Ministry Institute (May 4, 2016). https://tinyurl.com/y6ghd776.

———. *Soul Stories: African American Christian Education*. Revised ed. Nashville: Abingdon, 2005.

Wolpert, Daniel. *Creating a Life with God: The Call of Ancient Prayer Practices*. Nashville: Upper Room, 2003.

———. *Leading a Life with God: The Practice of Spiritual Leadership*. Nashville: Upper Room, 2006.

Wong, Janelle. *Immigrants, Evangelicals, and Politics in an Era of Demographic Change*. New York: Russell Sage Foundation, 2018.

Zikmund, Barbara Brown, Adair T. Lummis, and Patricia Mei Yin Chang. *Clergy Women: An Uphill Calling*. Louisville: Westminster John Knox, 1998.

Index